body ART

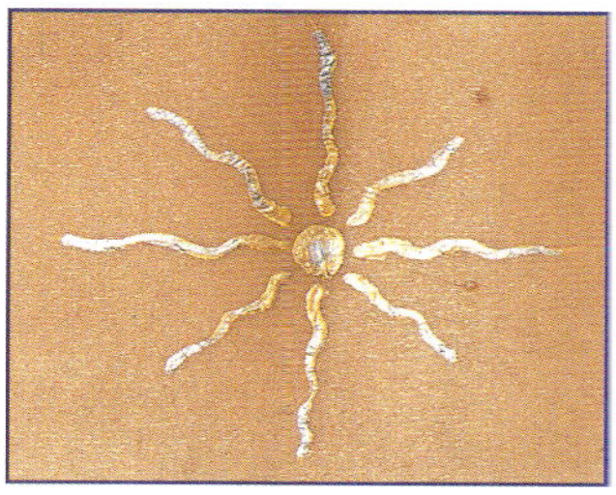

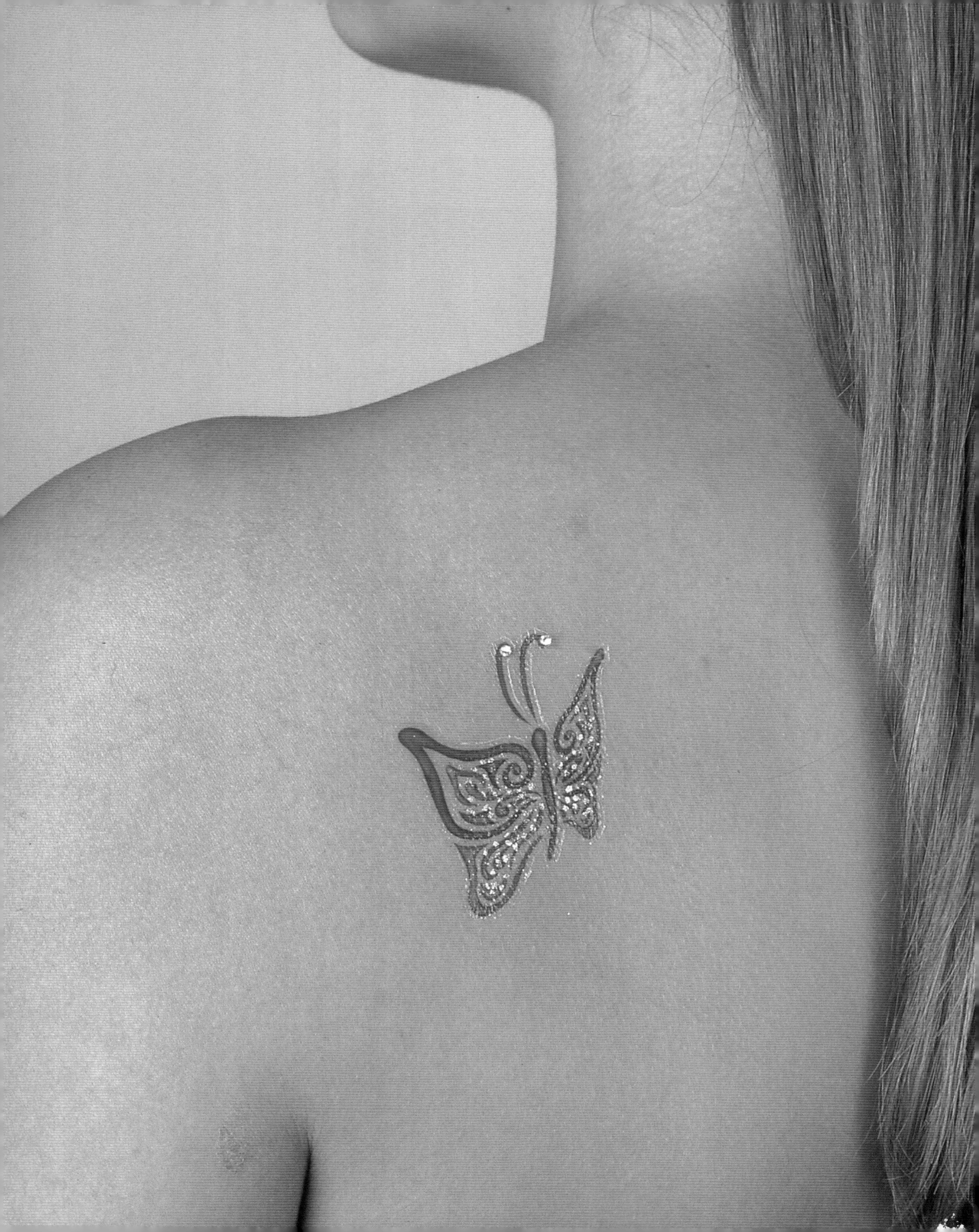

body ART

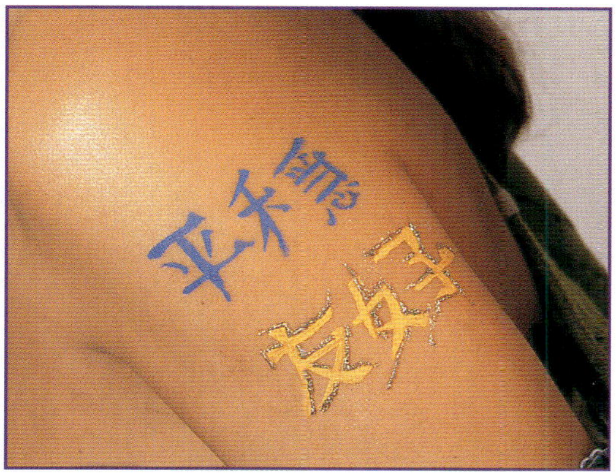

MARIE MINGAY

D&S BOOKS

First published in 2001 by D&S Books

D&S Books
Cottage Meadow, Bocombe,
Parkham, Bideford
Devon, England
EX39 5PH

e-mail us at:-
enquiries.dspublishing@care4free.net

This edition printed 2001

ISBN 1-903327-31-8

Creative Director: Sarah King
Editor: Clare Haworth-Maden
Project Editor: Yvonne Worth
Designer: Axis Design
Photography: Paul Forrester

Distributed in the UK & Ireland by
Bookmart Limited
Desford Road
Enderby
Leicester LE9 5AD

Distributed in Australia by
Herron Books
39 Commercial Road
Fortitude Valley
Queensland 4006

1 3 5 7 9 10 8 6 4 2

contents

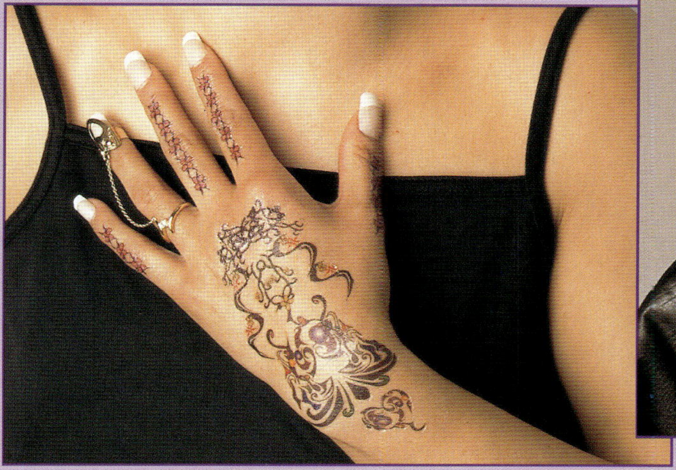

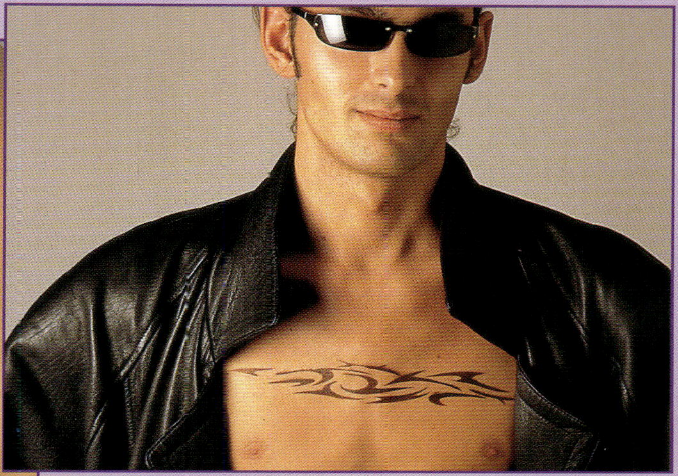

Introduction

Body art has been around for centuries and appears in many different cultures. It has been used in tribal warfare, to honour power, strength and position, to celebrate love and marriage, as well as simply to decorate the body. During the last decade, it has become a fashion accessory popularised by such celebrities as Madonna.

Body art includes bindi, a product based on henna powder which is mixed with water, the designs being hand-drawn by means of a piping method, as if you were icing a cake, or, for the less artistic, being applied around stencils placed on the skin. To enhance these designs, bindi adornments in a variety of designs, colours and sizes can be added. A special range of coloured paints can add definition and depth to your design, while a less permanent technique is airbrushing, which uses water-based paints over stencils that are available in a wide range of designs, from Celtic and floral motifs to dolphins, to name but a few. Another option is water-based inks (similar to eyeliner), which are usually applied in a freehand style, although stencils can also be used. The simplest and easiest forms of body art are water-based transfers, which are sold in a range of designs and colours and can be shaped and cut to adorn your body, and self-adhesive jewels, with which you can decorate any part of your body, including your eyebrows, eyelashes, finger- and toenails (you can further enhance your feet with toe rings and ankle chains).

Equipment & materials

There are different types of body art available from many shops and outlets, and your choice will largely depend on how long you wish your design to last.

For easily removable temporary body art, body paints are best as they are soluble in water. Semi-permanent tattoos or transfers will need some washing to remove, while henna tattoos can last several weeks depending on how careful you are with them.

Ink stencils

Ink stencils can be bought as kits (normally containing four stencils) in a wide range of designs, including flowers and butterflies, a range of armbands and Kanji symbols and ornaments. The kits also contain a small, thimble-like pad and pots of coloured inks, sometimes pearlised.

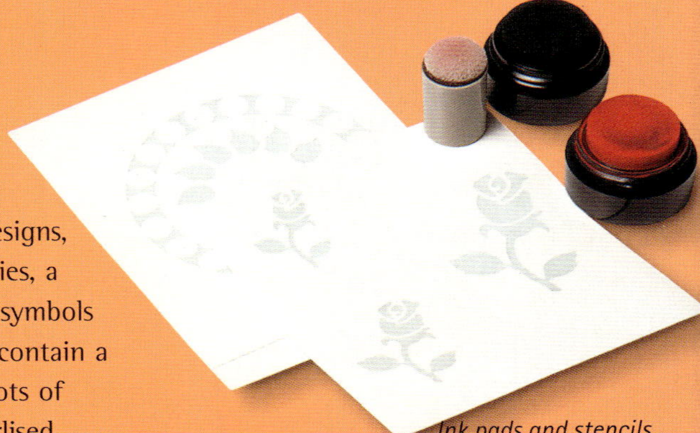

Ink pads and stencils.

DESIGNING YOUR OWN STENCILS

Not only can you unleash your creativity by designing your own stencils, but using stencils is a particularly helpful solution if you don't feel confident drawing freehand.

Draw or mark out your design onto a piece of thin waxed card. Using masking tape, tape your stencil to a craft or chopping board to reduce the risk of it moving while you are cutting it. Using a craft knife, carefully cut out the design. (This is a time-consuming task – don't rush it.) Using the glue stick, glue the stencil to the designated skin area, which should be clean and dry. Try to buy a skin-friendly glue from a body-art specialist as this type of glue comes off easily when you remove the stencil.

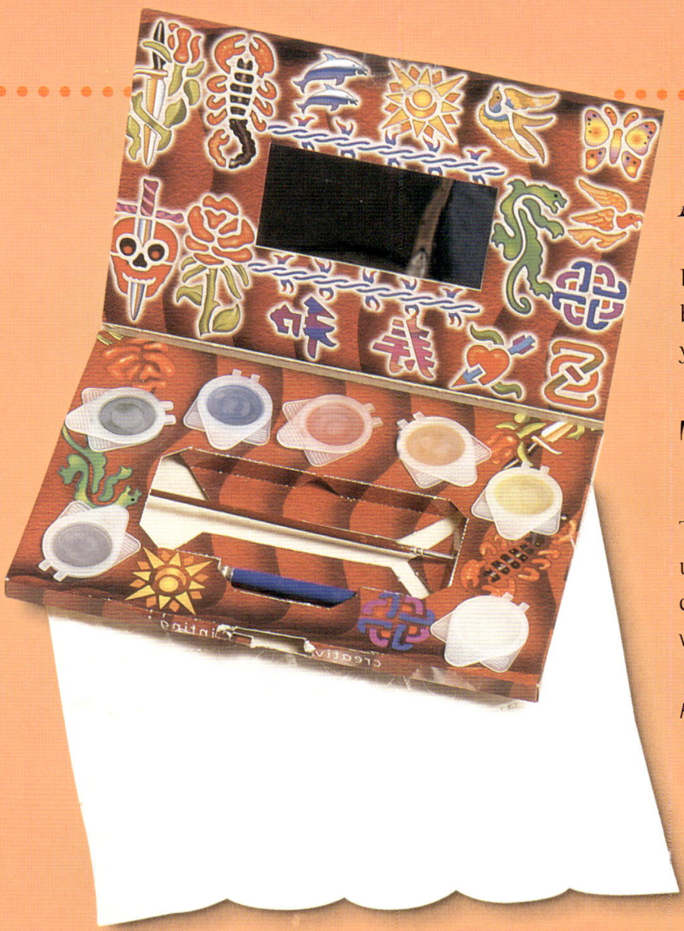

Art pencils and inks

Instead of using an ink pad, you can also use special pens and brushes to apply body ink. These can be used with a stencil, or, if you're feeling brave, you can paint freehand!

Tattoo inks

Tattoo inks, which resemble liquid eyeliner in their packaging, are usually brown or black. They can be applied either freehand or in conjunction with a stencil. You can use tattoo inks and pencils with other designs and materials to create different looks.

Painting kit.

Glitter dust

Glitter dust, which is sold in a variety of colours and forms, including loose powder and sprays, will give extra sparkle to your body art.

Tattoo pens

Sold in an array of colours, tattoo pens can be used either freehand or with a stencil. Dermatologically tested, they usually last for up to sixty hours. You can wash them off with soap and water and they will generally also wash out of fabrics. Tattoo pens are reusable and their effect varies in depth and colour according to your skin's natural pigmentation.

Body sprays

Body sprays are a fun way of decorating your body. Make your skin shimmer by simply spraying them on or use them with stencils to create eye-catching designs.

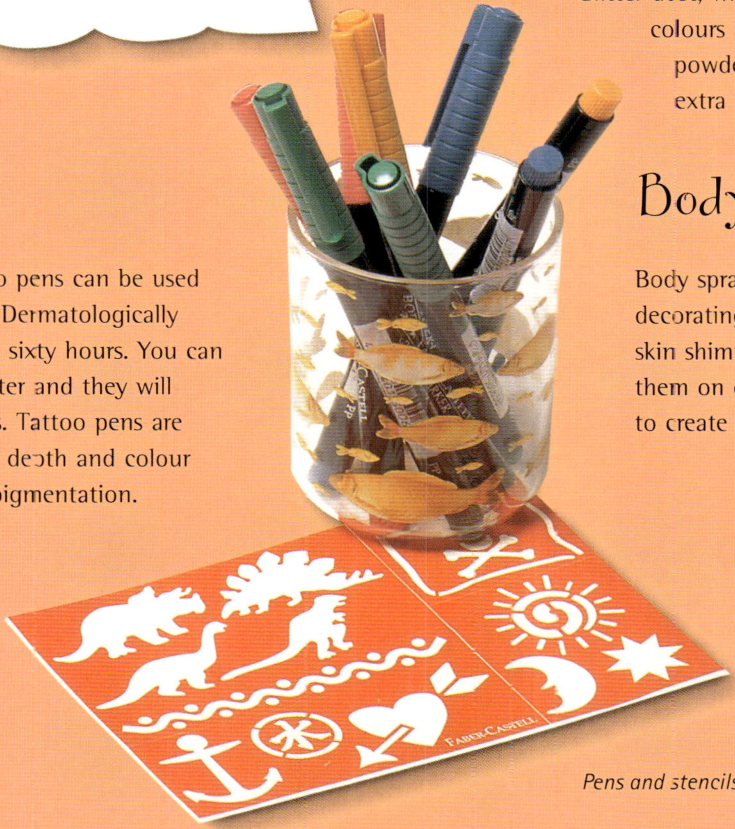

Pens and stencils.

Airbrushing

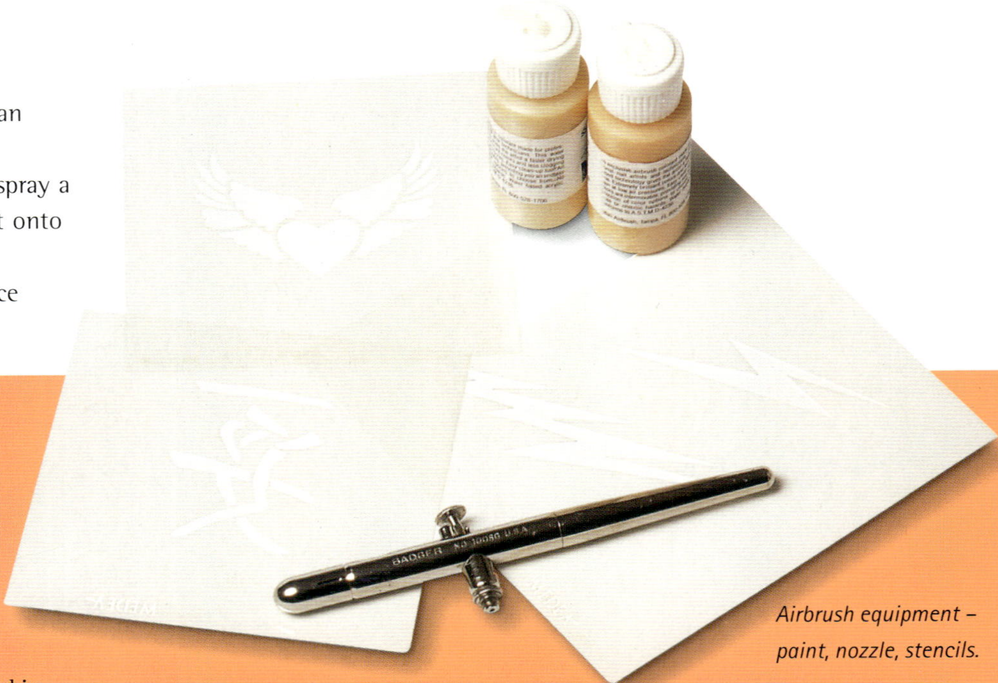

Airbrushing usually involves using an airbrush in conjunction with a compressor, which enables you to spray a very fine mist of water-based paint onto your skin to create shaded effects comprising two to three tones. Once you have perfected your spraying action, you'll find that the paint dries very quickly.

Before airbrushing the skin, it is essential that it is clean, oil-free and dry – you can buy special alcohol-free liquids or wipes with which to prepare it. Airbrushed designs will only last for two or three days, depending on the oiliness of your skin.

Airbrush equipment – paint, nozzle, stencils.

Semi-permanent tattoos

Semi-permanent tattoos are sold in many colours, ranging from soft pastel tones through shades of brown to black, as well as all sorts of designs, often with additional body jewellery.

Remember that these tattoos will last longer if they do not come into contact with lotions, creams and suntan products.

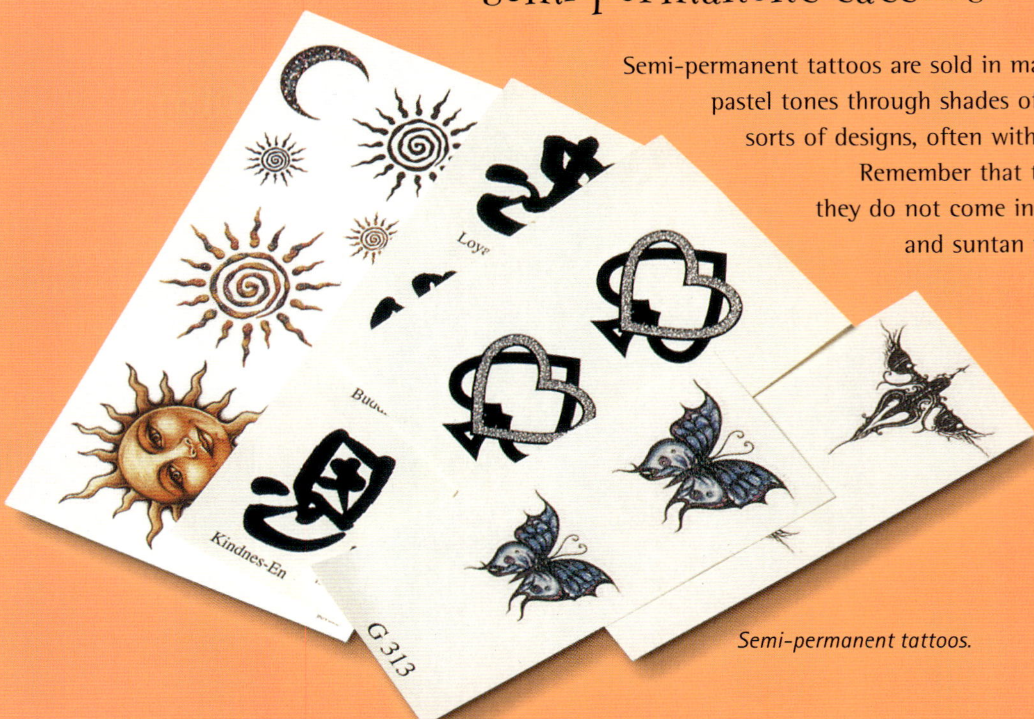

Semi-permanent tattoos.

Henna

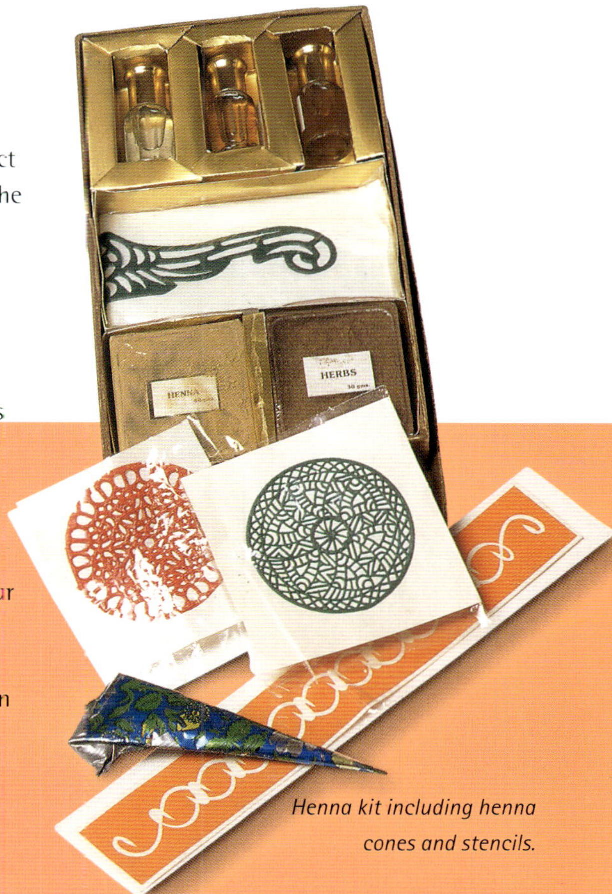

Henna kit including henna cones and stencils.

There can be confusion over the difference between Henna and Mehndi. In fact the only difference is the name – henna is the Arabic name, while Mehndi is the Indian name. As the name Henna is generally more widely recognised, this is what we refer to throughout the book.

Henna is an organic powder derived from the leaves of a plant, Llawsonia inermis. Best known as a hair colourant, henna can be used in a number of ways, including staining the skin, which is usually called henna tattooing, but has more recently become known as bindi. In order to produce the best results in terms of depth of colour, henna paste must be warm and moist when it is applied to the skin to enable the active ingredient within the henna, hennotannic acid (which is released when dry skin reaches a pH level of 5.5), to react with the skin's cells.

The henna dye does not penetrate the skin, only staining the first layer: your skin pigmentation and rate of exfoliation will determine how long the henna tattoo lasts, but it will usually be for a couple of weeks. (The skin cells are replaced over a period of one to twelve weeks, depending on whether your skin type is dry, normal or oily.) Henna designs last longest on certain parts of the body, such as the soles of your feet, where the skin is thicker, while a design applied to thinner parts of your skin will fade faster.

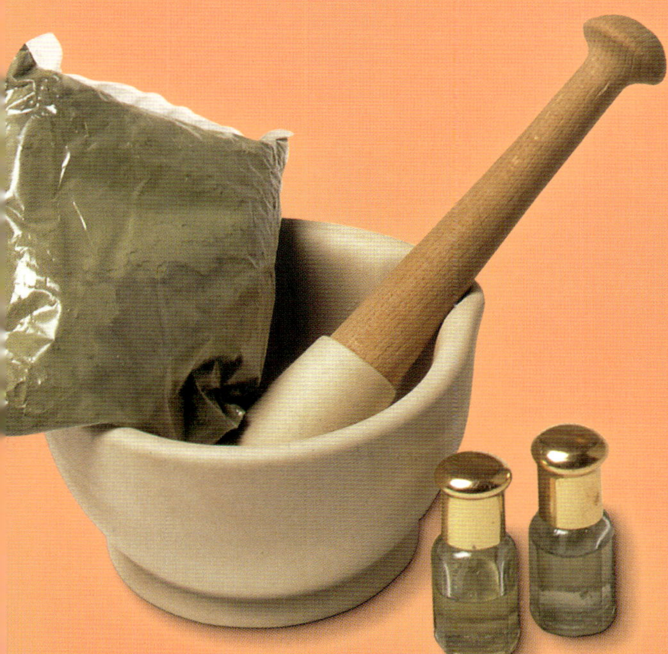

Material for making henna.

Skin tones

When staining the skin with henna, remember that if the skin tone is fairly dark, the colour obtained will range from red to rusty brown, while a henna design on a fairer skin tone will range from gold to a pale, rusty copper. Bold patterns show up better on dark skin tones, while fine, intricate patterns complement paler skin tones.

Precautions

It is unlikely that you will have an allergic reaction to henna, but if you are concerned about this, carry out a patch test on your skin first to be on the safe side. If you are pregnant, always carry out a patch test and only use pure, natural henna. Never use henna on children under the age of six months, as their skin is extremely delicate and thin.

Henna quality

There are a number of henna powders on the market, and in order to avoid being disappointed with the colour, I advise you to buy pure, natural henna which has had no chemicals or other ingredients added to it. Steer clear of stale henna, which you can recognise by its pale-orange colour.

Different-coloured hennas

It is difficult to adjust the colour of your henna mix if you want to stain your skin naturally, without the use of chemicals. For extra depth of colour, you could add reheated percolated coffee to dry henna powder or else reheated beetroot juice or the juice of any other dark root vegetable. Do not use fabric dyes, however, as these may contain chemicals.

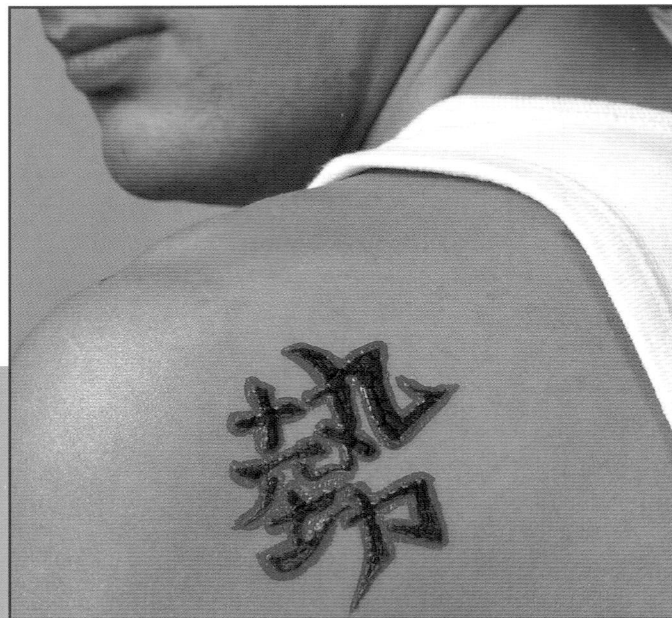

Henna designs can be enhanced with body paints.

Henna to avoid

Black henna is considered more beautiful than the Indian red henna, which comes from the same plant, but is gathered slightly differently. Because heat deepens the colour of the henna, if fresh henna is applied during very hot weather and is then left overnight (cover the henna for added heat), the combination of the heat and perspiration will naturally darken the henna until it becomes almost black. The effect is best seen on the hands and feet.

Creating very black henna is extremely hazardous because the chemicals that are required to turn henna black are highly processed and could both cause permanent skin damage and endanger your health.

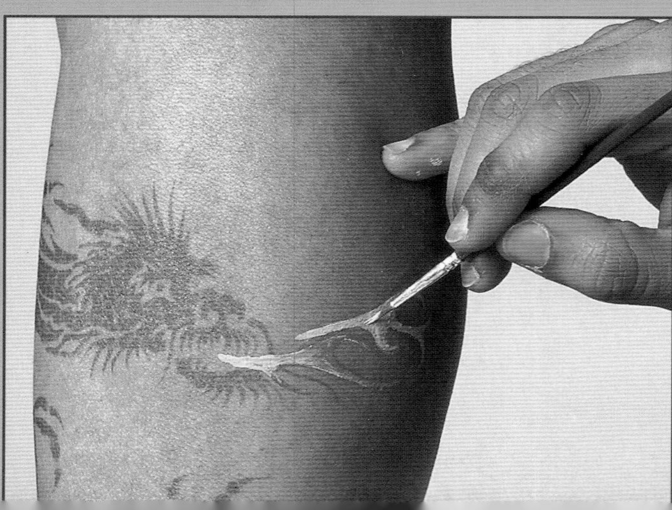

Henna on holiday

Henna reacts with chlorine and fades more quickly if you spend a lot of time in the swimming pool. If you've been swimming in salt water, the henna design may become dry, which you can correct with a good moisturiser.

The design will fade as the skin exfoliates, and because henna acts as a total sun block, once the skin has been exfoliated, you will be left with an untanned area where the design was.

Drawing your designs

There are several different ways of creating a henna design. When you begin you will probably want to use a stencil, as this will enable you to get used to the henna applicator.

Once you have gained confidence you can create designs freehand. There are pattern books available to copy, or you could try following designs in fashion books and magazines.

Once you have practised your technique you will probably want to design and try out your own patterns. It is really up to you how far you go!

Pre-mixed henna paste

You can create your own designs freehand using pre-mixed henna paste in an easy-to-use application bottle made from flexible, squeezable plastic. Not only are application bottles reusable, but you can fit different-sized tips to them to give anything from a very fine to a heavy flow.

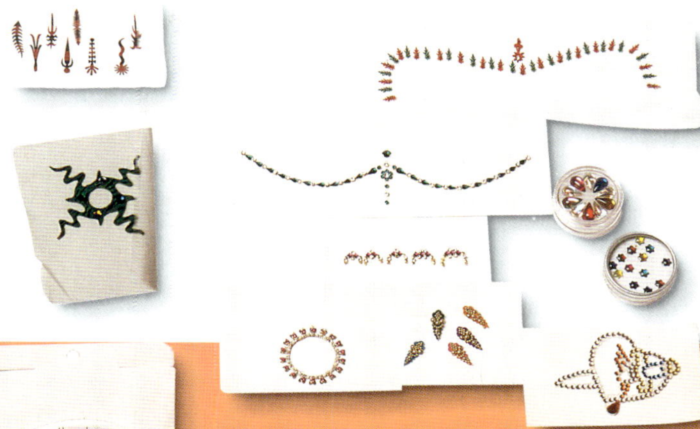

Bindis and stick-on jewellery.

Removing a henna design

If your design has not turned out as you wished, or you have grown tired of it, you can remove it by exfoliating the skin with a facial scrub and lemon juice mixed to a paste. Another tip is to use exfoliating mitts or gloves.

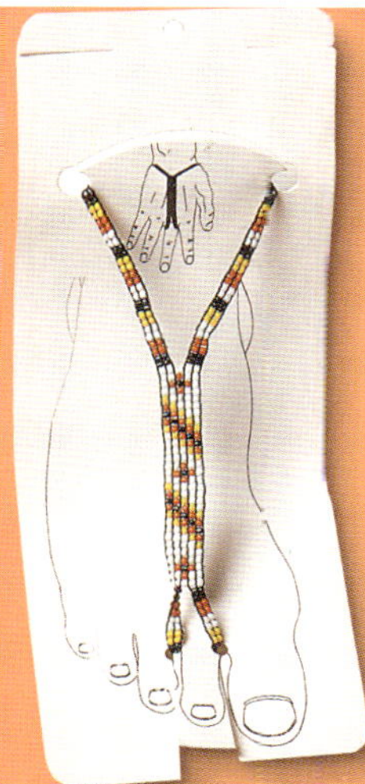

Body badge, bindis, anklet.

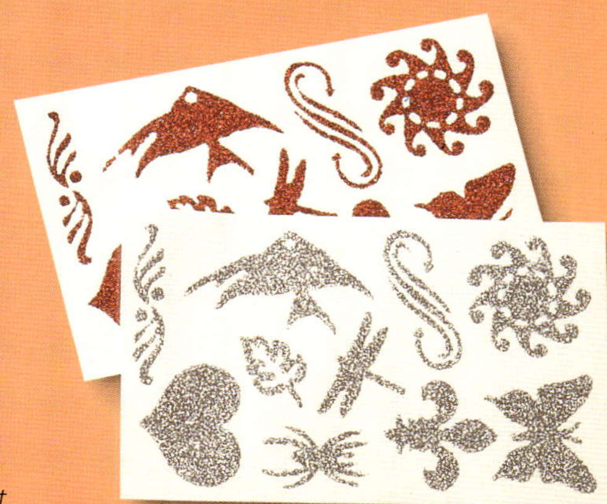

Hair tattoos.

Body jewellery

There are a number of self-adhesive body jewels available, ranging from single stones to ornate designs. These can be mixed and matched as you wish, and can be used for fun or even for more formal occasions.

Jewellery and bindis.

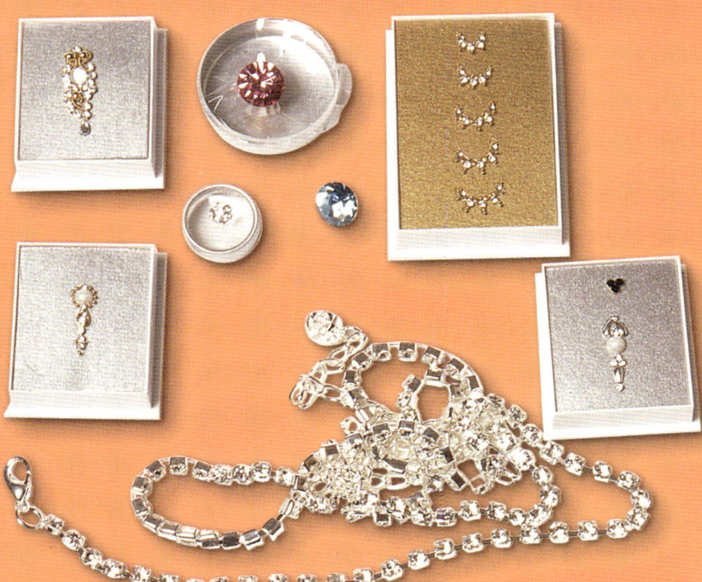

Other equipment

Finally you will need a selection of other items for preparing your skin, and removing body art. These include cotton pads, paper towels, cotton buds, alcohol solution and talcum powder.

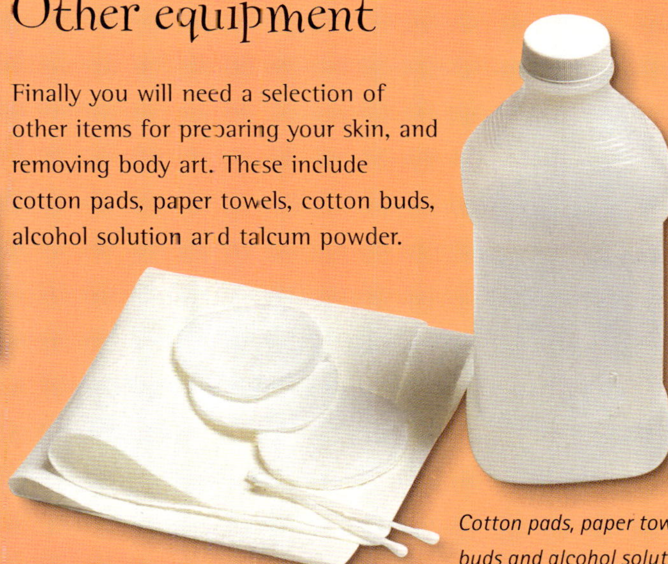

Cotton pads, paper towel, cotton buds and alcohol solution.

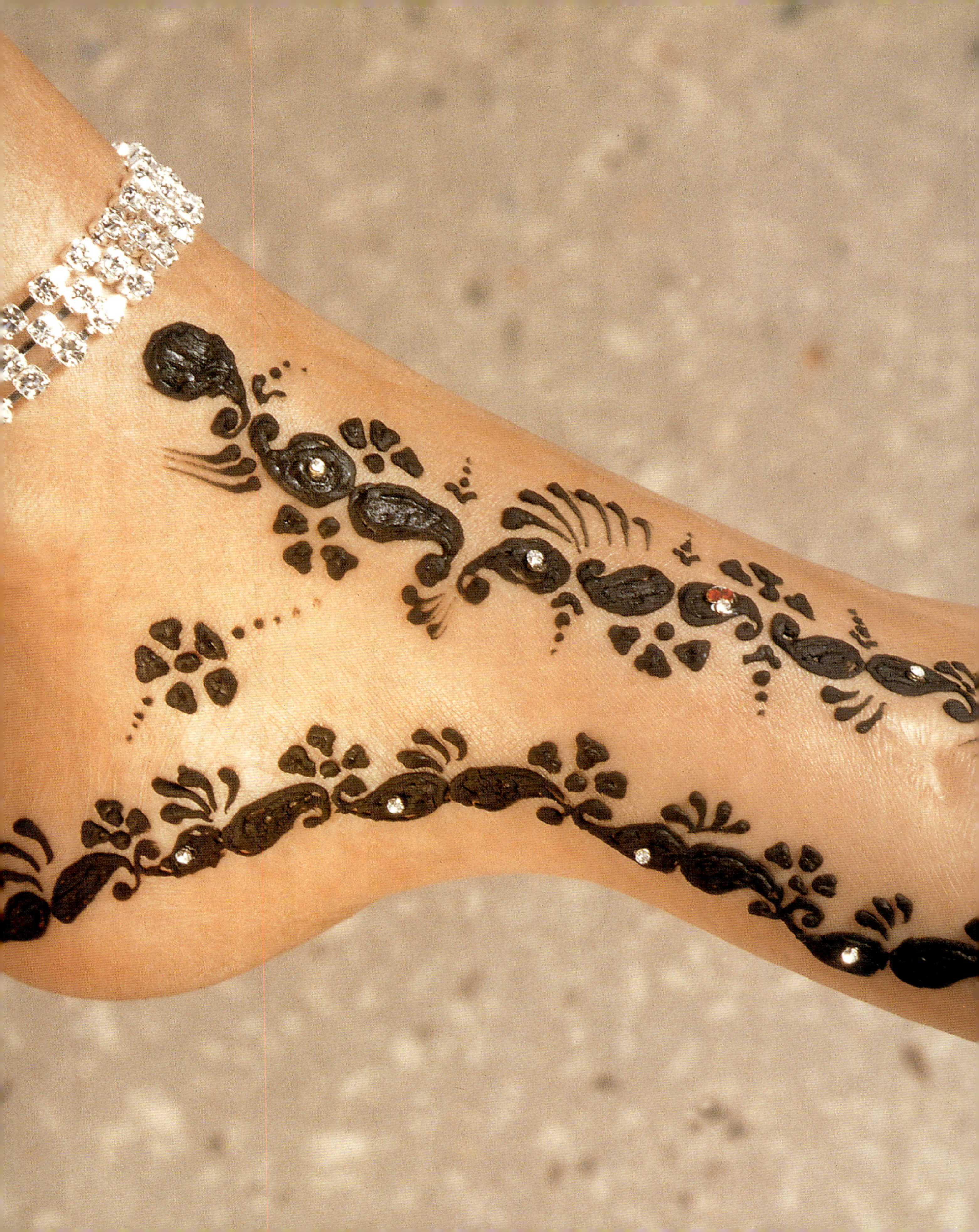

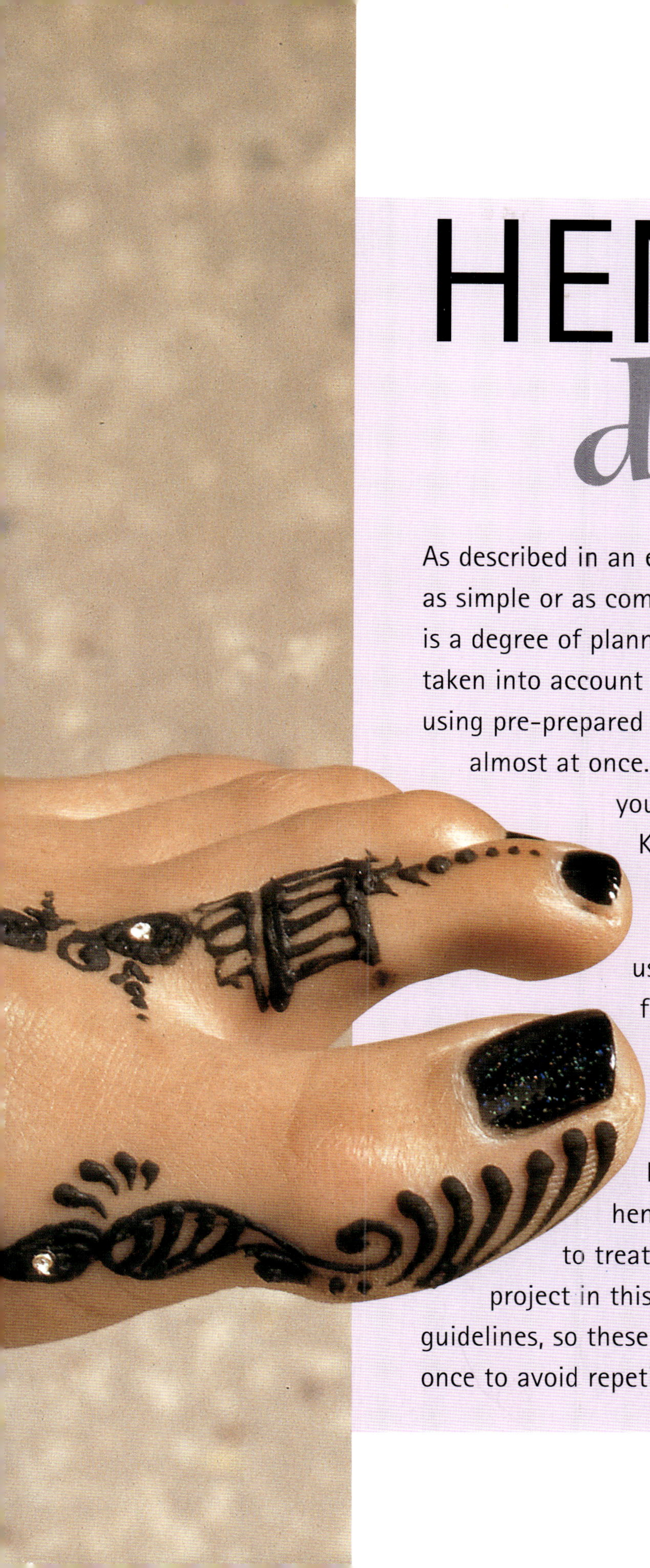

HENNA designs

As described in an earlier chapter, henna designs can be as simple or as complicated as you wish. However, there is a degree of planning and preparation that must be taken into account before you can proceed. If you are using pre-prepared henna, you can begin your design almost at once. If you are mixing the henna yourself, you will need time to mix the powder. Kits are available containing everything you need.

Your henna designs can be created using stencils, or drawing them freehand. Designs can be embellished at various stages with coloured paints, glitter and gems.

The first part of this chapter looks at how to prepare and use henna, how to seal your design and how to treat your skin before applying. Every project in this section will follow the same guidelines, so these instructions will be provided only once to avoid repetition.

Preparing and using henna

YOU WILL NEED
- Henna powder
- Strainer or sieve
- Large mixing bowl (not plastic)
- Wooden spoon
- Strained juice of two lemons or limes
- Cloth
- Hot, concentrated coffee (optional)
- Boiling water (optional)
- Icing bag or freezer-bag cone or ready-prepared henna-kit cone
- Paper towel
- Stencil (optional)
- 'New Skin' spray
- Soft tissues
- Sticky tape
- Clingfilm
- Cotton wool (optional)
- Lemon juice (optional)
- Sugar (optional)
- Distilled water

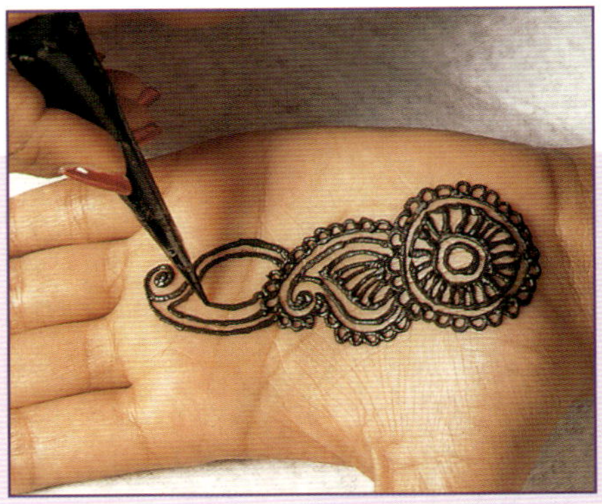

1 Empty part of the contents of the packet of henna into a strainer or sieve and sift the henna into a large mixing bowl, continuing the process until you have sifted as much as you want. Sift just enough henna powder – usually around 25g (1oz) – for the design that you want to create.

2 Make a well in the centre of the henna. Using a wooden spoon, mix in sufficient strained lemon or lime juice until the mixture has the consistency of mashed potato. Cover the bowl with a dry cloth and leave it in a cool place overnight to enable the hennotannic acid to be released.

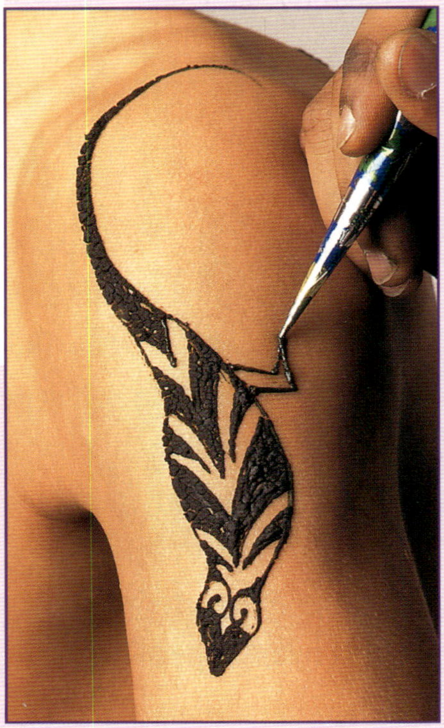

3 To achieve a smoother consistency, gradually add strained lemon juice, a few drops of hot, concentrated coffee and boiling water to the henna paste. The desired texture should resemble royal icing (i.e., not too runny).

4 Using a wooden spoon, spoon the henna paste into an icing bag, freezer-bag or henna-kit cone. (One or two spoonfuls, depending on the size of your design.)

5 Make sure that the area of skin that you are going to embellish is clean, oil-free and completely dry. Now squeeze out a few practice strokes from the icing bag onto a paper towel to ensure that the henna paste is of the correct consistency.

6 If you are feeling artistic, you could create your own design freehand, otherwise place a stencil over the area to be tattooed. Once you have completed your design, seal it by spraying on 'New Skin' (a preparation that is generally used to protect small cuts and open wounds). This will help to prevent any smudging over the next two to six hours while the henna remains on the skin.

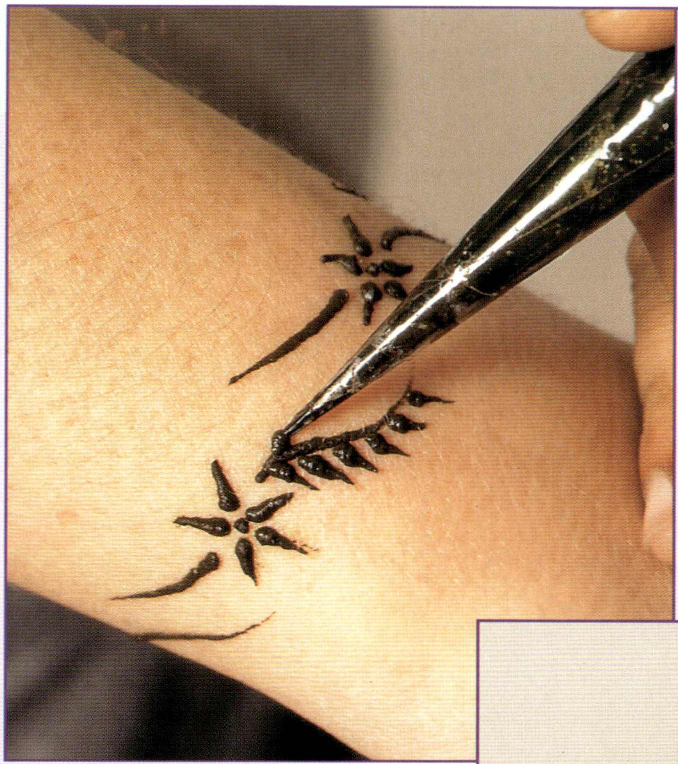

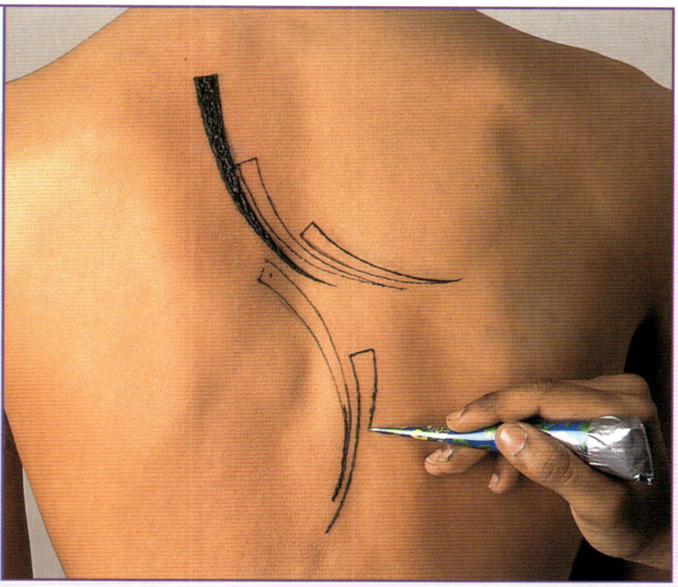

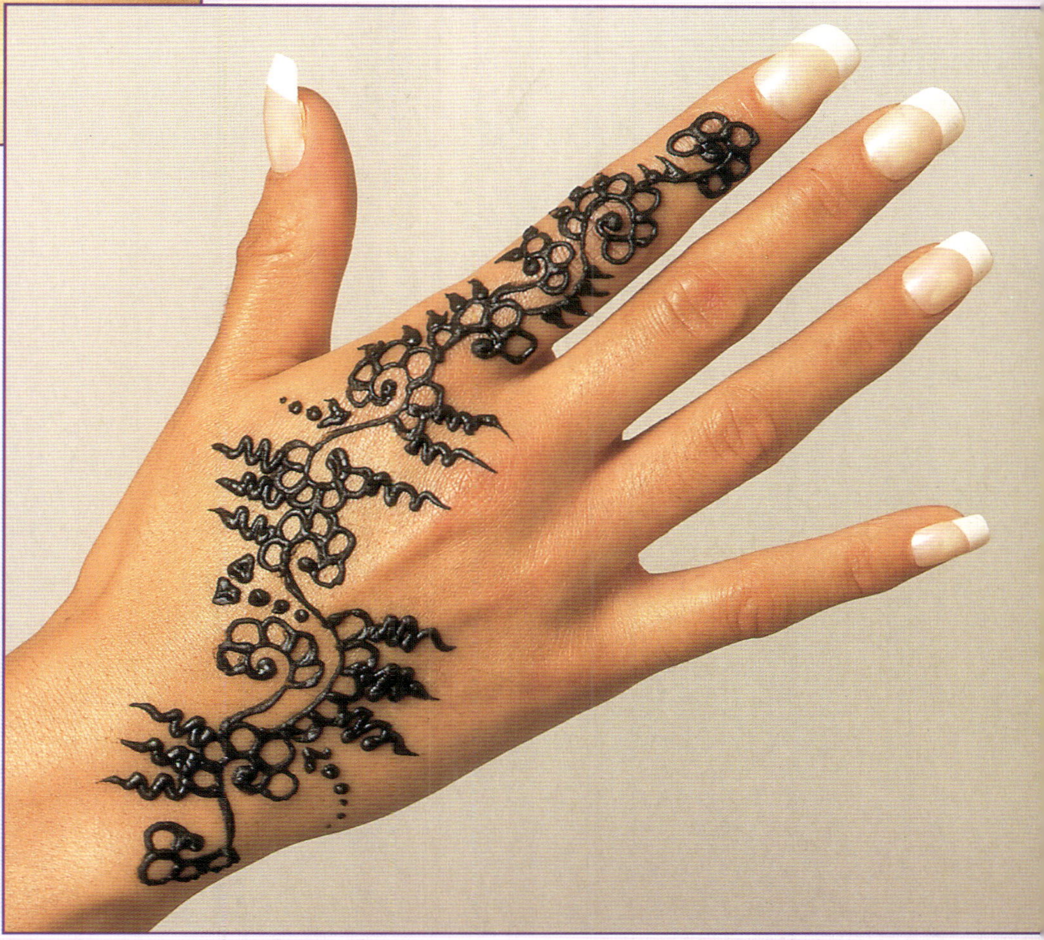

7 Gently place a soft tissue over your design and then secure it with sticky tape. Carefully wrap clingfilm around the design to encourage a build-up of heat and thus depth of colour.

8 If the weather is too hot to wrap your design in clingfilm, another way to seal it is by dabbing it with cotton wool soaked in a mixture of lemon juice and sugar (boiled to a syrup and allowed to cool). Repeat the process several times until a crunchy coating covers the design.

9 The longer you keep the design sealed (ideally overnight), the darker and longer-lasting it will be. Remove the clingfilm and tissue and then gently brush off the dried henna. Finally, rinse the design with distilled water.

Preparing the body for henna application

Before you apply henna to the skin, you need to follow some preparation steps. These will apply to every project that uses henna.

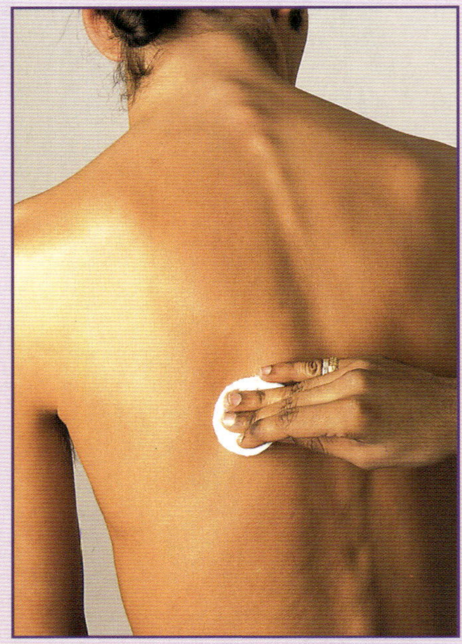

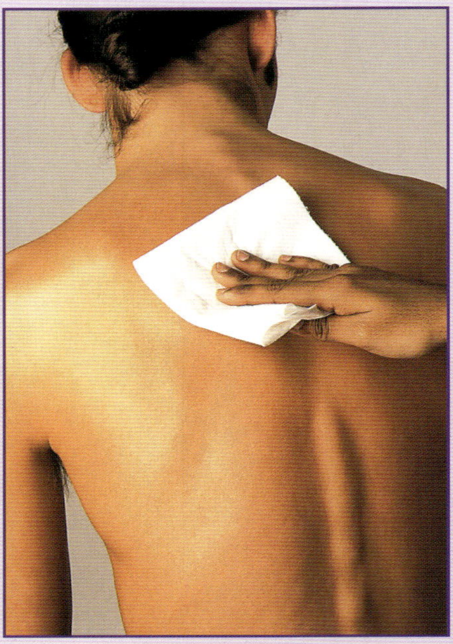

YOU WILL NEED
- Cotton pads
- Alcohol solution (witch hazel)
- Paper towels
- Henna (eucalyptus) oil

1 Cleanse the area on which you are going to place your design.

2 Pat the skin dry – it must dry completely before moving on to the next step.

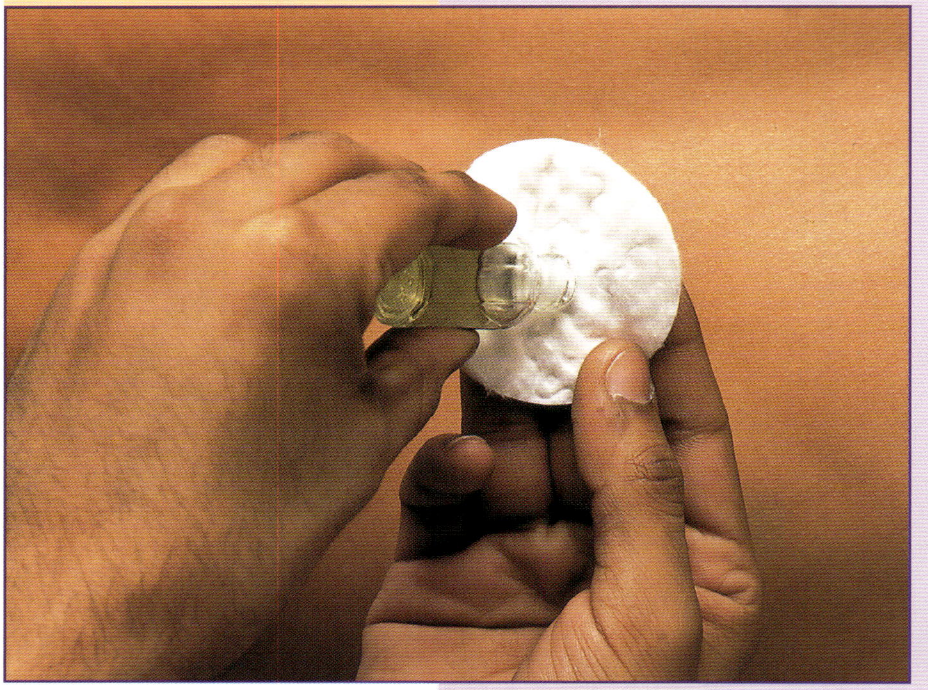

3 Apply a few drops of henna oil to a cotton pad and then dab it onto the area of skin on which you want to create your design.

4 Prepare the henna powder (as described on pp14–15) and then transfer it to the cone applicator.

Henna application method

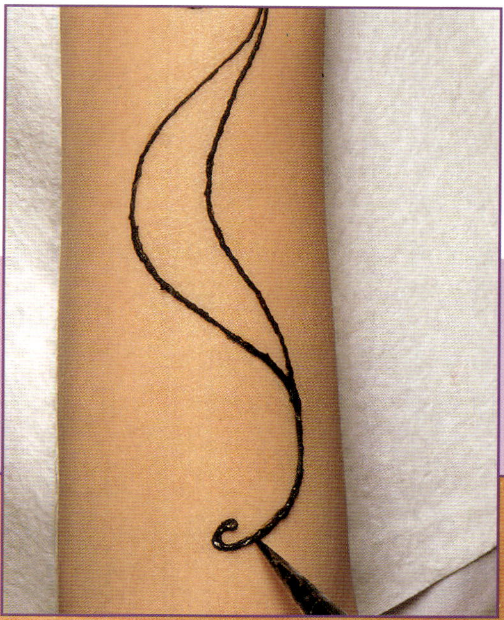

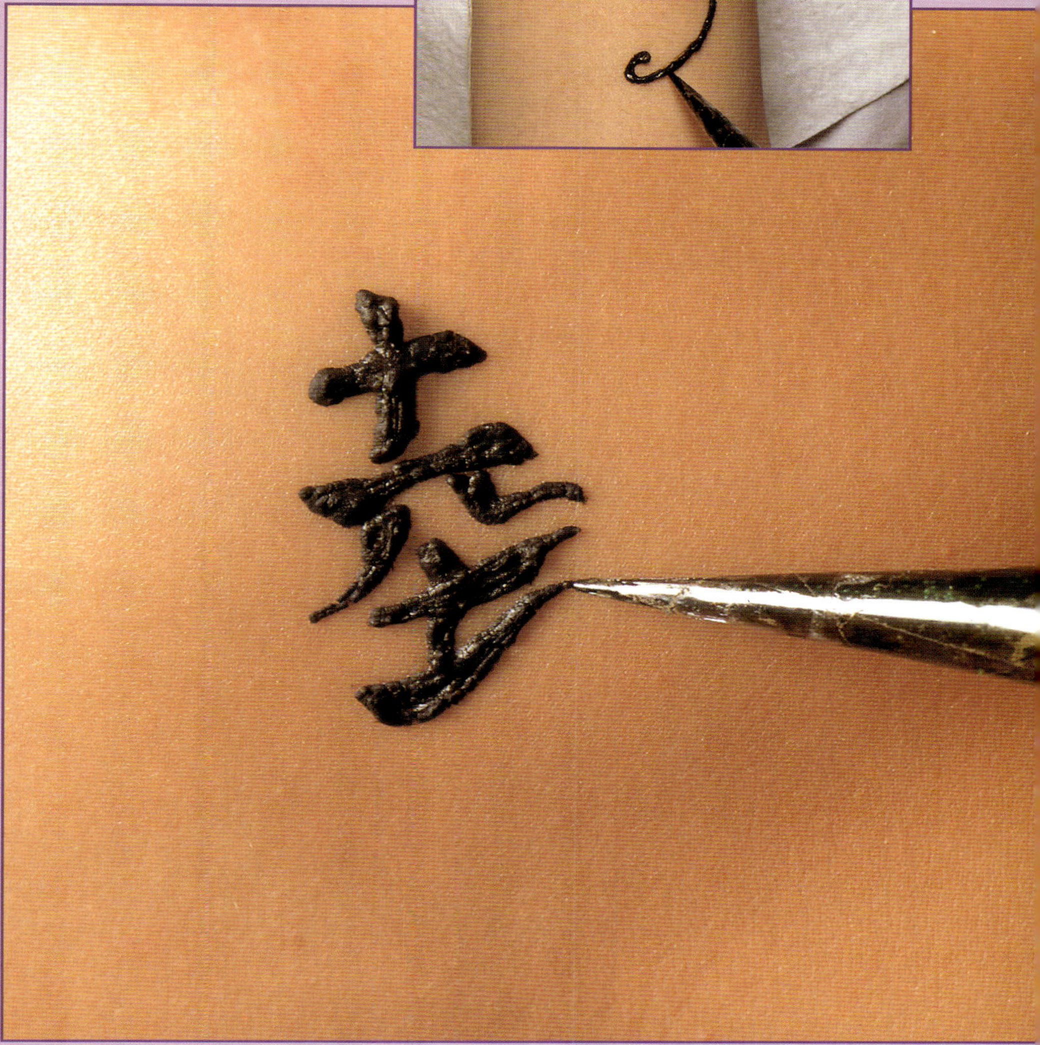

This technique will apply to all the henna projects in this section. Practice until you are confident before trying any of the designs.

1 Prepare the henna powder as in the previous project, and then transfer it to the bottle applicator.

2 Slowly draw the outline of your design, either freehand or with the help of a stencil, using even pressure to squeeze out the henna mixture. Allow fifteen to thirty minutes for the henna to dry. If you are using a stencil, then carefully remove and clean it.

3 Using a cotton pad, lightly apply the sealant to your design (see p15).

4 To avoid diluting its intensity of colour, do not wash the design for at least twenty-four hours, although you can lightly wipe it with moist-tissue or baby wipes. It can take from anything from twenty-four to forty-eight hours for henna to darken.

Daisy chain

This is a pretty design that is easier than it first appears. For all wrist and arm designs, you may find it easier to mark around the arm before you begin so that the design stays even.

YOU WILL NEED
- Cotton pads
- Alcohol solution (witch hazel)
- Henna (eucalyptus) oil
- Henna and applicator
- Sealant

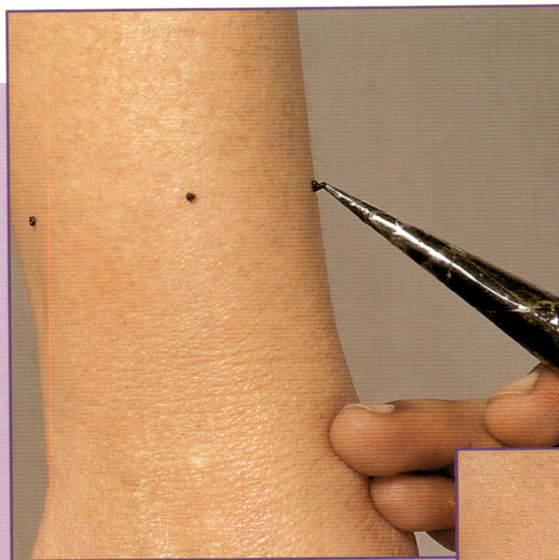

1 First mark up the position of your design around the arm using small dots of henna.

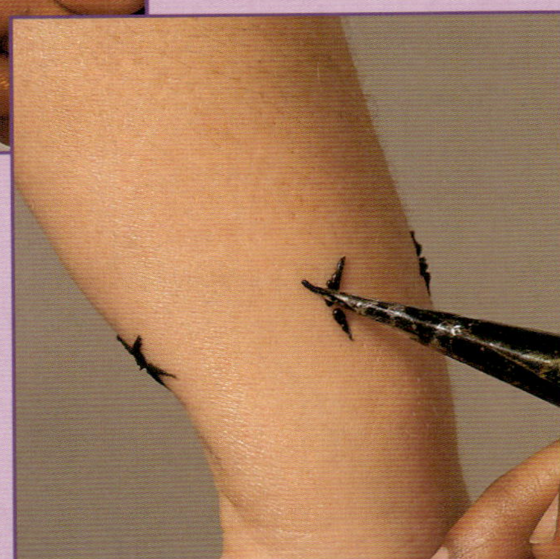

2 Begin drawing your daisies. Use slow, gentle strokes.

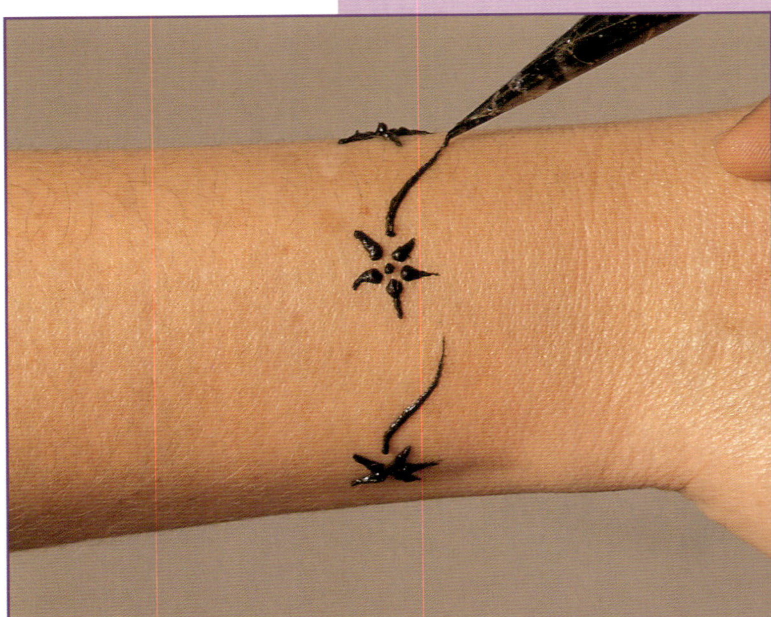

3 Now add the first row of stems.

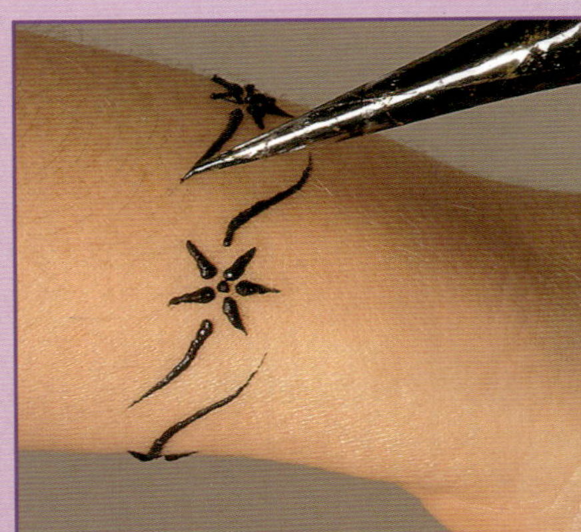

4 Continue the design further by adding another row of stem lines.

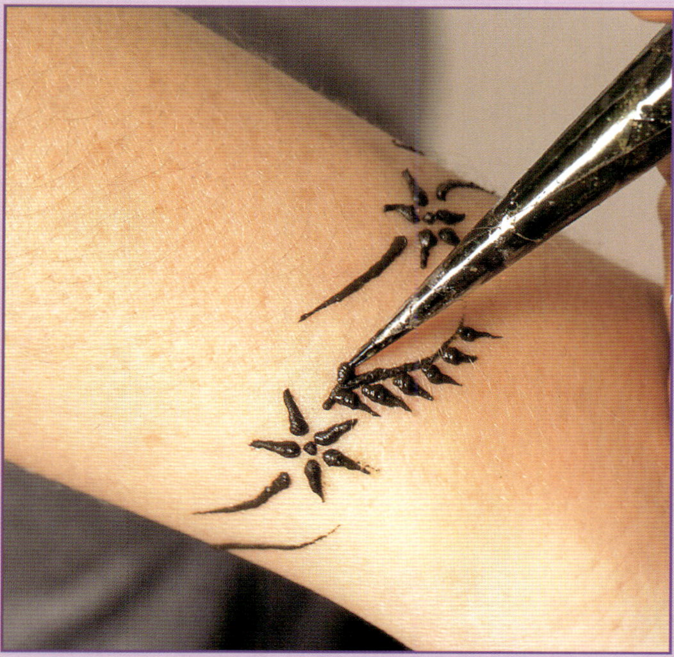

5 Add lines for the leaves at the top and bottom of each stemline.

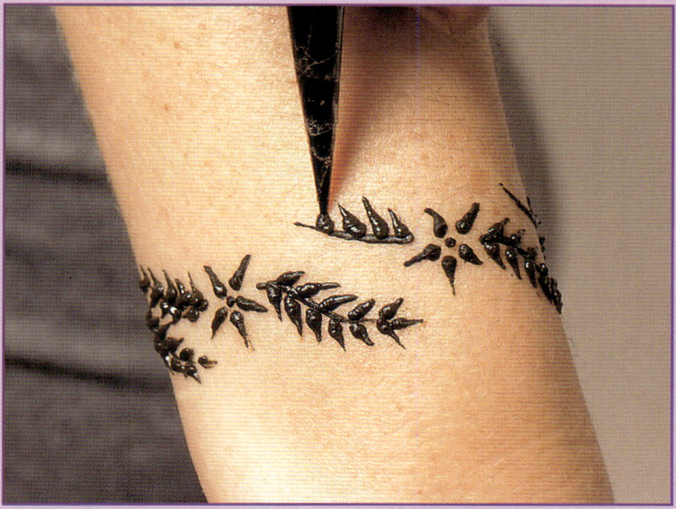

6 Add more if required. Keep the strokes steady to maintain an even pattern.

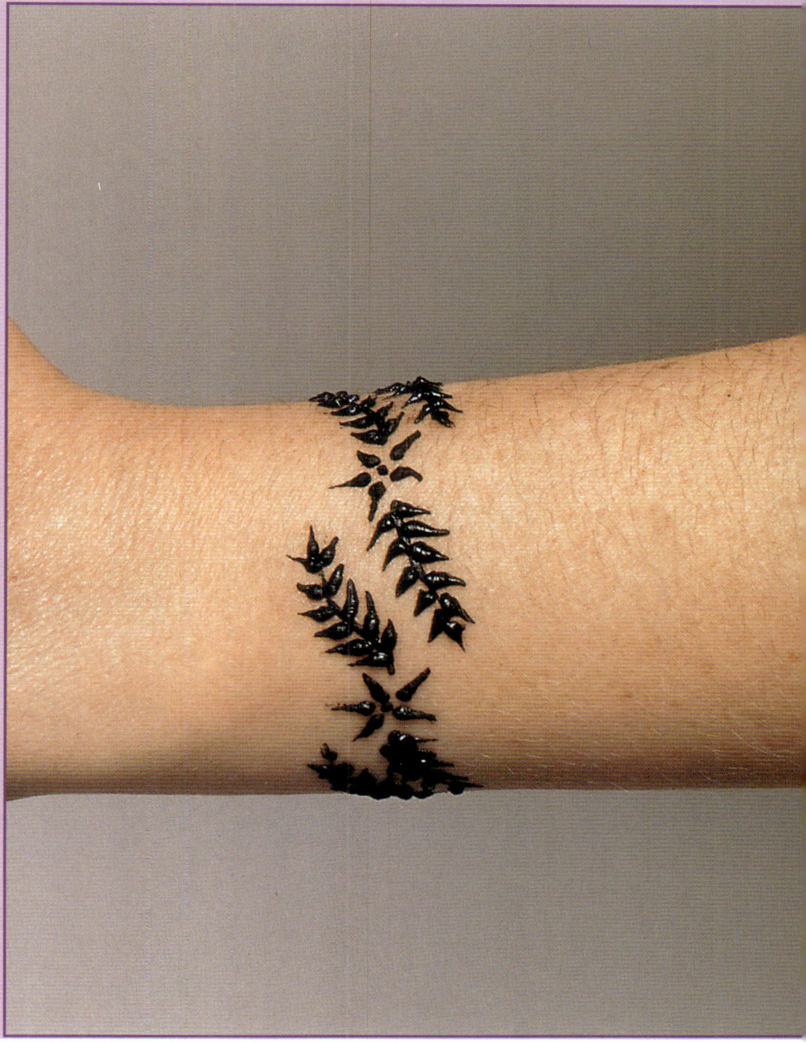

Lizard

The lizard is a popular design, particularly with men. You can buy a stencil, or you can draw the design freehand. After some practice, following a design from a pattern book or drawing can be quite easy.

YOU WILL NEED
- Cotton pads
- Alcohol solution (witch hazel)
- Henna and applicator
- Sealant

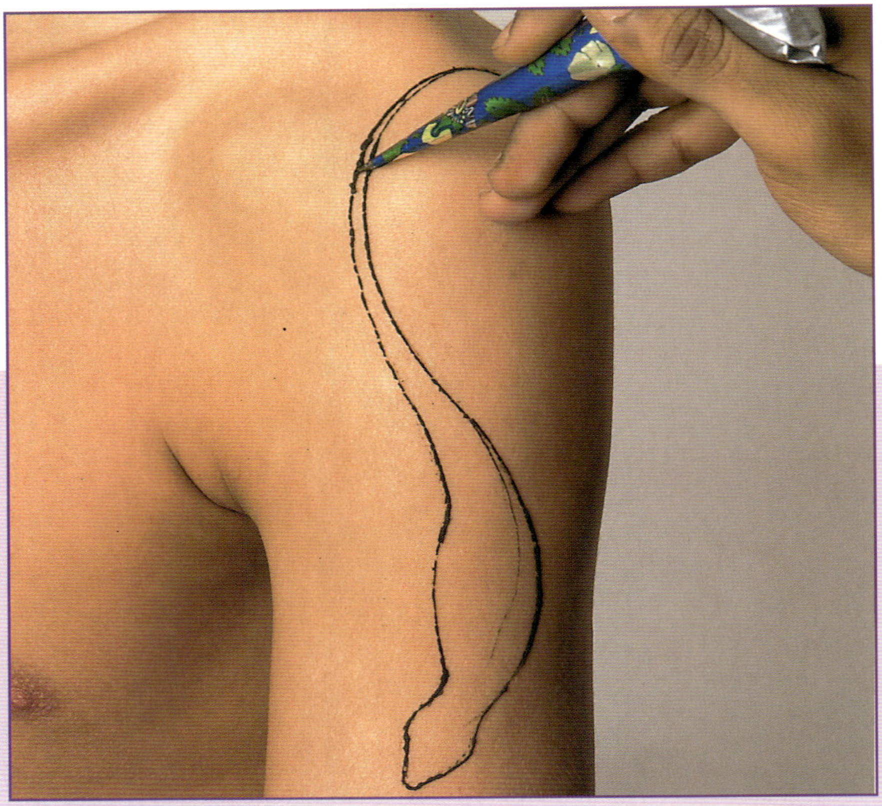

1 Ensure that the area on which you are going to place your design is oil-free by cleansing, drying and dabbing with henna oil. Slowly draw the outline of your design, using even pressure to squeeze out the henna mixture.

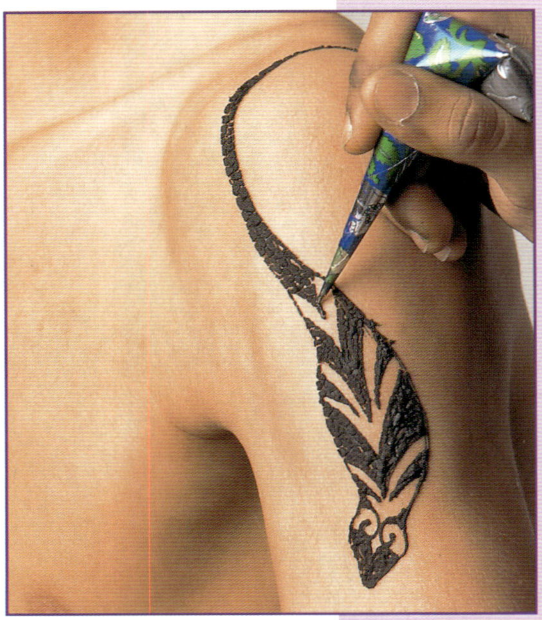

2 Carefully complete the body of your lizard.

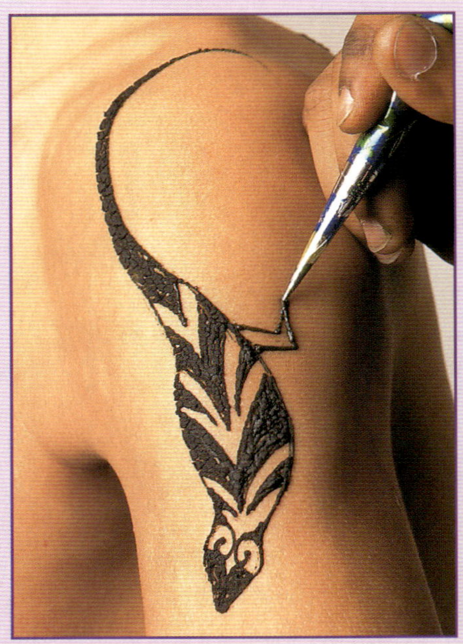

3 Now begin to draw the legs.

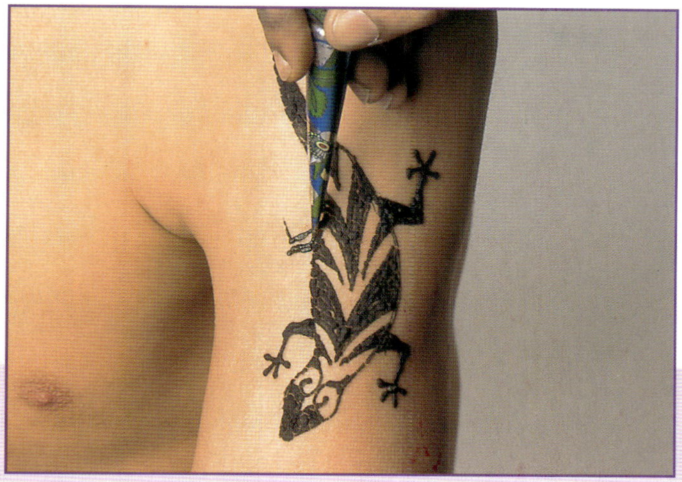

4 Make sure you keep the legs evenly spaced.

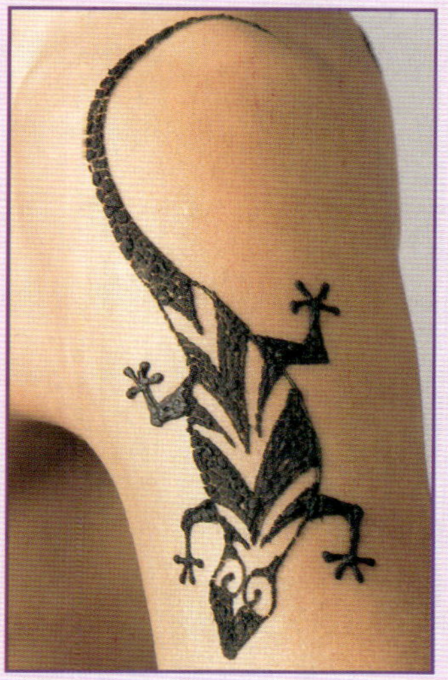

5 Once the design is finished, apply the sealant.

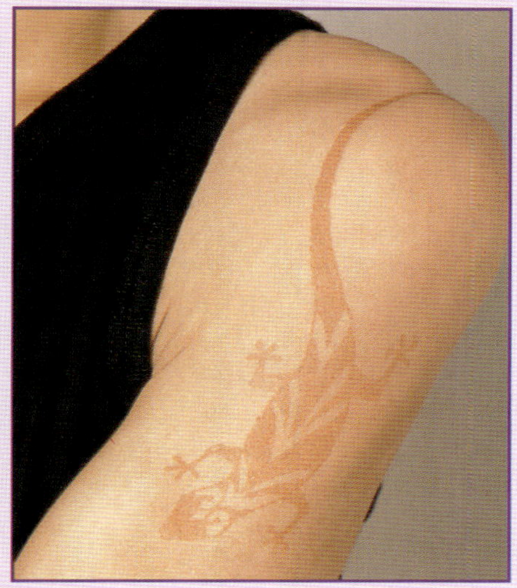

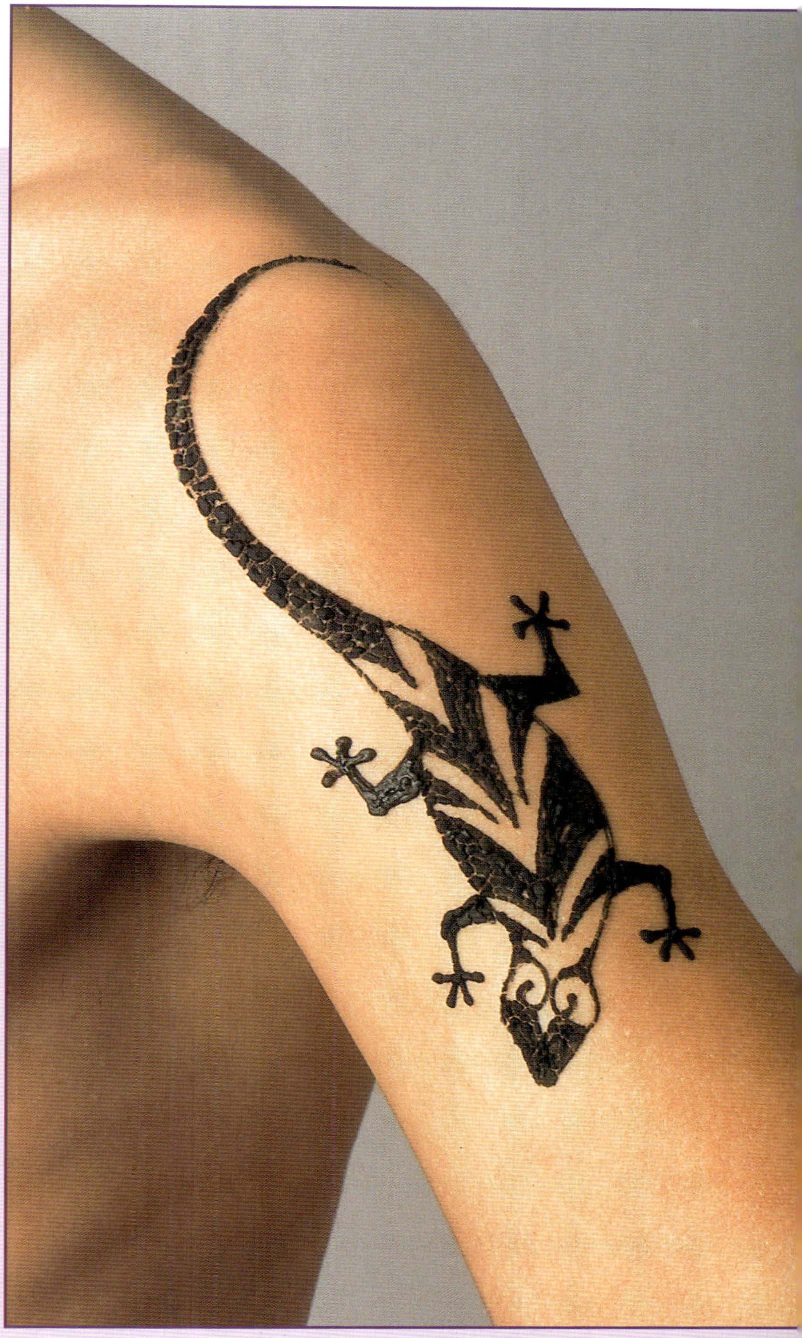

6 This is the design after 24 hours.

Hand design

Here is another beautiful and intricate pattern. You will find it is quite easy to follow, but do take care and keep your hand steady. If you are uncertain about creating the full design first time, why not try a small section of the design as a pattern on its own?

YOU WILL NEED

- Cotton pads
- Alcohol solution (witch hazel)
- Henna (eucalyptus) oil
- Henna and applicator
- Sealant

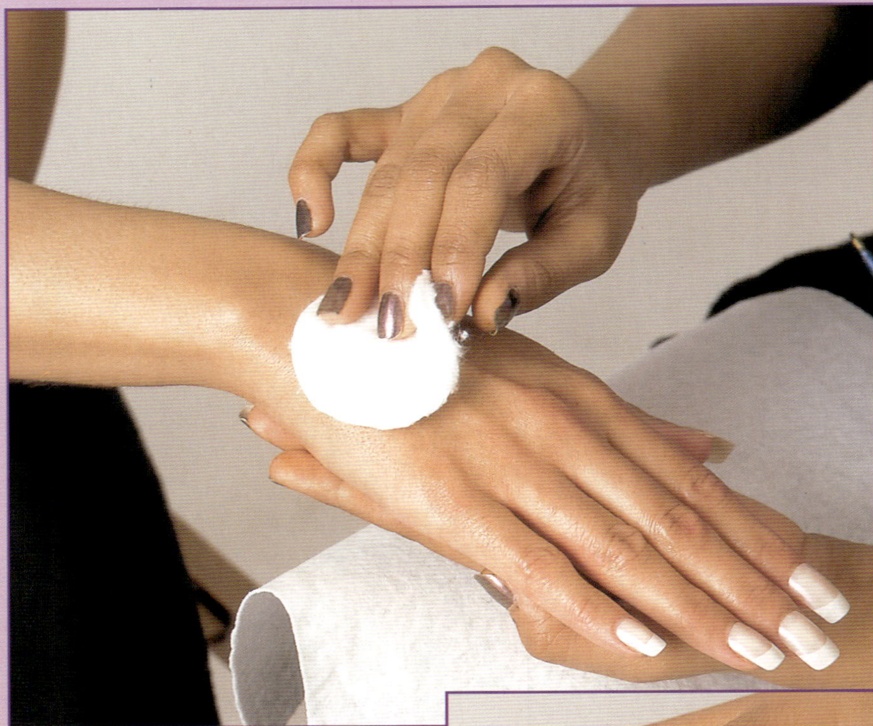

1 Cleanse the area on which you are going to place your design by wiping it with a cotton pad dipped in alcohol solution.

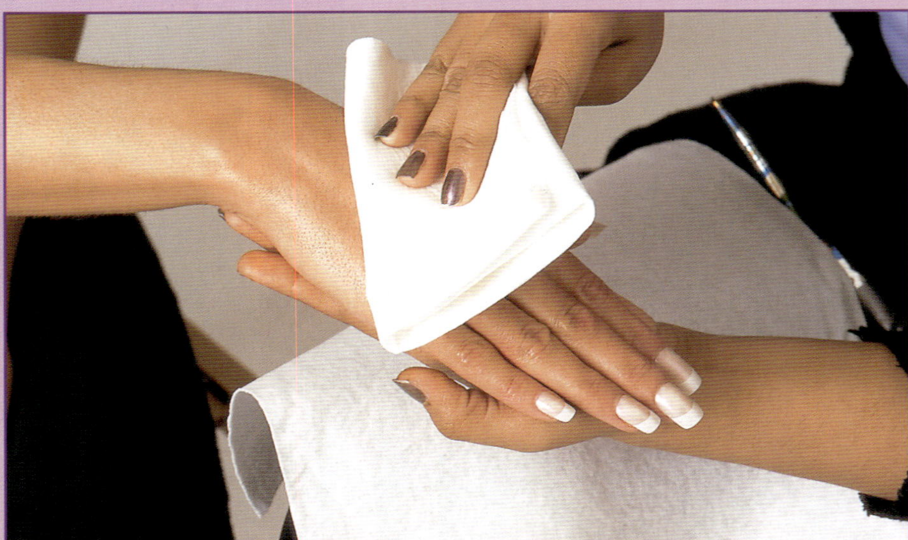

2 Pat the skin dry using a paper towel.

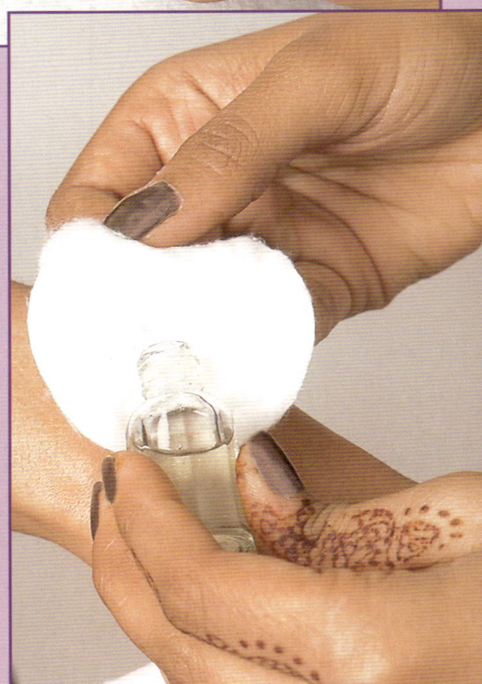

3 Apply a few drops of henna oil to a cotton pad and then dab it onto the area of skin on which you want to create your design.

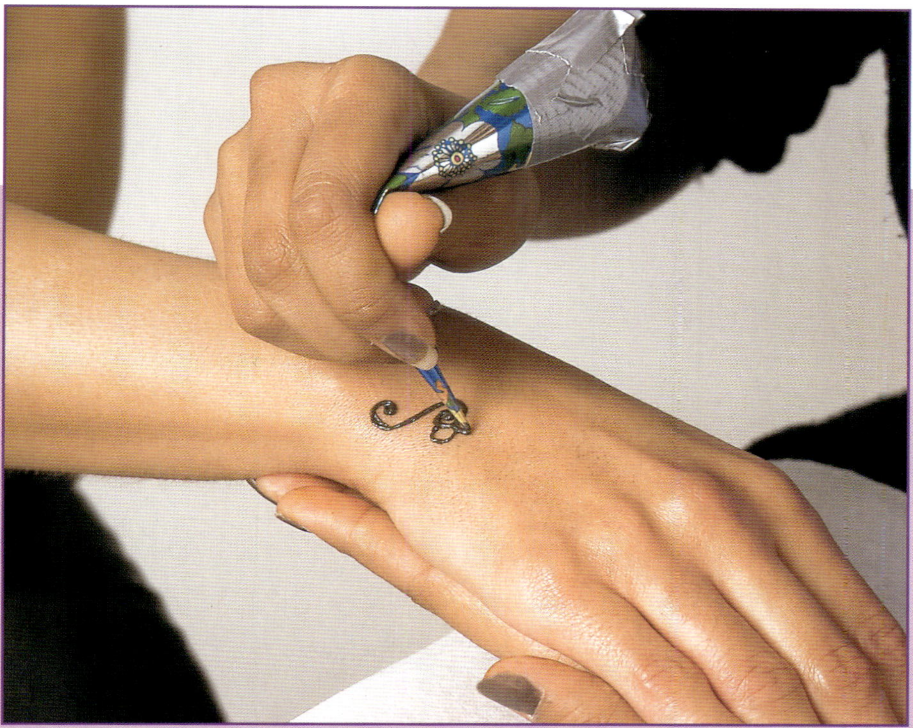

4 Begin the design. It is a good idea to begin in the centre of the hand so that you can keep the design balanced.

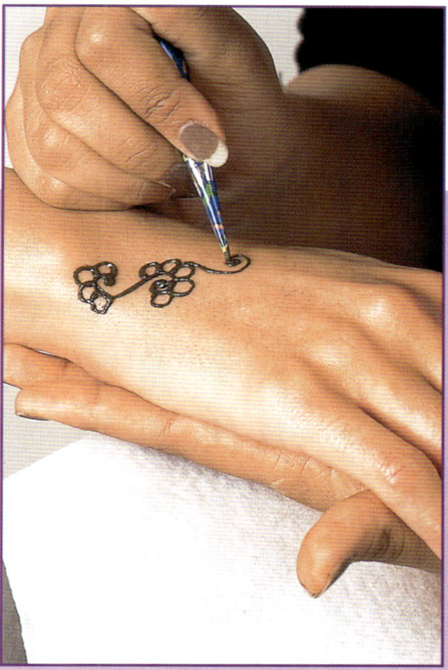

5 Work on the main part of the design first.

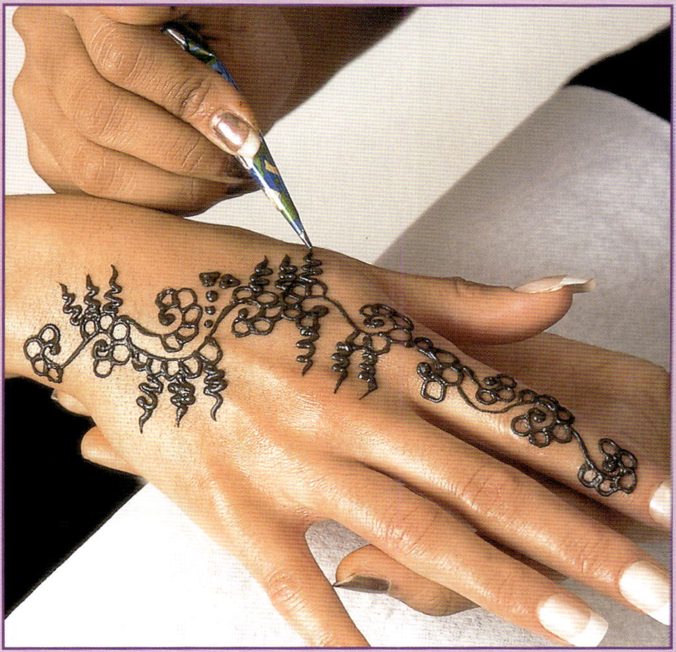

6 Once your basic design is complete, embellish with additional patterns as you wish.

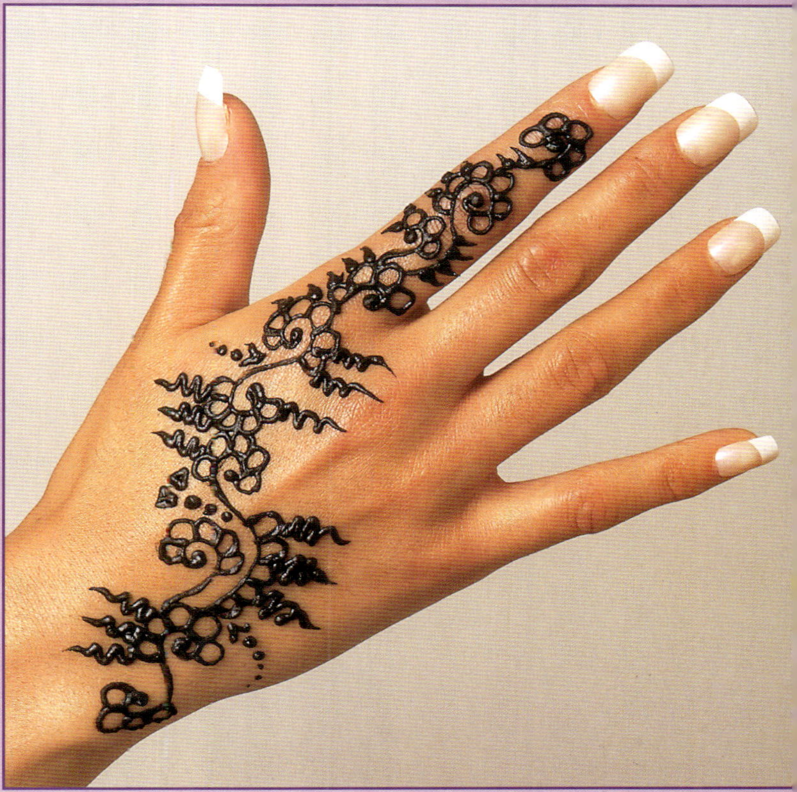

Jewelled foot

This is a pretty henna design which covers the top and side of the foot. Here we are using gems to enhance the finished design. This is quite a short-lived decoration, as even with care the henna will brush off. As it does so, you will have to be careful not to lose the gems!

YOU WILL NEED

- Cotton pads
- Alcohol solution (witch hazel)
- Henna and applicator
- Sealant
- Gems

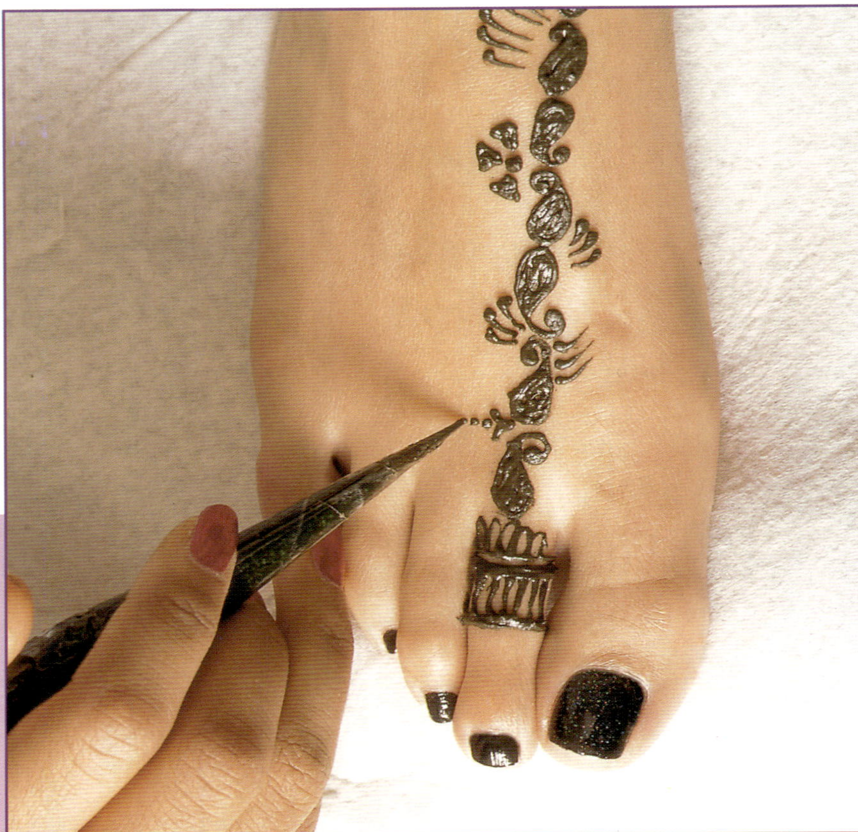

1 Cleanse, dry and oil as described on p16.

2 Begin the design across the top of the foot.

3 Continue design onto the side of the foot, using slow, delicate movements.

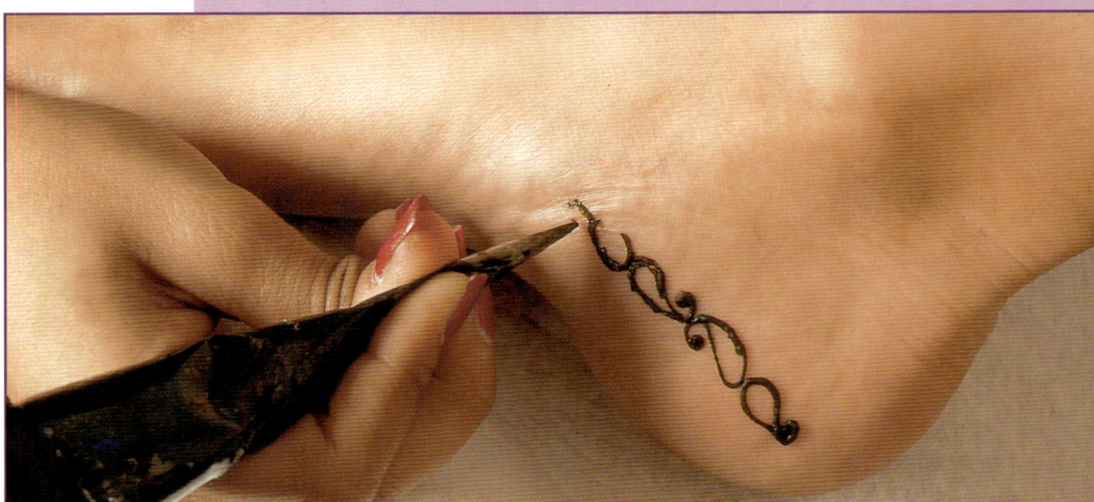

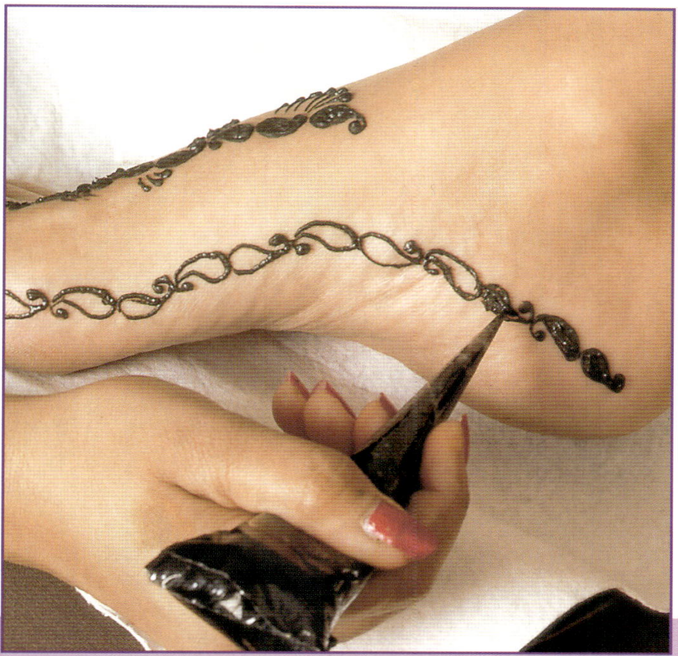

4 Fill in the pattern at the side of the foot to match the top.

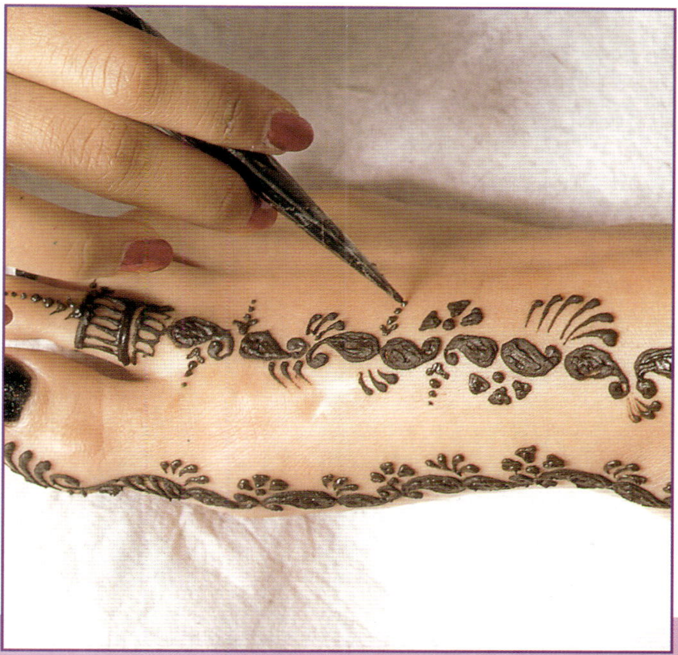

5 Add final embellishments as you wish before adding gems.

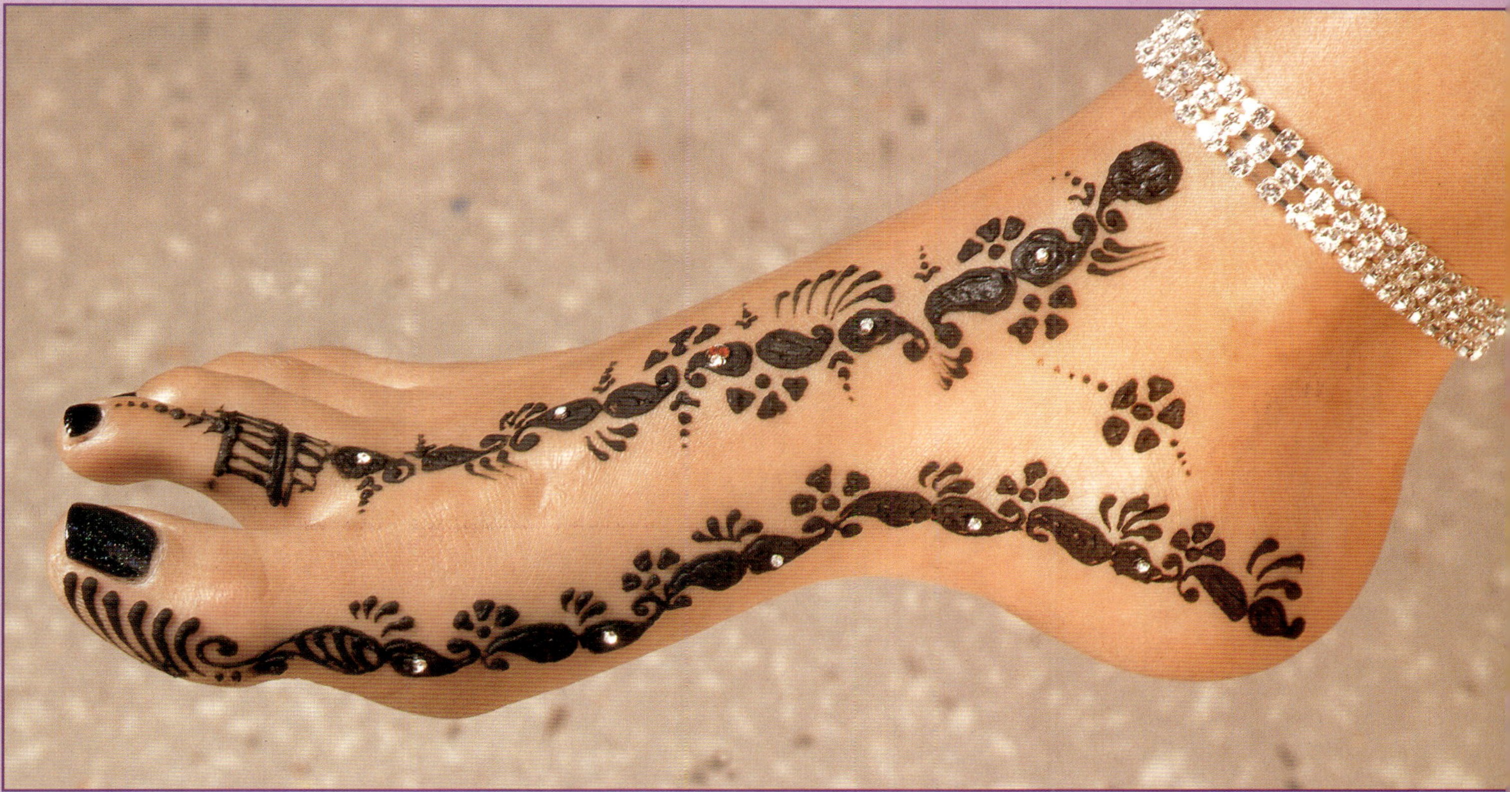

Barbed wire

Barbed-wire designs can be created in almost any size. For example, to make an armband, bracelet, ring or choker.

YOU WILL NEED

- Cotton pads
- Alcohol solution (witch hazel)
- Henna (eucalyptus) oil
- Henna and applicator
- Sealant

1 Cleanse, dry and oil the skin as described on pp16–17.

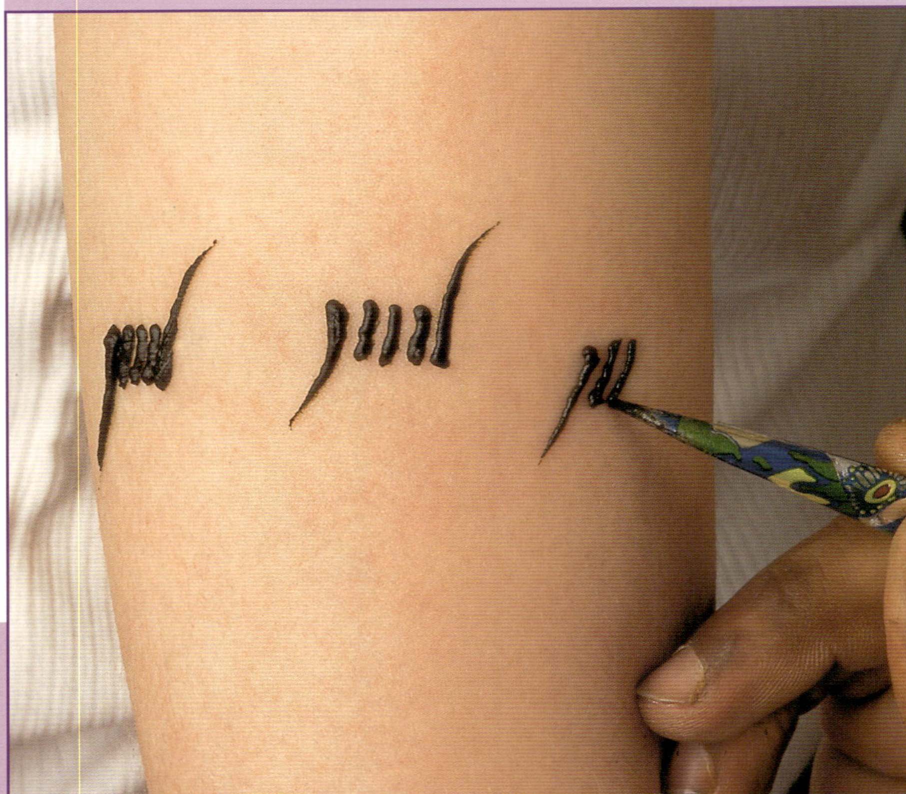

2 Begin the design by drawing vertical strokes at regular intervals.

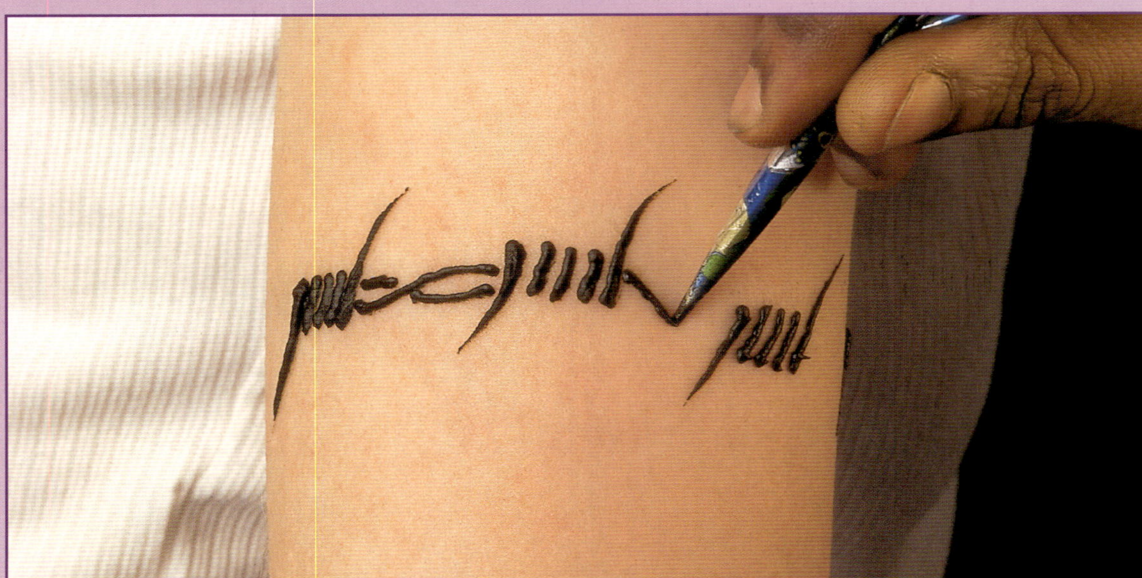

3 Now add horizontal curves between the vertical lines.

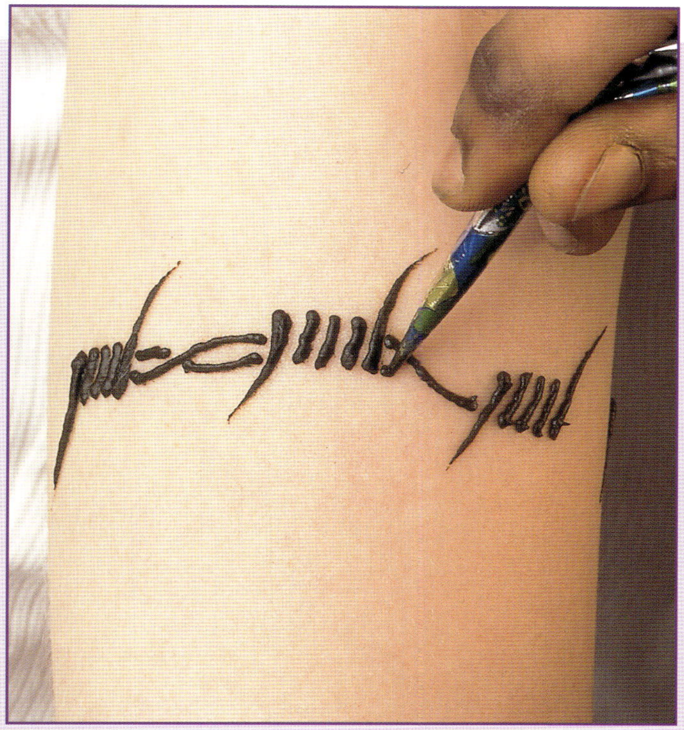

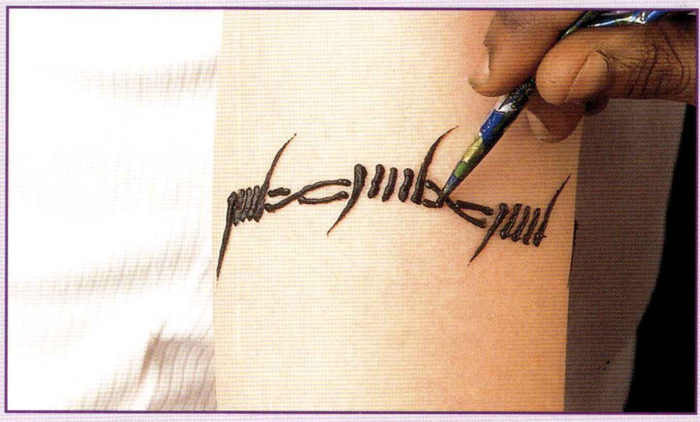

5 Finish off by filling in any remaining gaps.

4 These curves show how easily the design is created.

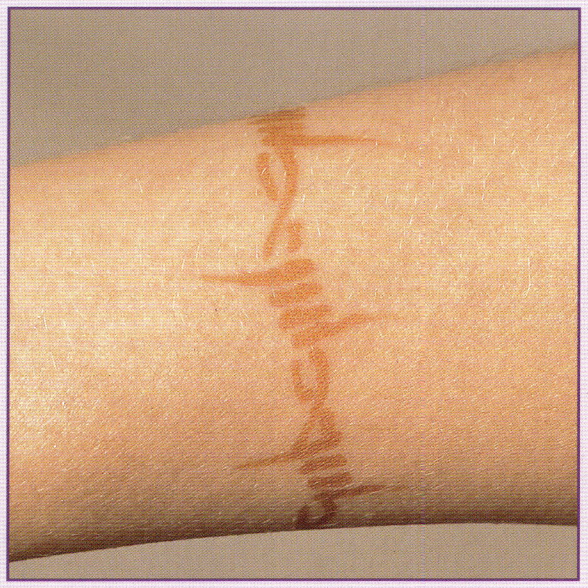

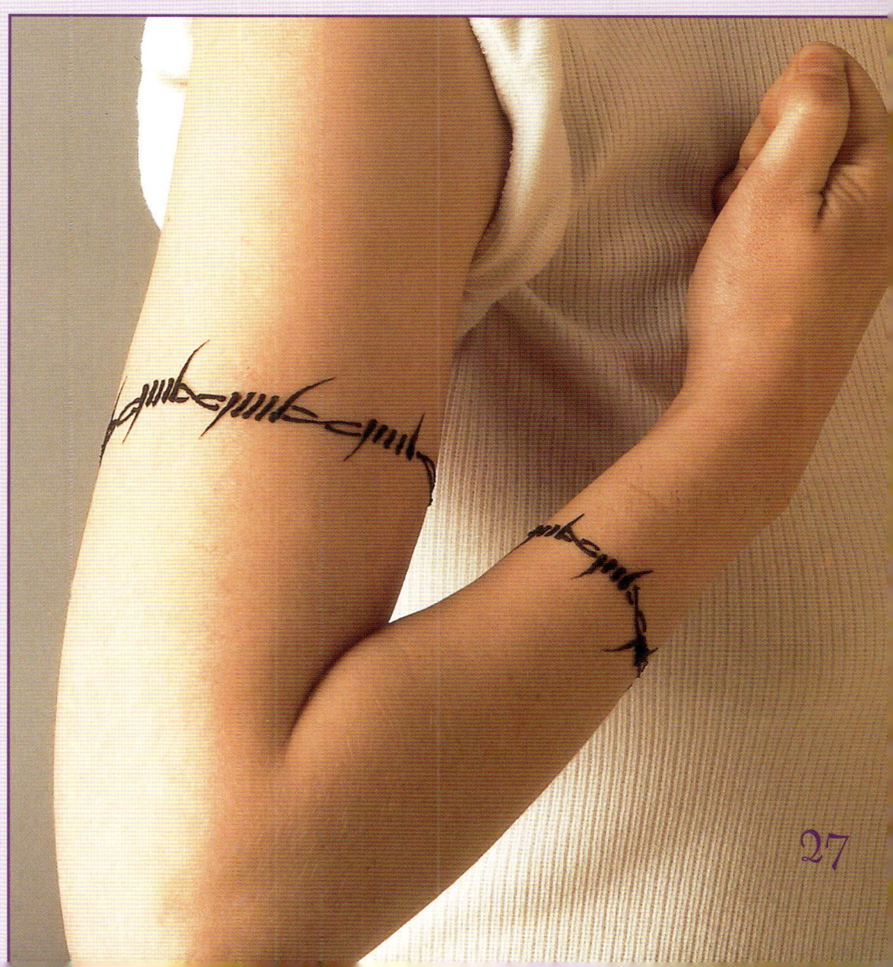

6 This is the design after 24 hours.

Henna palm design

Many of the traditional henna or mehndi designs use intricate patterns on the hands. Here we are drawing on the palm for a discreet, yet beautiful effect.

YOU WILL NEED
- Cotton pads
- Alcohol solution (witch hazel)
- Sealant
- Henna and applicator

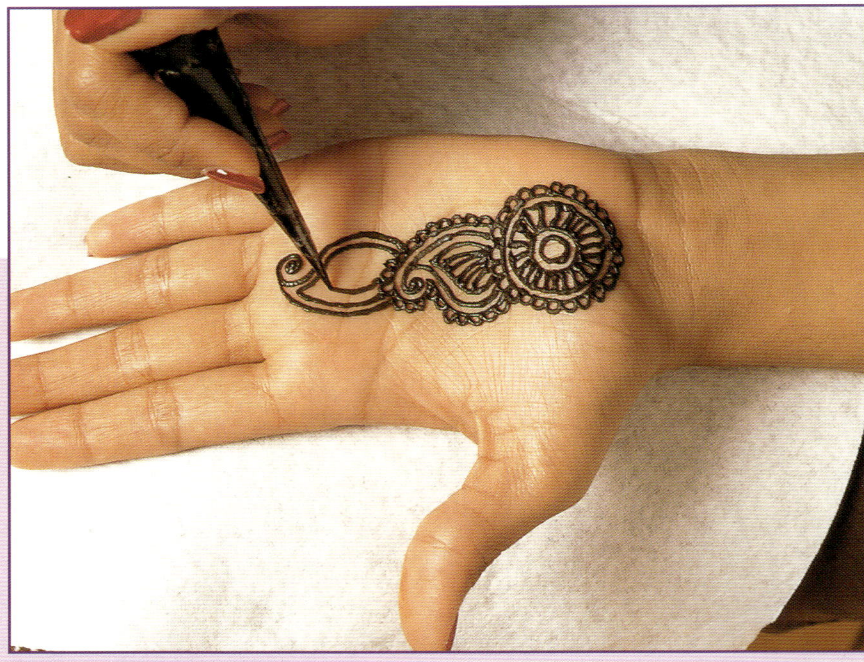

1 Following the instructions on pp16-17, begin your freehand design.

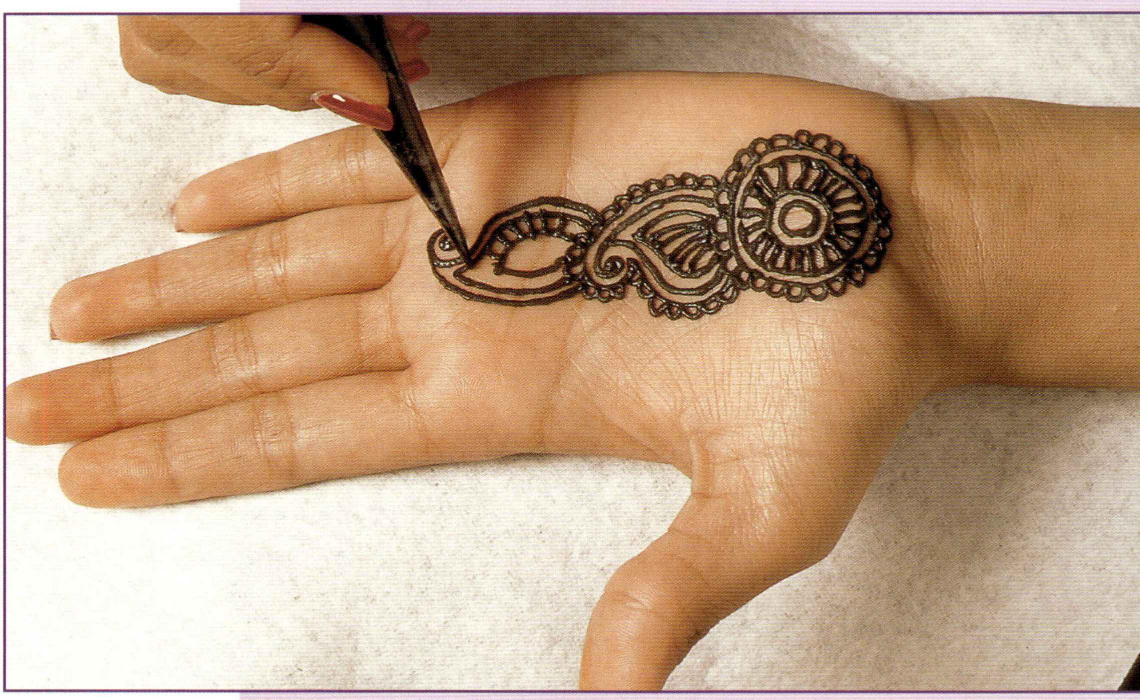

2 Slowly continue the pattern.

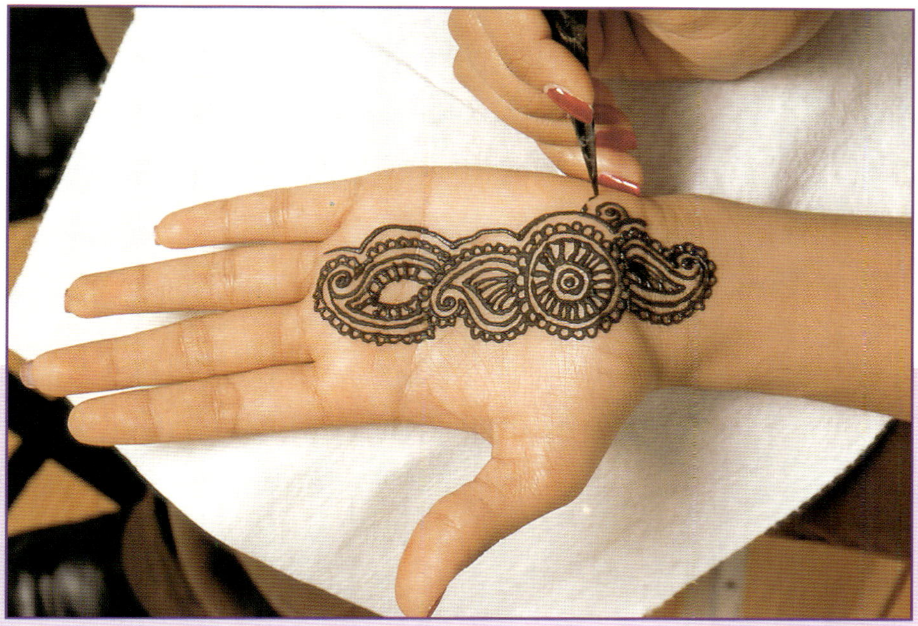

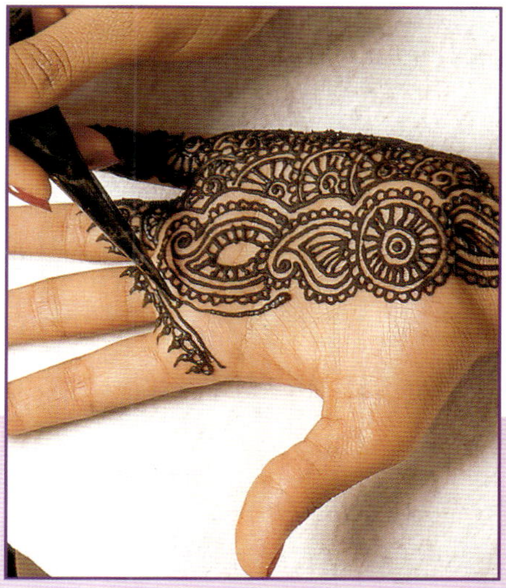

4 Finish the design so you have covered the palm as evenly as possible.

3 Let the henna flow smoothly onto your skin – try to avoid creating blobs.

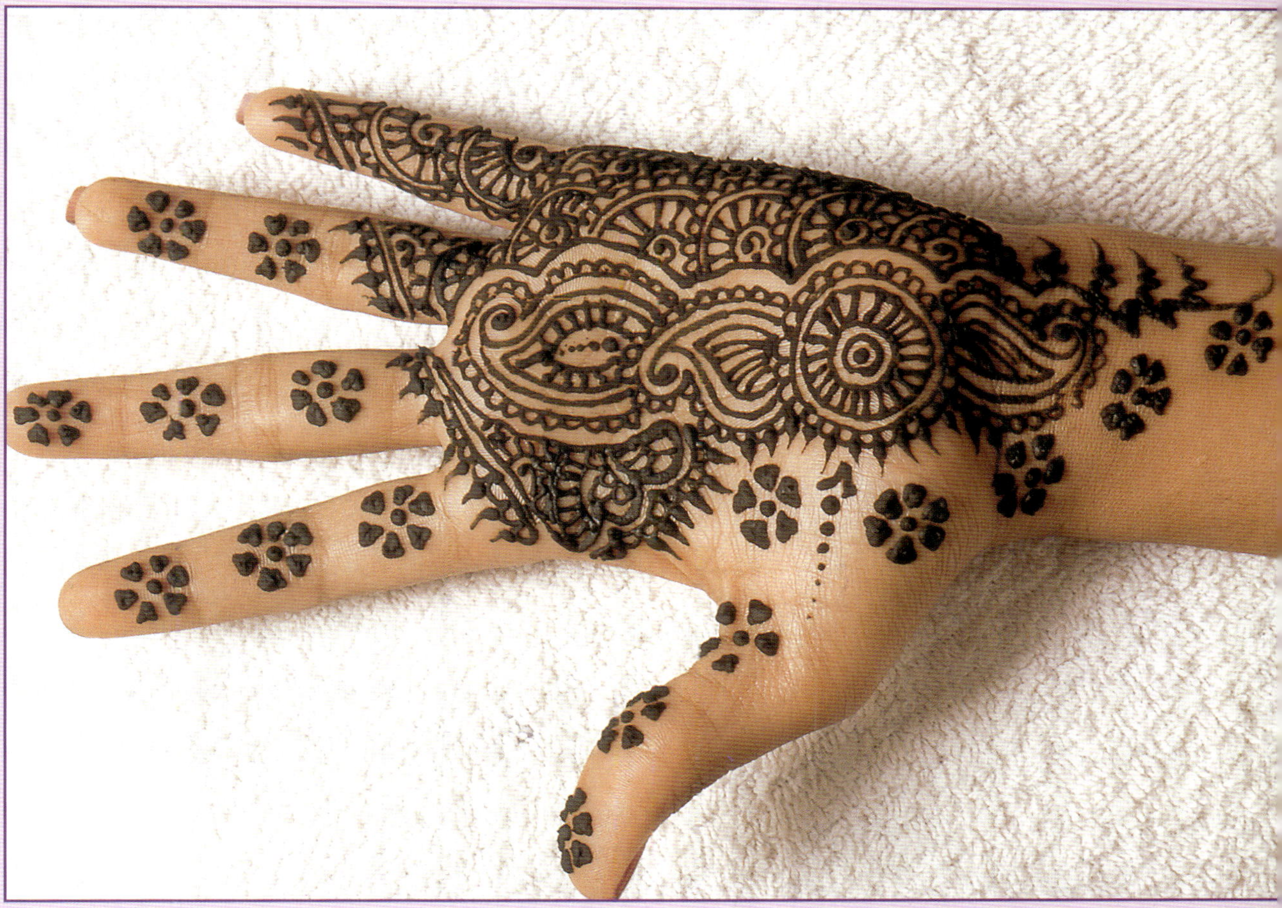

Oriental designs

Inspired by Chinese and Japanese characters, these symbols represent concepts ranging from love, peace and happiness to astrology. If you see one that you like, try to discover its meaning before applying it to your body. You can either outline these designs using a stencil or draw them freehand. The character shown here means 'Power'. Body paints can be used to enhance the henna design.

YOU WILL NEED
- Cotton pads
- Alcohol solution (witch hazel)
- Henna and applicator
- Sealant

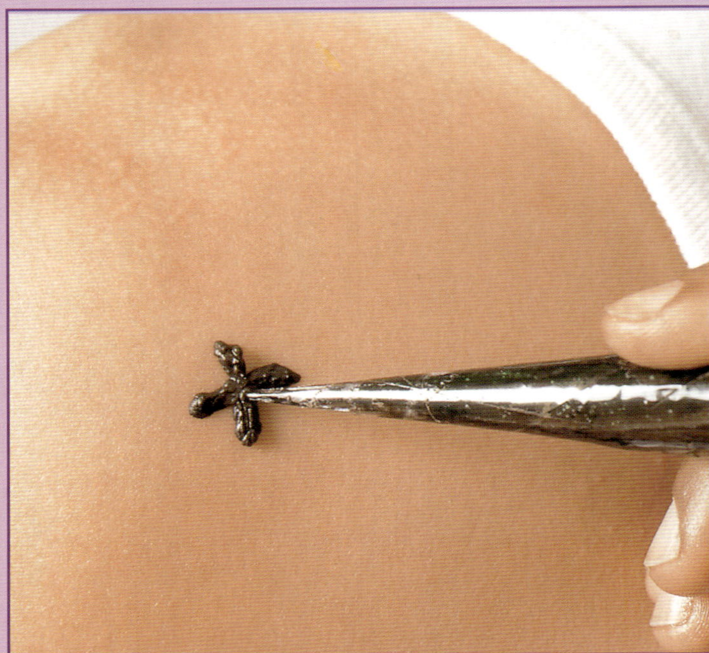

1 Cleanse, dry and oil the skin as for previous projects. Begin the design, applying henna consistently.

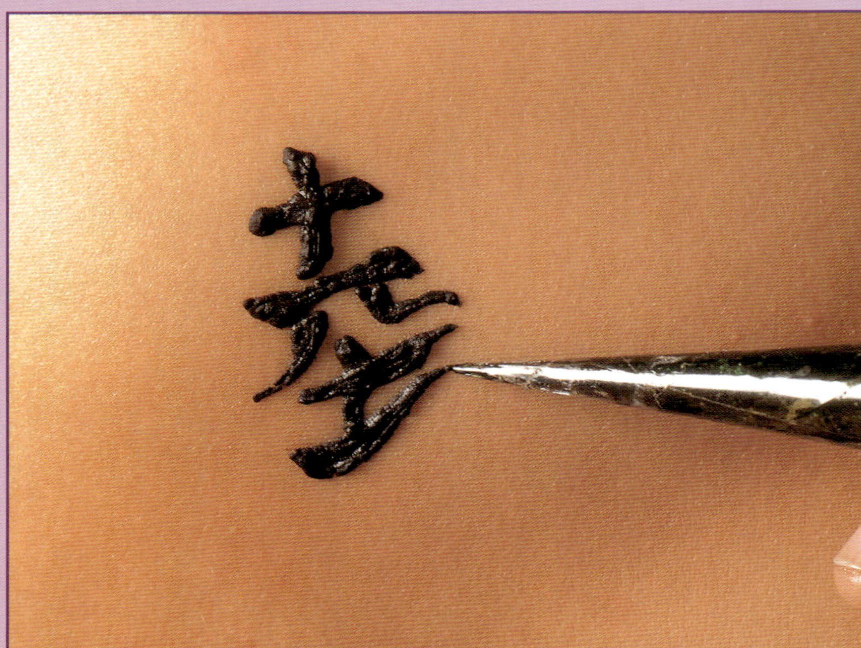

2 Carefully continue the design, making sure the henna does not smear or blob.

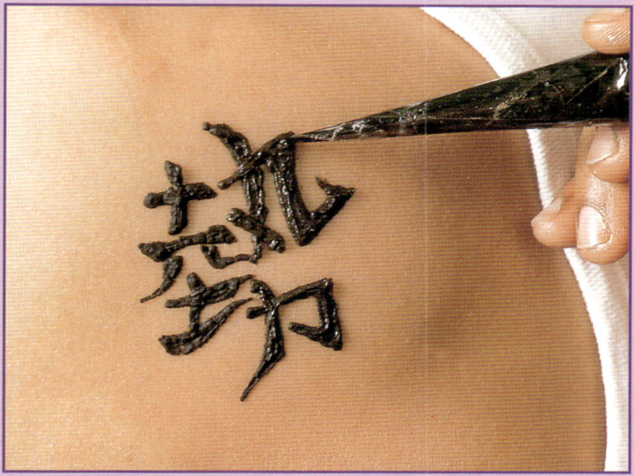

3 Finish the design evenly.

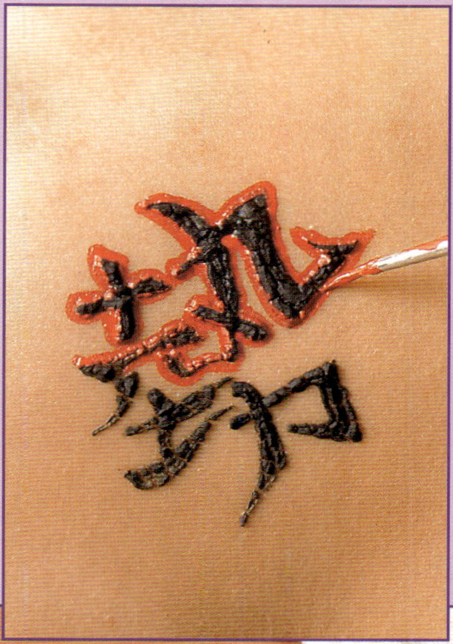

4 To add a final, dramatic touch to your design, why not outline parts of the character in a suitable colour?

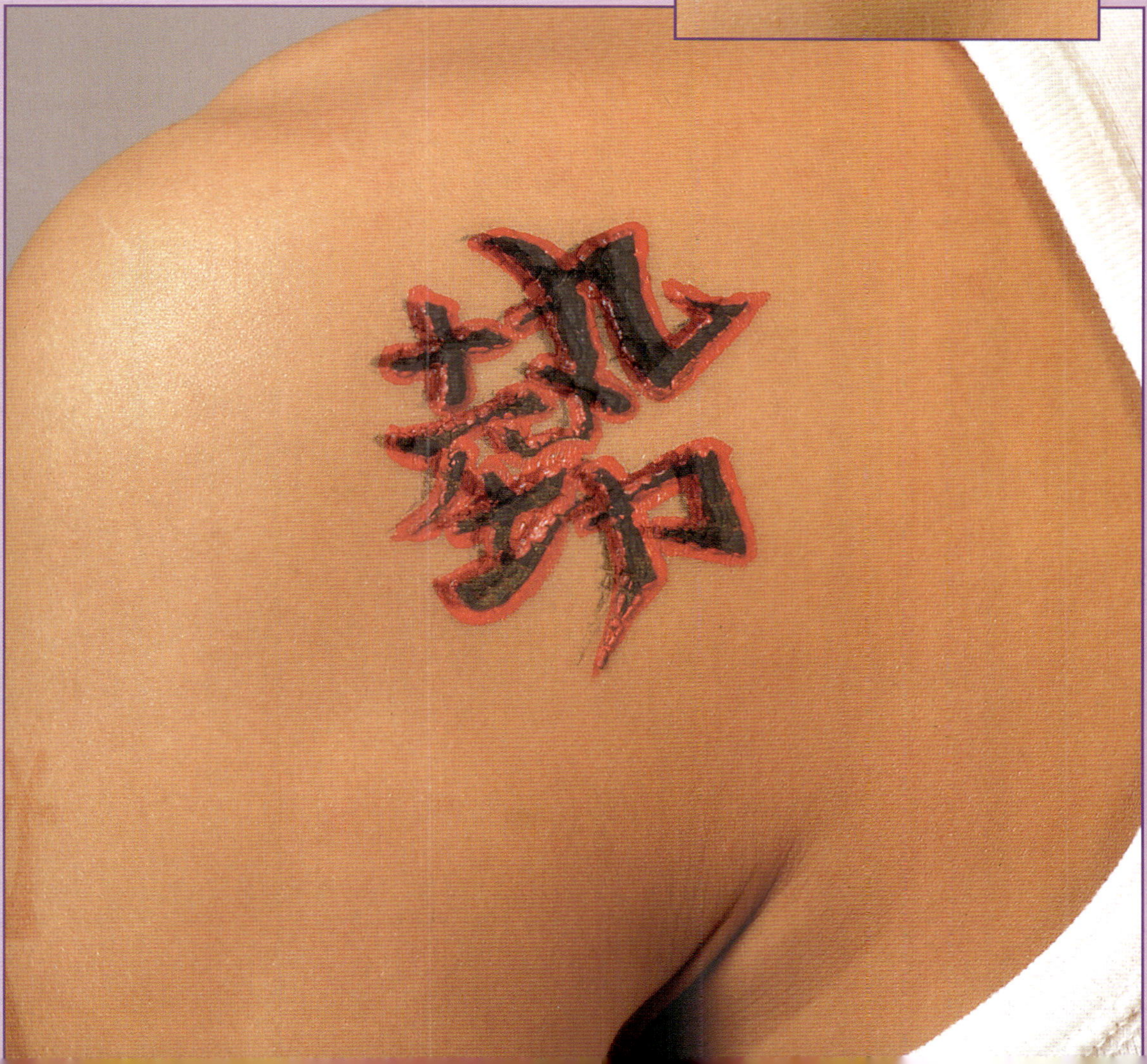

Sheer lace

This is a pretty, delicate design in the style of a traditional Hindi wedding design. It is very ornate, but balanced, so once you have confidence you should be able to recreate the design easily, and even embellish it with your own patterns.

YOU WILL NEED
- Cotton pads
- Alcohol solution (witch hazel)
- Henna (eucalyptus) oil
- Henna and applicator
- Sealant

1 Cleanse, dry and oil the skin as described on pp16–17.

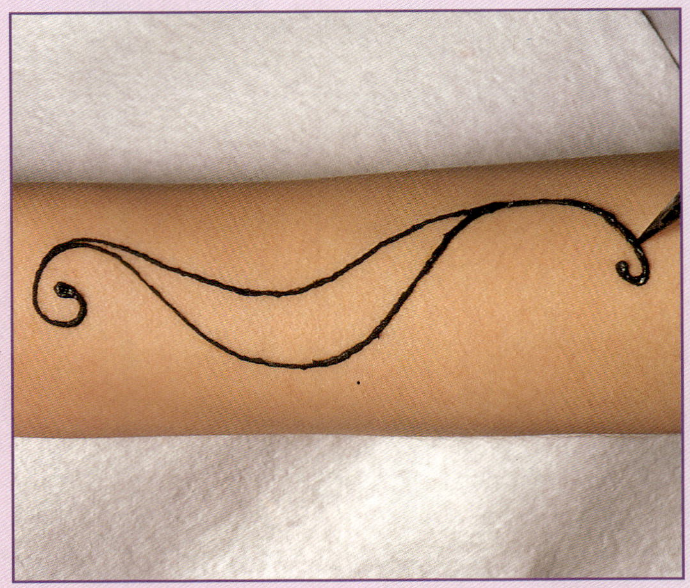

2 Begin the design with a curved pattern on the forearm.

3 Work down the arm, creating the main pattern, and continue on to your finger.

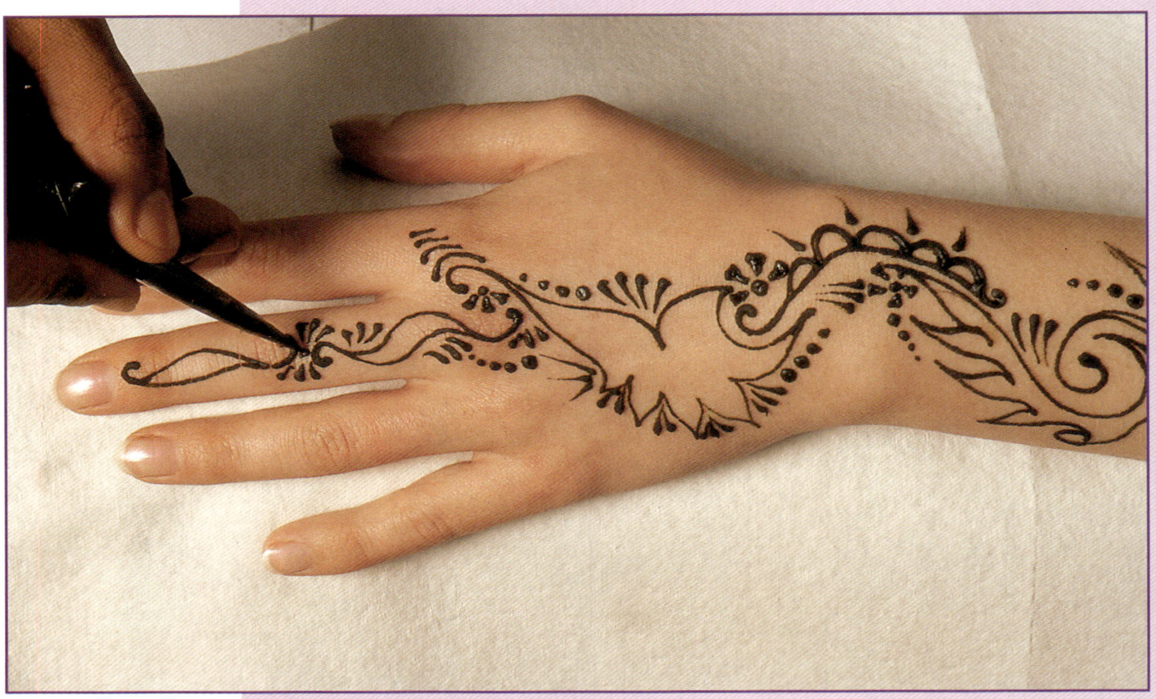

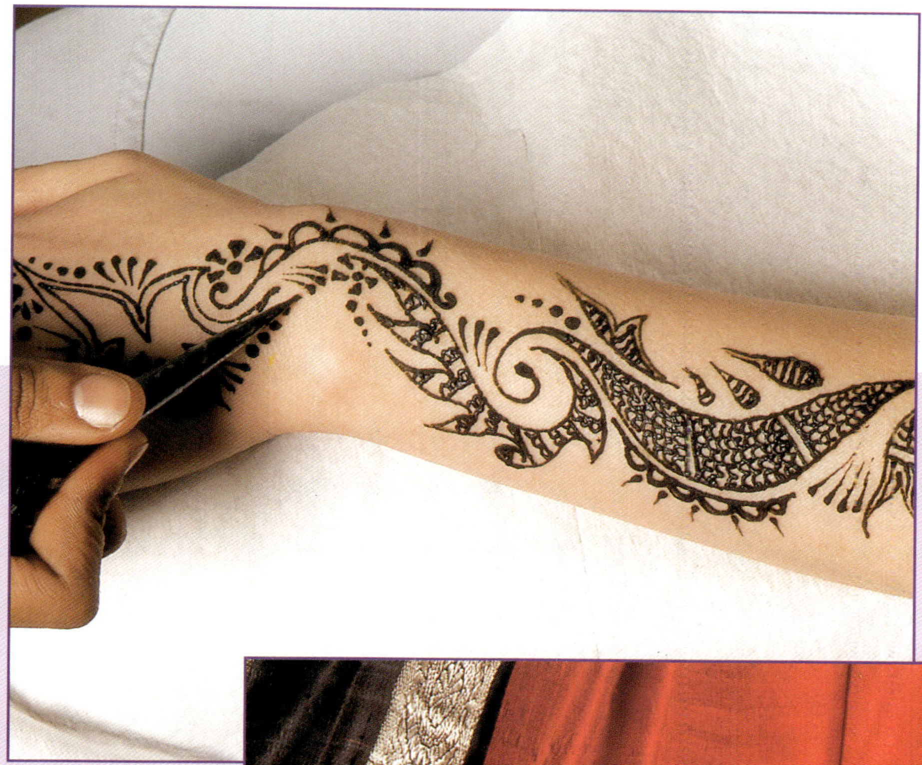

4 Finish the design by filling in and embellishing your original outline pattern.

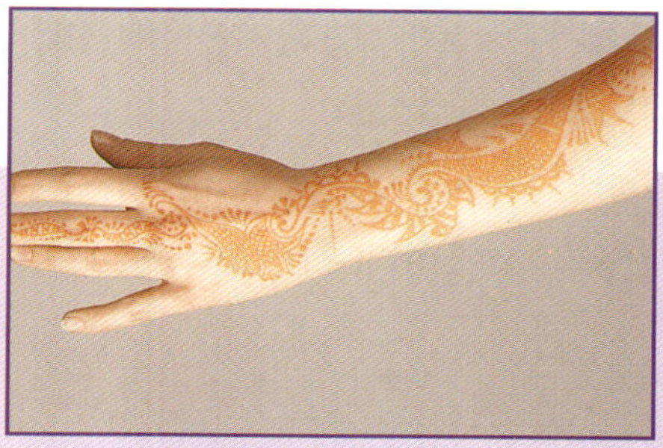

5 Here is the design after 24 hours.

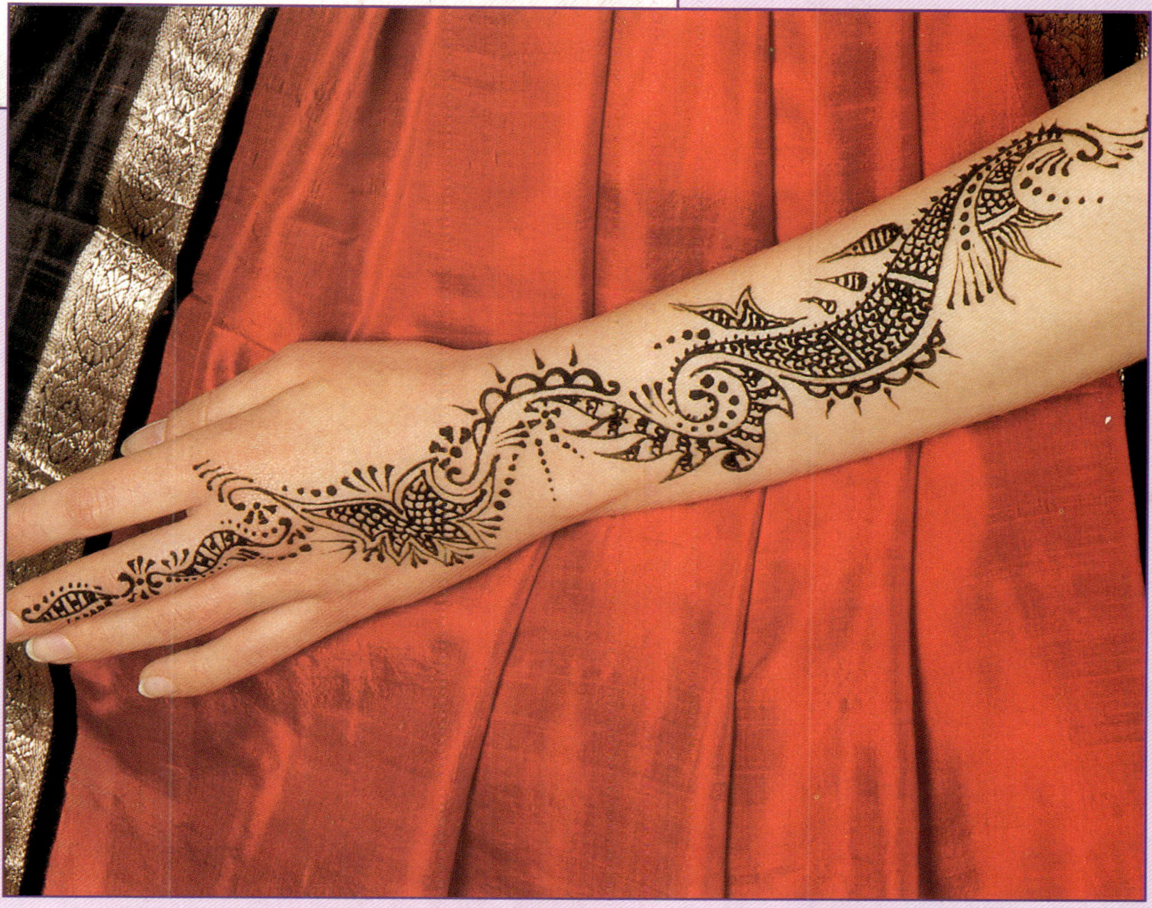

Arabic lotus flower

This design, based on Arabic illustrations, is beautiful on any part of the body, but the width of the foot makes the flowers stand out especially well. Apply some bindi jewellery for extra effect.

YOU WILL NEED

- Cotton pads
- Alcohol solution (witch hazel)
- Henna and applicator
- Sealant

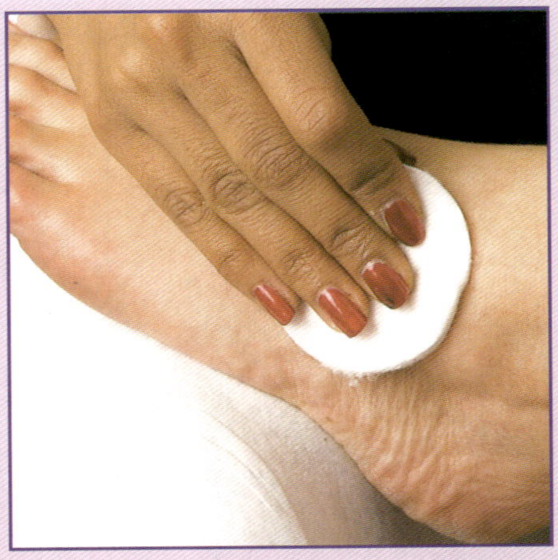

1 Cleanse your foot with a cotton pad dipped in alcohol solution and then pat dry. Apply a few drops of henna oil to a cotton pad and then dab it on to your foot.

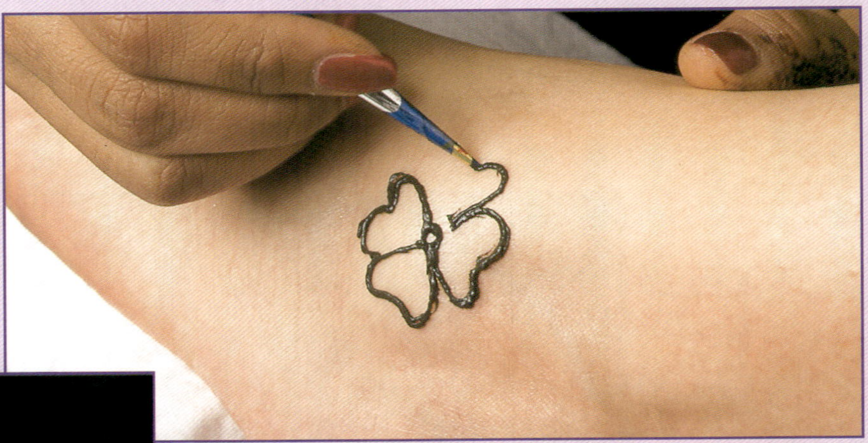

2 Following the instructions on p17, begin drawing the first flower.

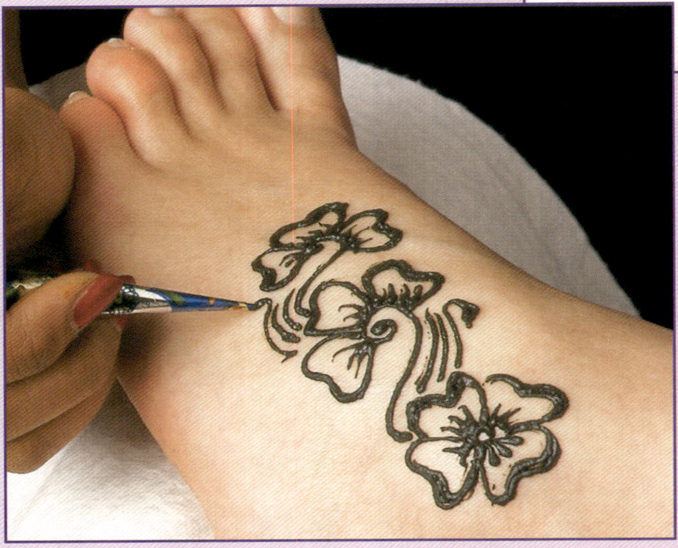

3 Continue the design with further flowers and stem details.

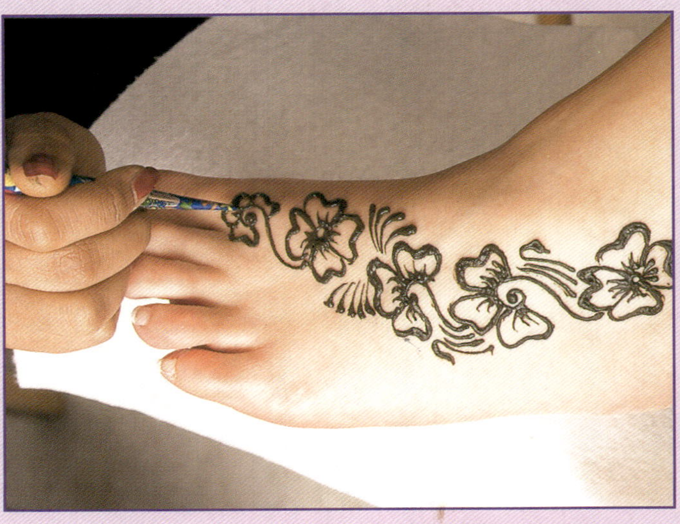

4 Finish the main design.

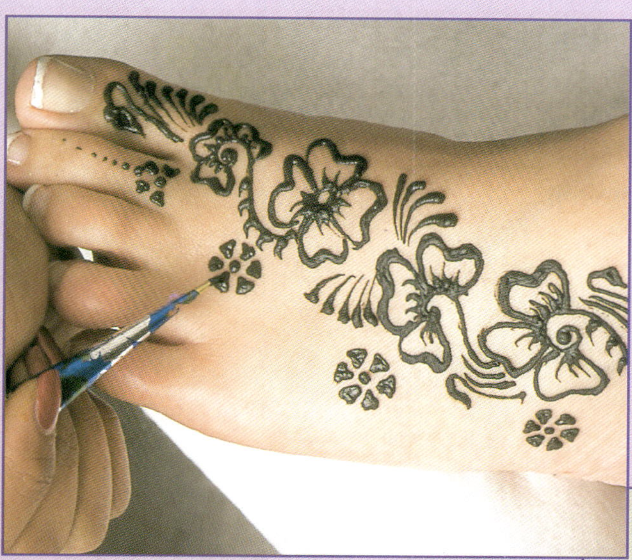

5 Add the final details. You will need a steady hand to keep the pattern even.

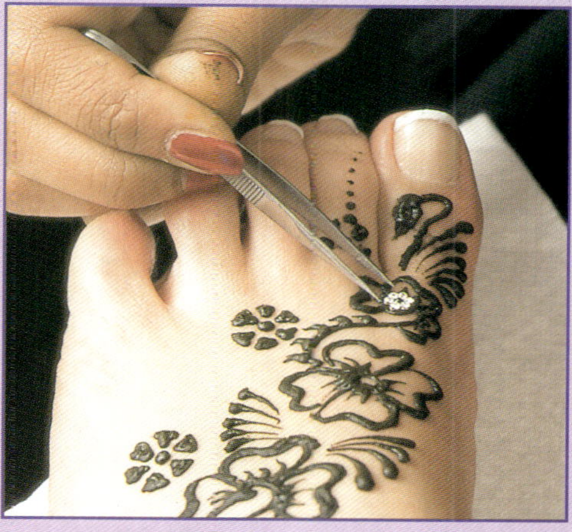

6 Add bindi jewellery.

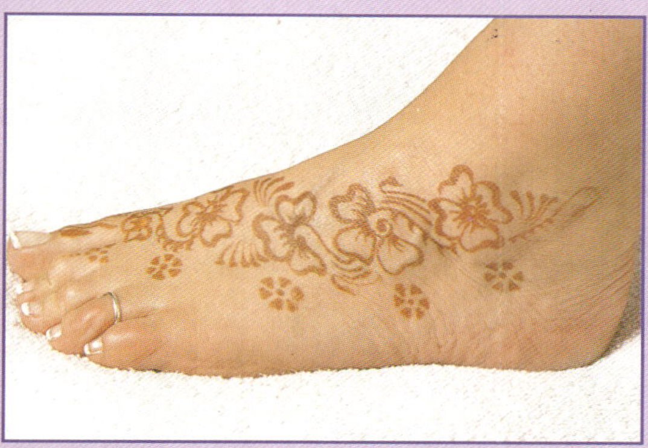

7 This is the design after 24 hours.

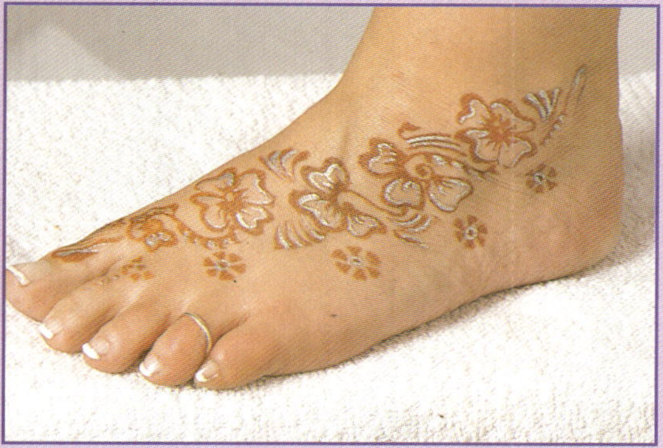

8 Now you can embellish the design if you wish. Here we have used silver body paint.

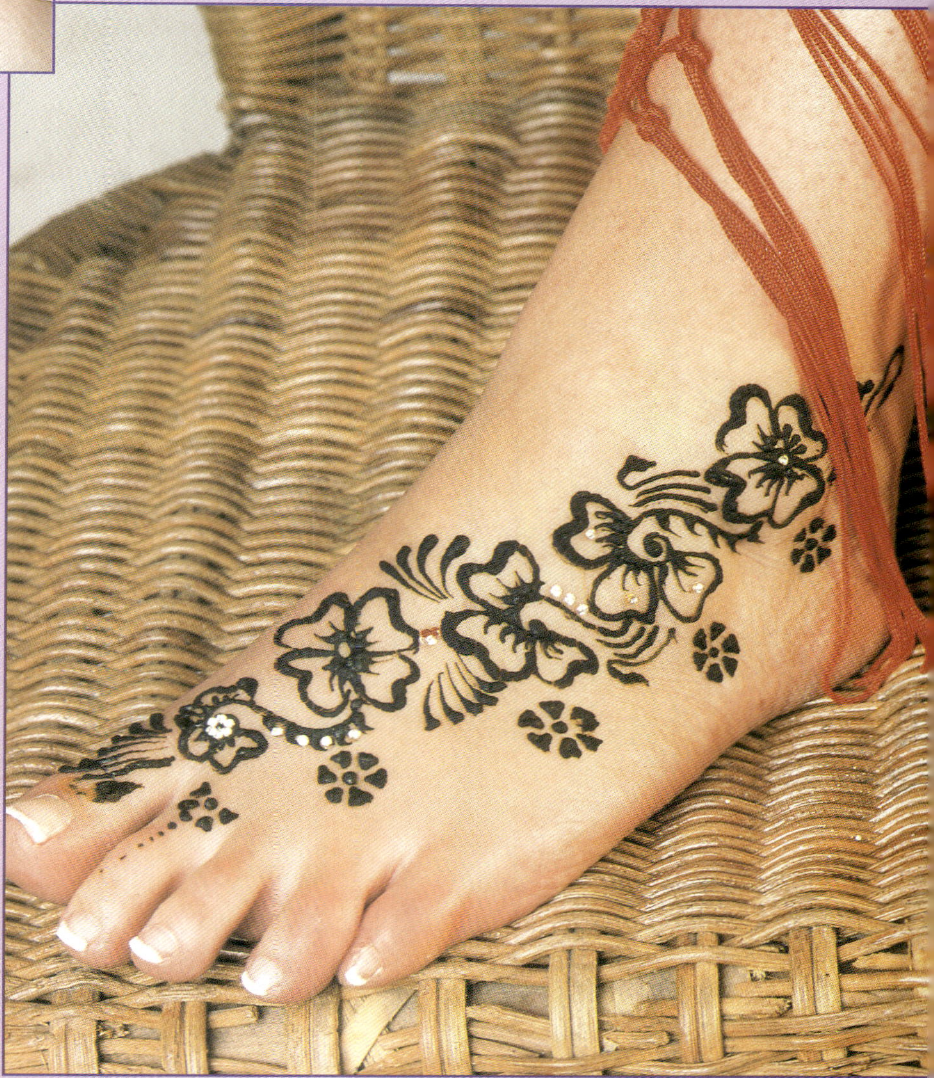

New Age ankle

New Age designs are often slightly heavier in finish than more traditional ones, and the ankle is a particularly good area to apply one as it will complement the contours of both the ankle and the foot.

YOU WILL NEED
- Cotton pads
- Alcohol solution (witch hazel)
- Sealant
- Henna and applicator

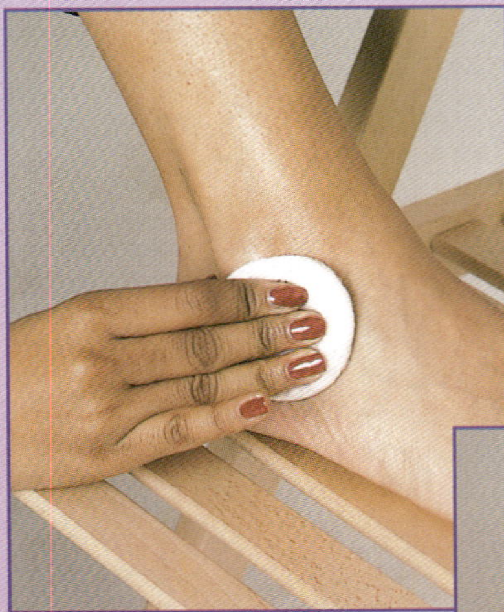

1 Cleanse your ankle by wiping it with a cotton pad dipped in alcohol solution and then letting it dry thoroughly.

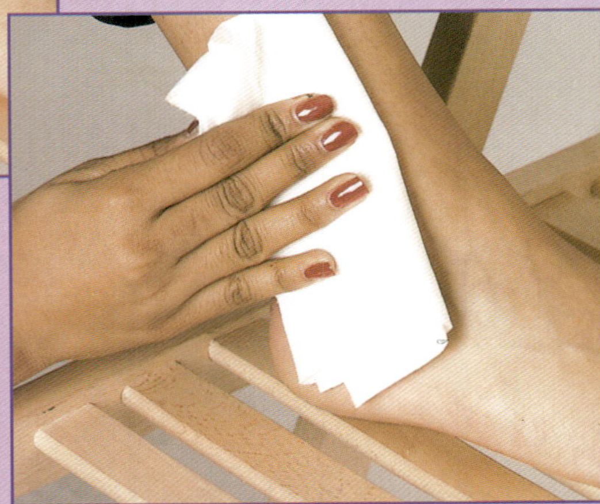

2 Us a paper towel to finish drying the skin.

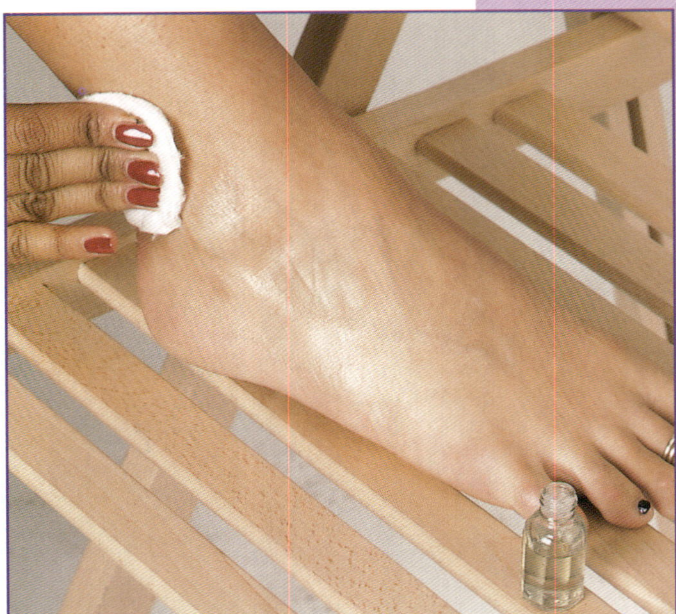

3 Apply a few drops of henna oil to a cotton pad and then dab it onto the area of skin on which you want to create your design.

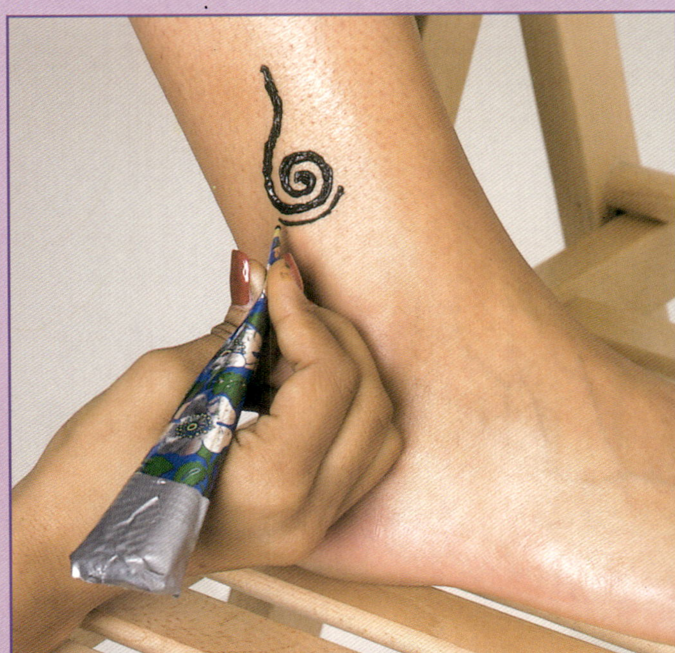

4 Following the instructions on pp16–17, begin your freehand design.

5 Continue the design down your ankle, making sure you don't blob or smear the design.

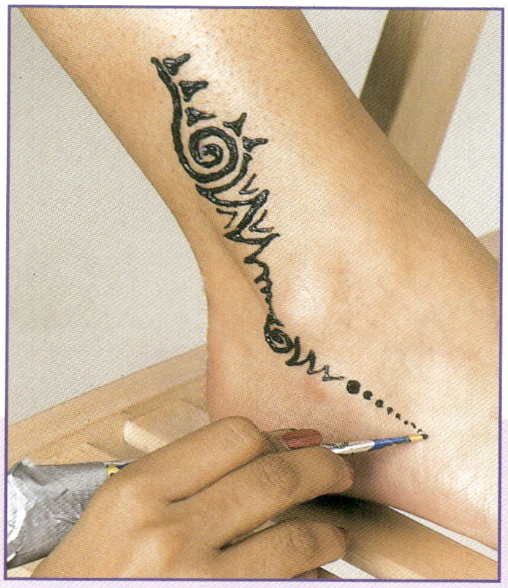

6 Finish off the design so that it looks evenly balanced.

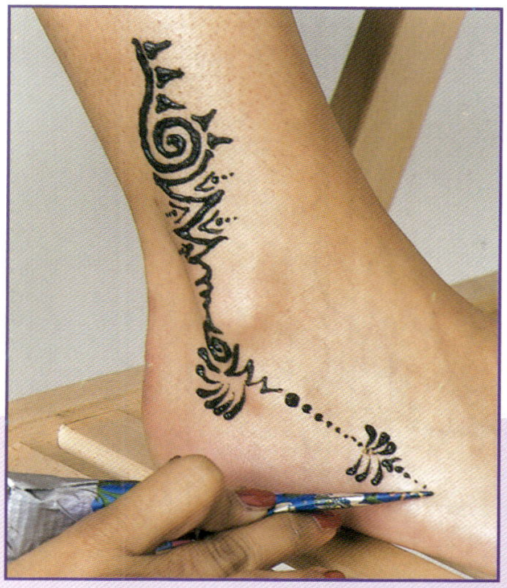

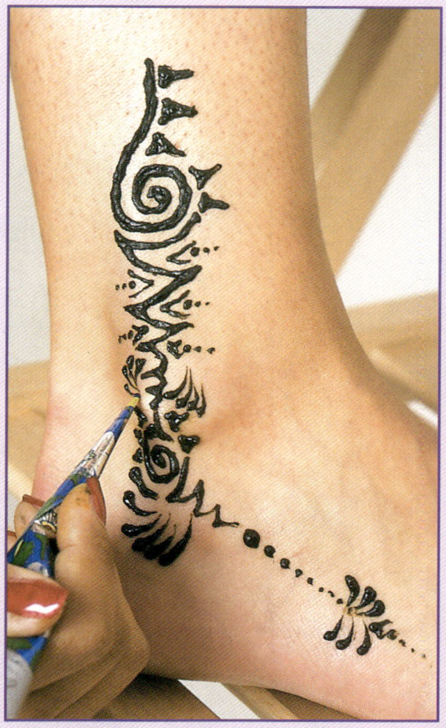

7 Finally, add another level of pattern for stunning effect.

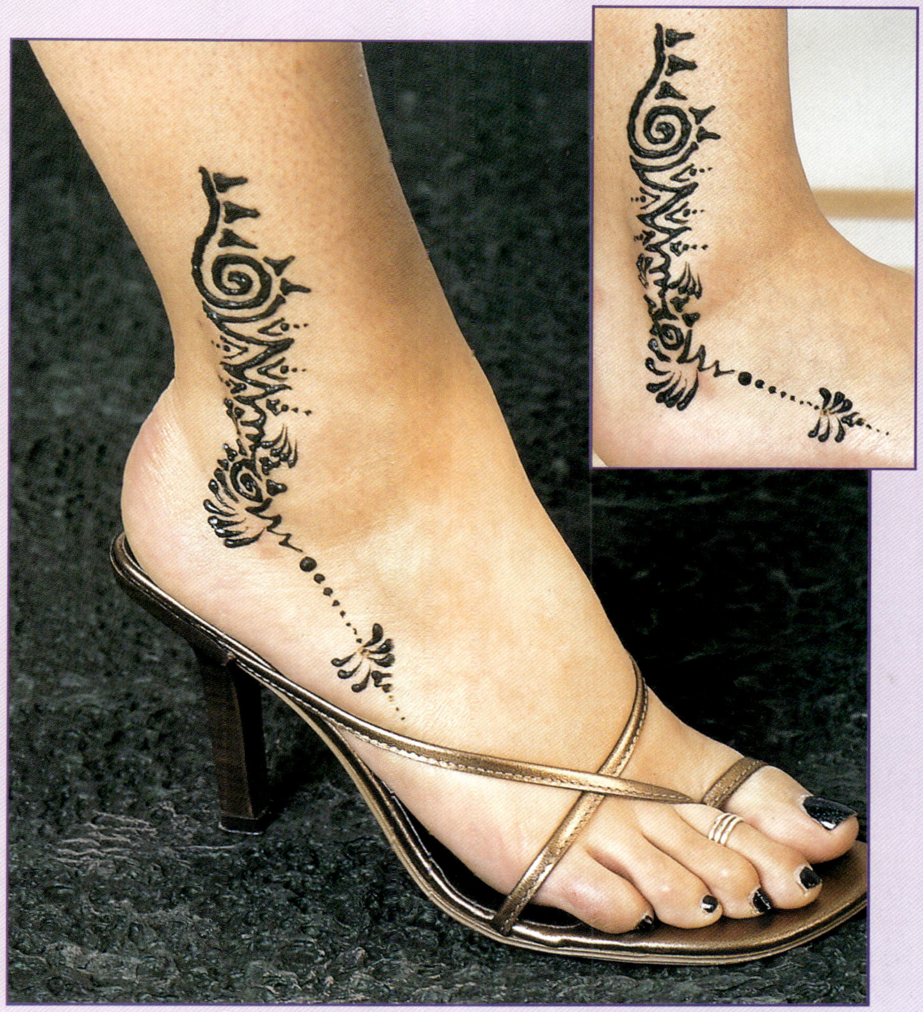

Abstract edge

This is a freehand design which we have chosen to create on the back. It can be scaled down for different parts of the body, but here the look is very dramatic. Cleanse dry and oil the skin as described on p16.

YOU WILL NEED

- Cotton pads
- Alcohol solution (witch hazel)
- Henna (eucalyptus) oil
- Henna and applicator
- Sealant (here we have used a lemon and sugar mix)
- Toothpick or cotton bud

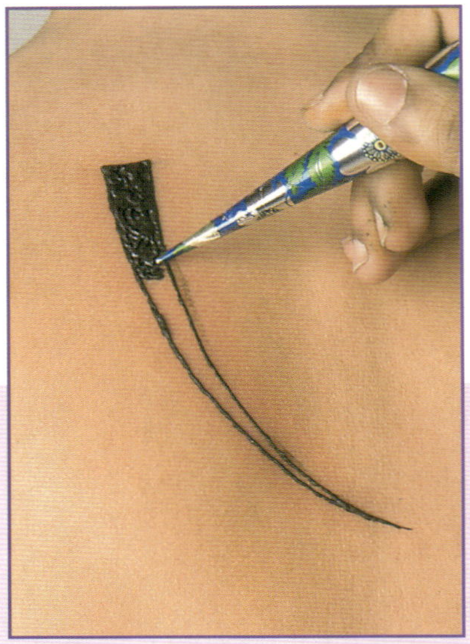

1 When creating this abstract design, outline the first crescent as illustrated and then fill in the inside area. Follow the contour of the back, as shown.

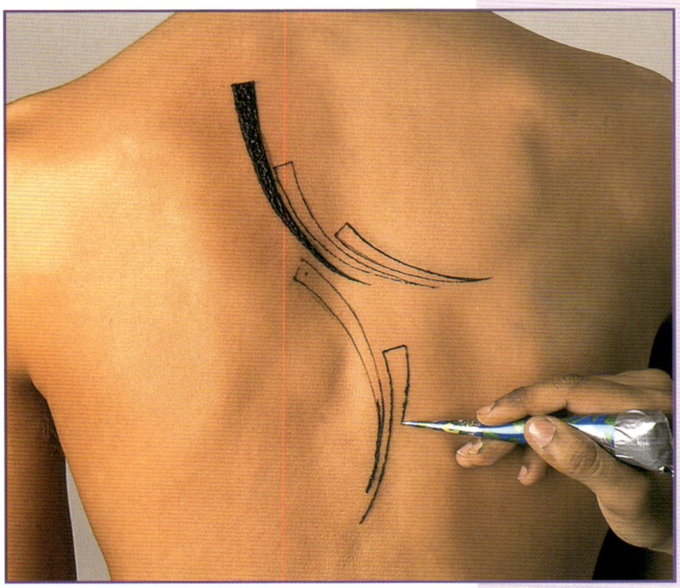

2 Carefully continue your design. Work slowly and do not rush.

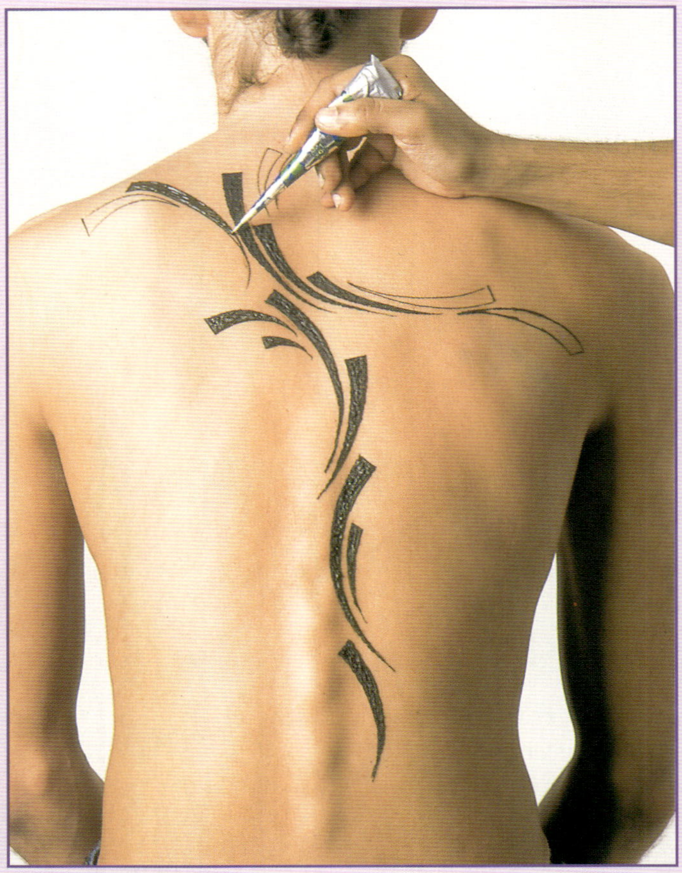

3 Beign to fill in the outline patterns.

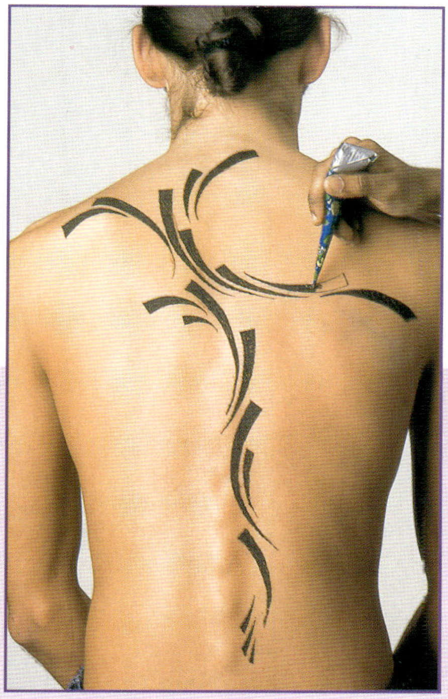

4 Finish the design by adding extra patterns to create a balanced effect.

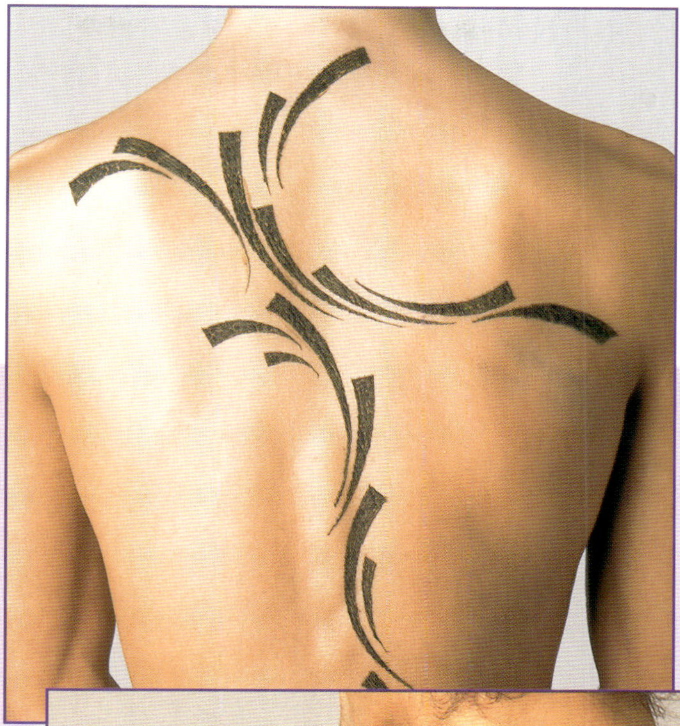

5 This shows how the finished design looks before applying sealant.

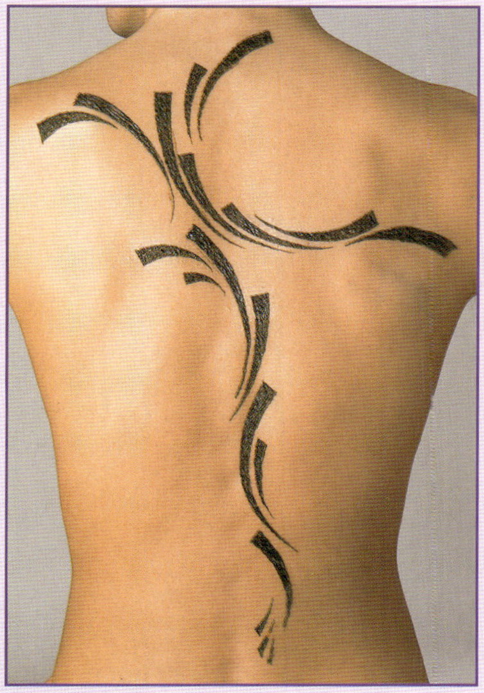

6 This is the finished design after sealing.

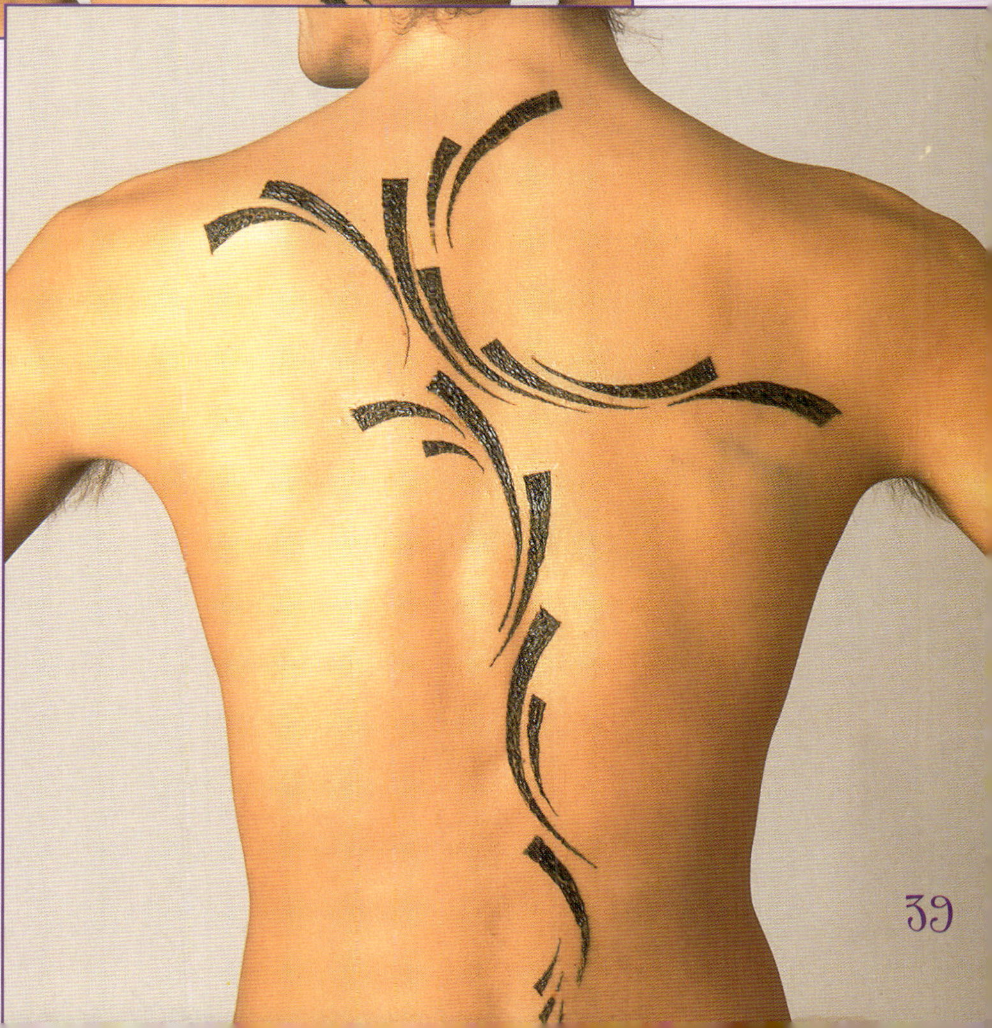

Glittering henna

This shows how you can liven up a henna design that is a few days old, by adding glittering paints.

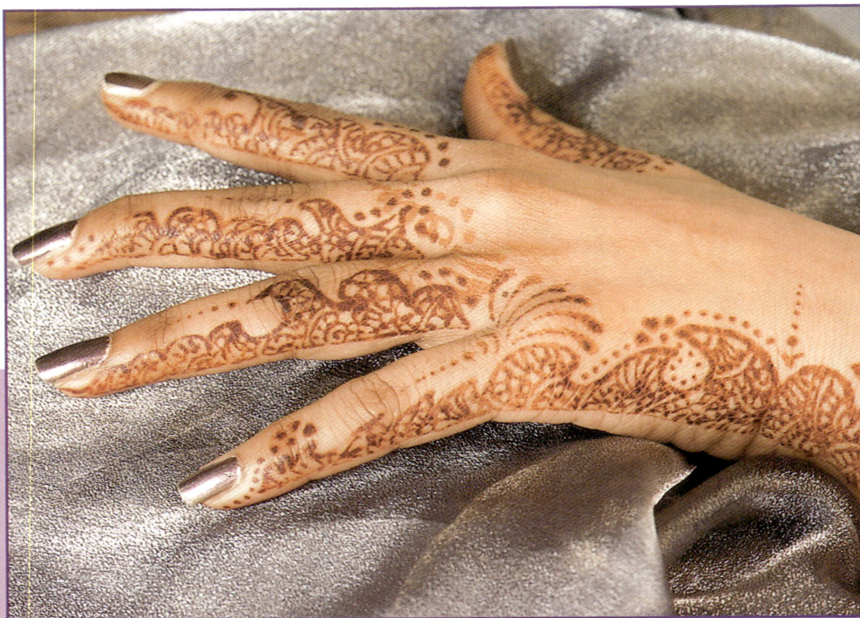

YOU WILL NEED

- Cotton pads
- Alcohol solution (witch hazel)
- Henna (eucalyptus) oil
- Henna and applicator
- Sealant

1 This henna design is now a few days old. It is very attractive, but we can make it even more special.

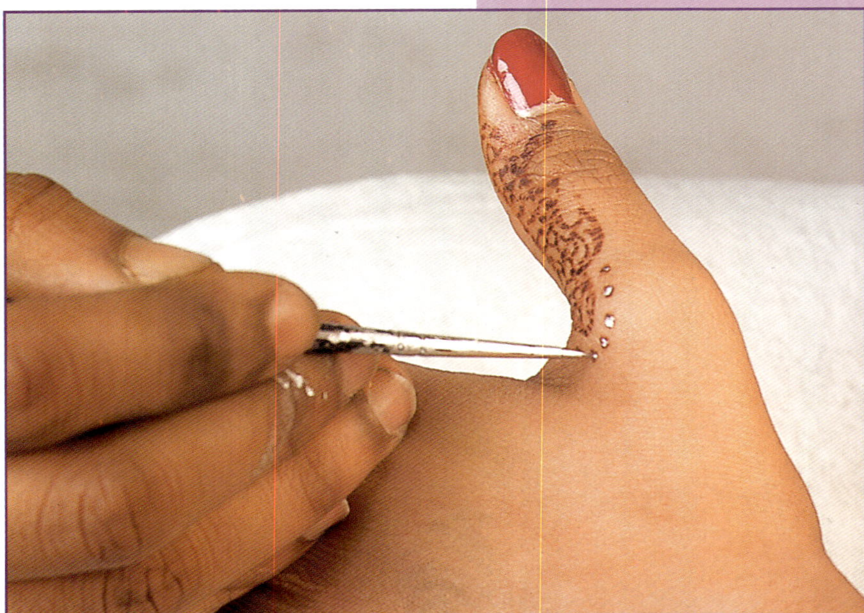

2 Use silver paint to gently outline the henna design.

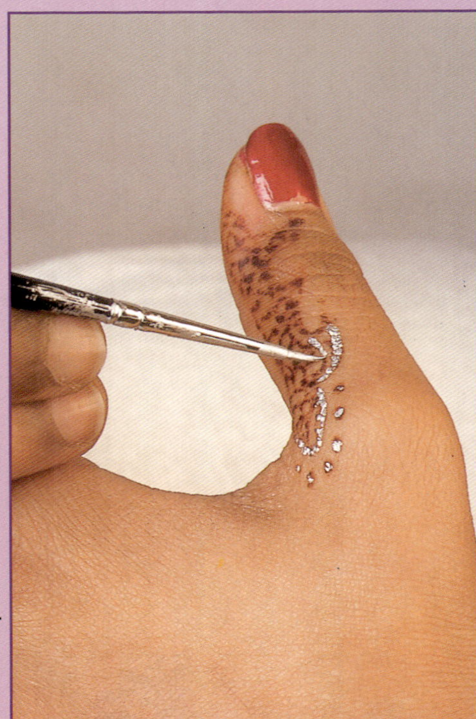

3 You don't necessarily want to outline every part of the design. The idea is to highlight, not overpower.

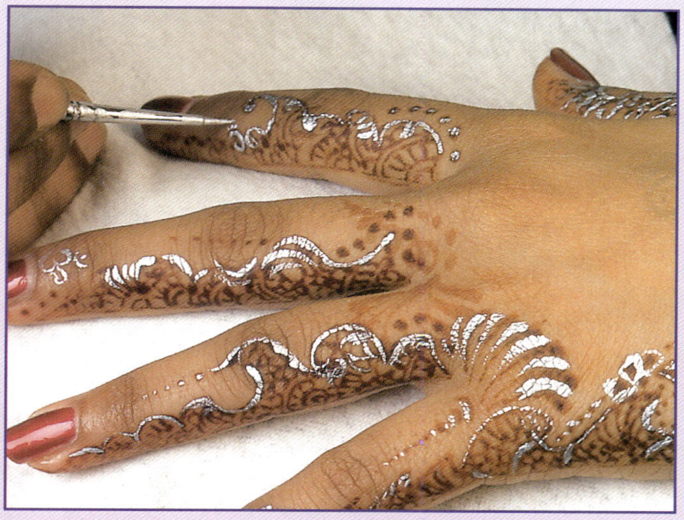

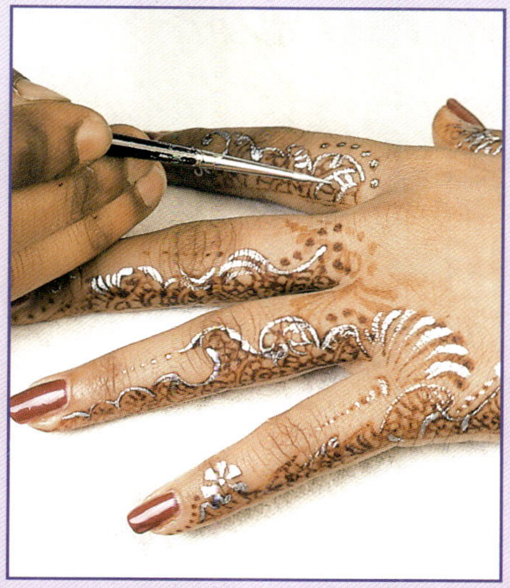

5 Finally, add any strokes to provide a balanced effect.

4 Gently work over each finger with a steady hand.

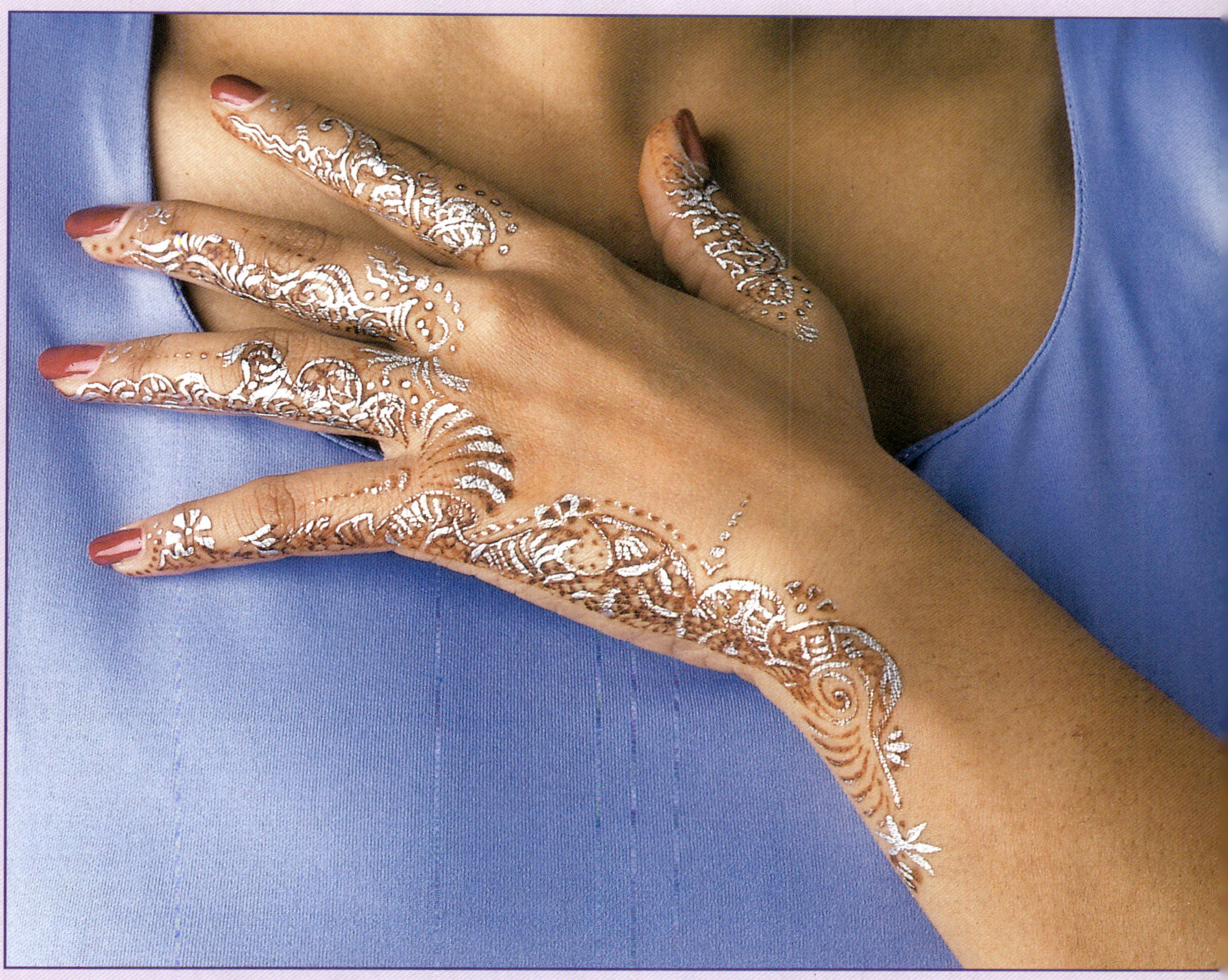

Pisces

Stencils can make creating henna patterns even easier. This project also shows how a simple design can be enhanced by some simple freehand body painting. Your freehand pattern can be simple wavy lines to represent the sea – or you can go all out as we have! The belly button is an idea place for a round design.

YOU WILL NEED

- Henna and applicator
- Stencil
- Body paints
- Brushes
- Gems

1 Cleanse, dry and oil the skin as described on p16.

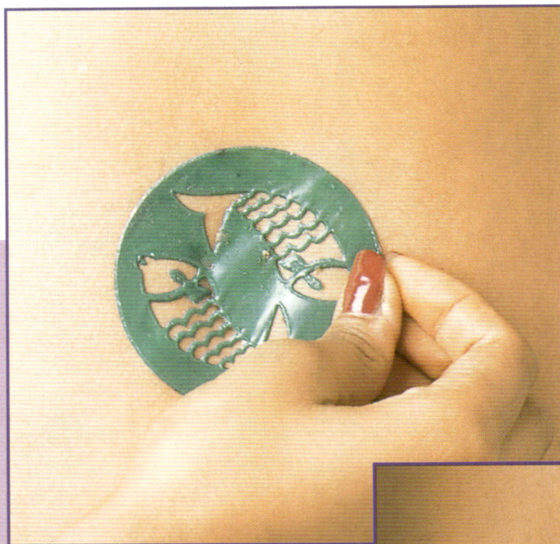

2 Position your stencil around the belly button.

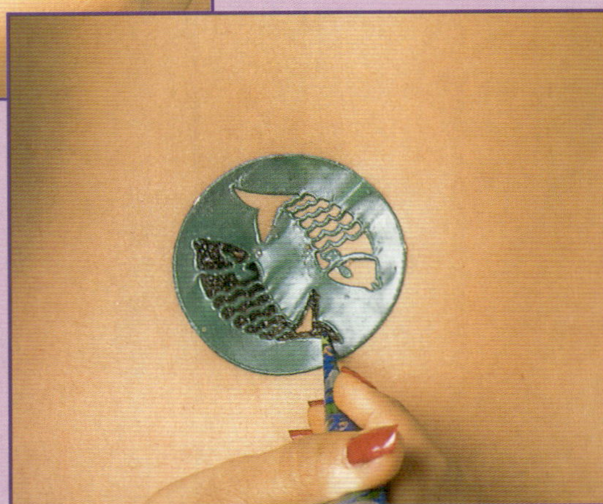

3 Begin to apply the henna through the stencil.

4 Apply some more to fill the stencil.

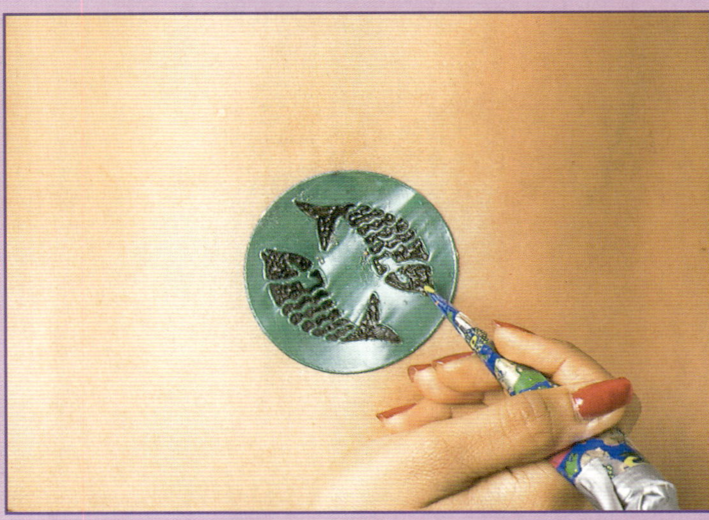

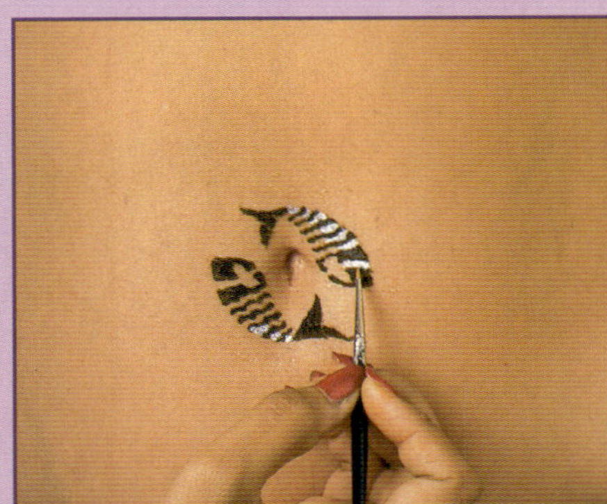

5 Once you have gently removed the stencil, embellish your design using body paints.

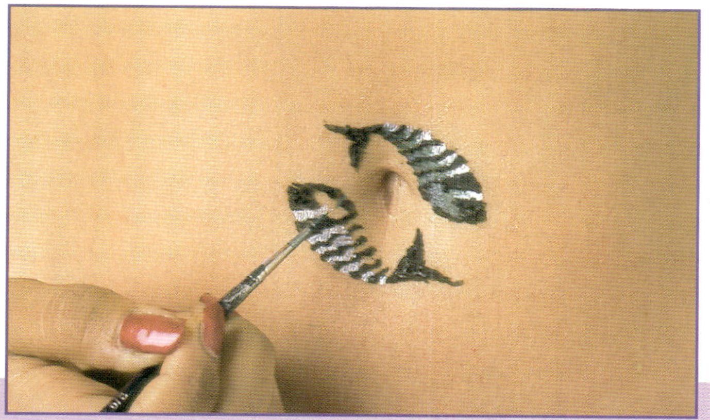

6 Use more colour if you wish.

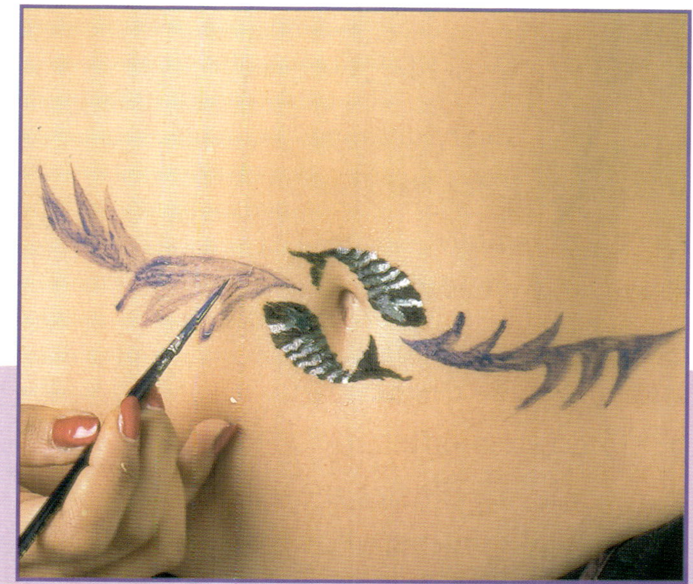

7 Begin to paint the waves.

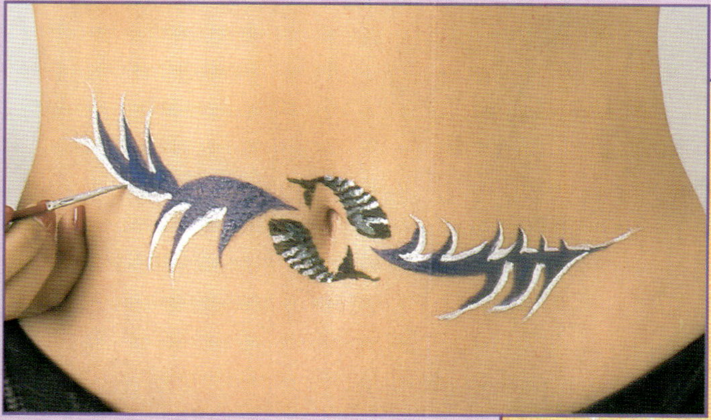

8 Enhance the waves using glittering body paint.

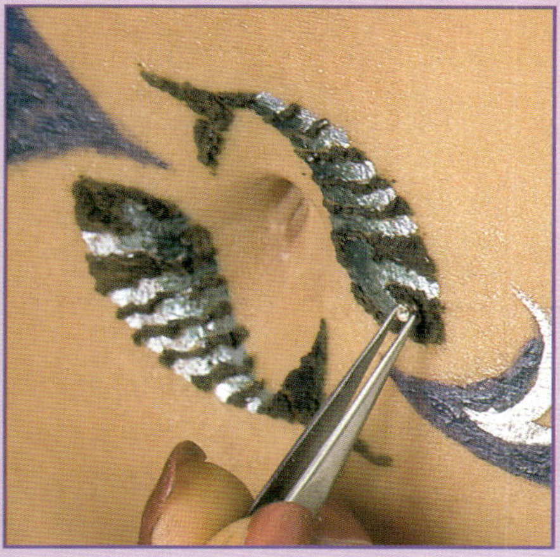

9 For added effect, why not add gems to the eyes?

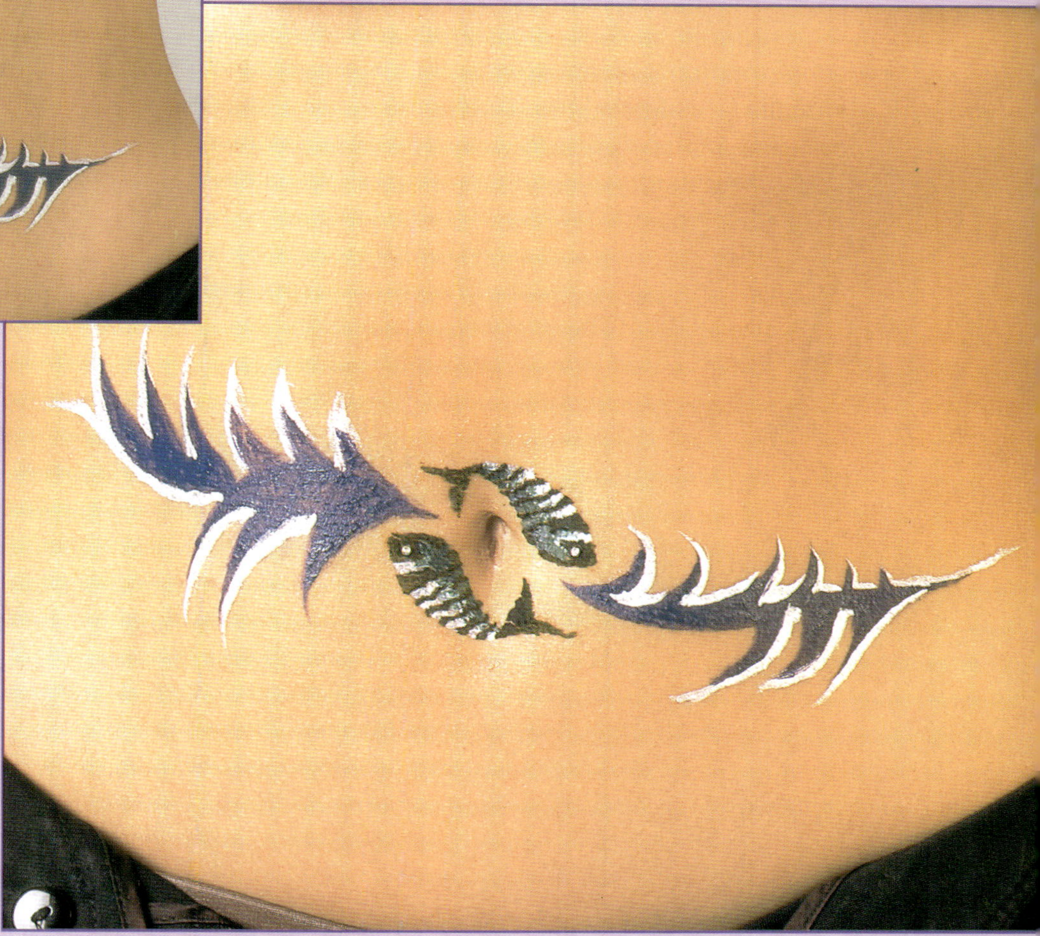

Chinese dragon

Because it is very detailed, this design is for the more advanced henna-tattooist. However, we have included it to show quite how stunning some designs can be! To create a different effect, you could paint the dragon with body paint.

YOU WILL NEED

- Cotton pads
- Alcohol solution (witch hazel)
- Henna (eucalyptus) oil
- Henna and applicator
- Sealant
- Body paints

1 Cleanse, dry and oil the skin as described on p16.

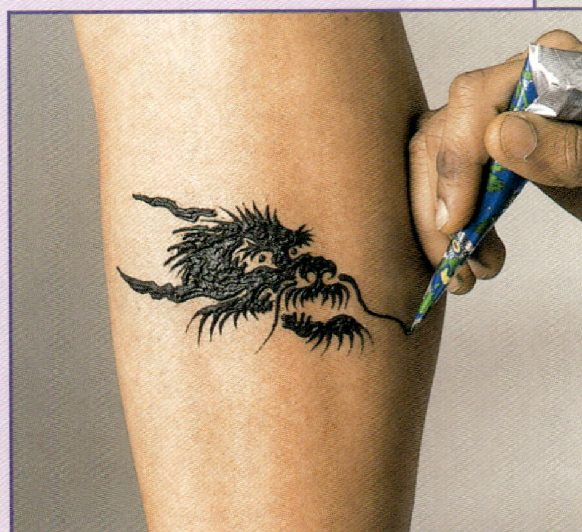

2 Your design will cover the whole of the lower part of the leg, so allow yourself space. First begin with the head.

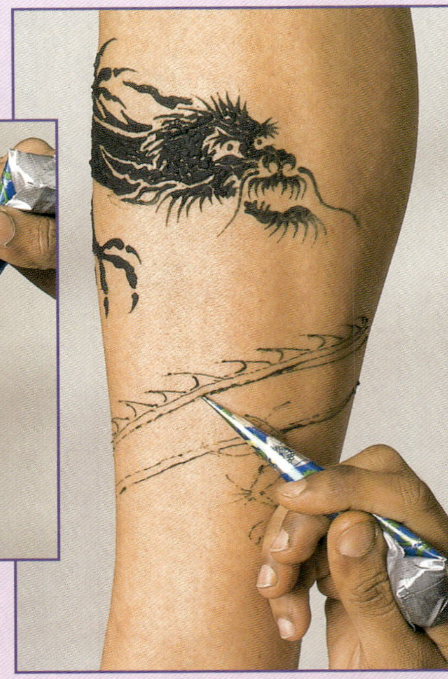

3 Next, move down the leg, drawing the main body outline.

4 At the ankle, begin the outline of the dragon's tail.

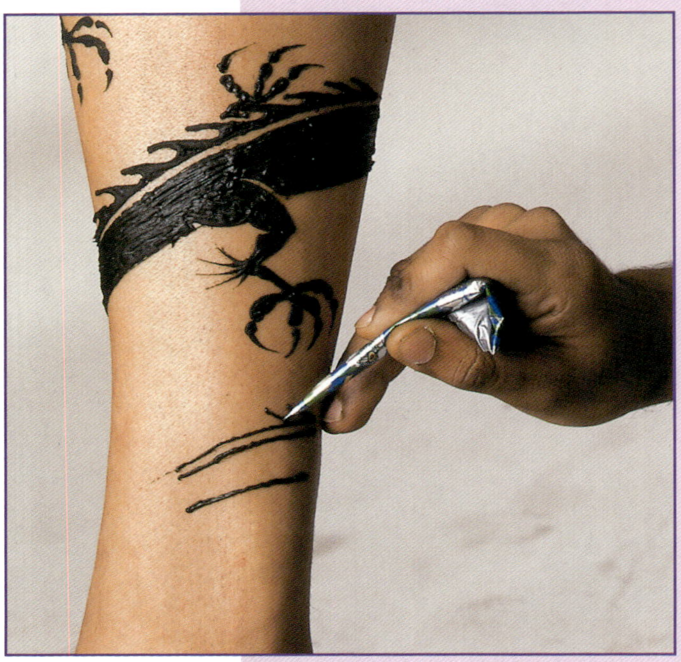

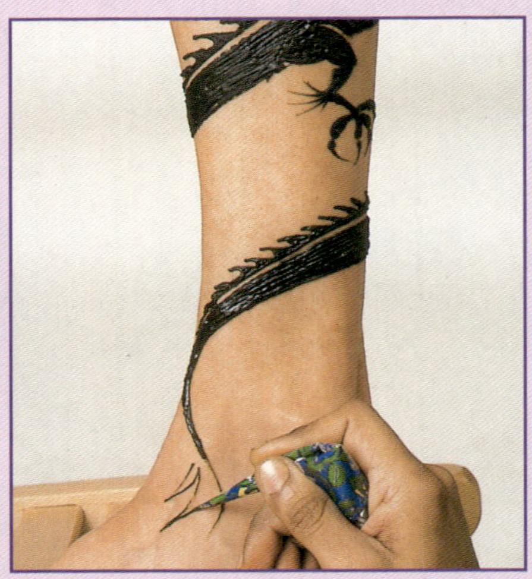

5 Take the tail design right down onto the foot.

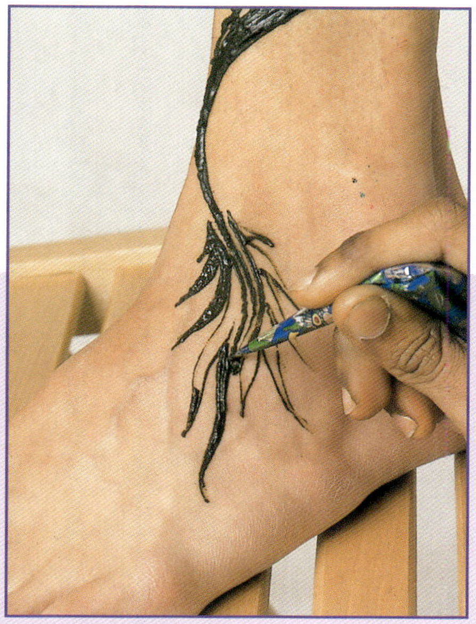

6 Fill in the final tail details.

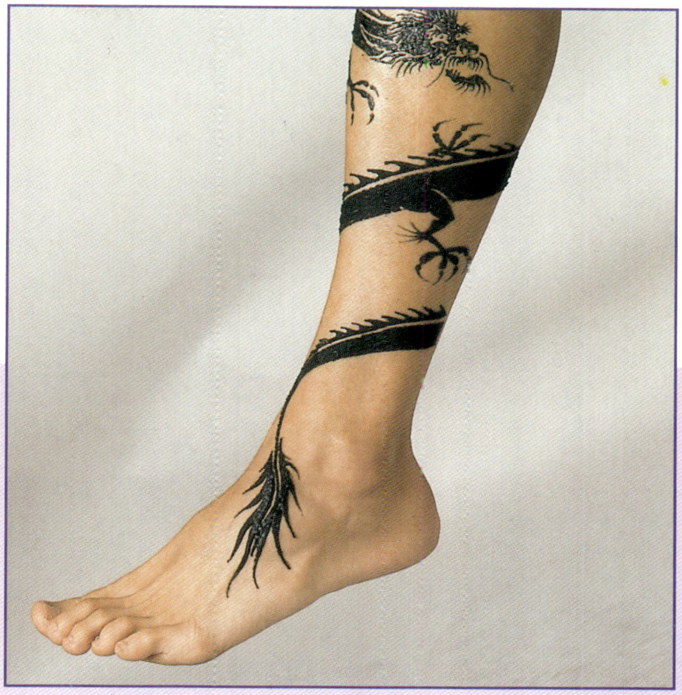

7 Finished effect before sealing.

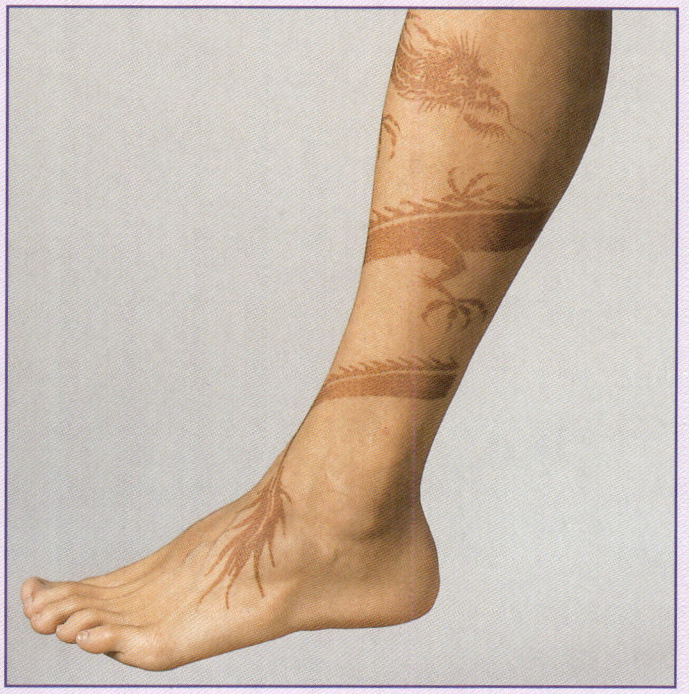

8 This shows the design after 24 hours.

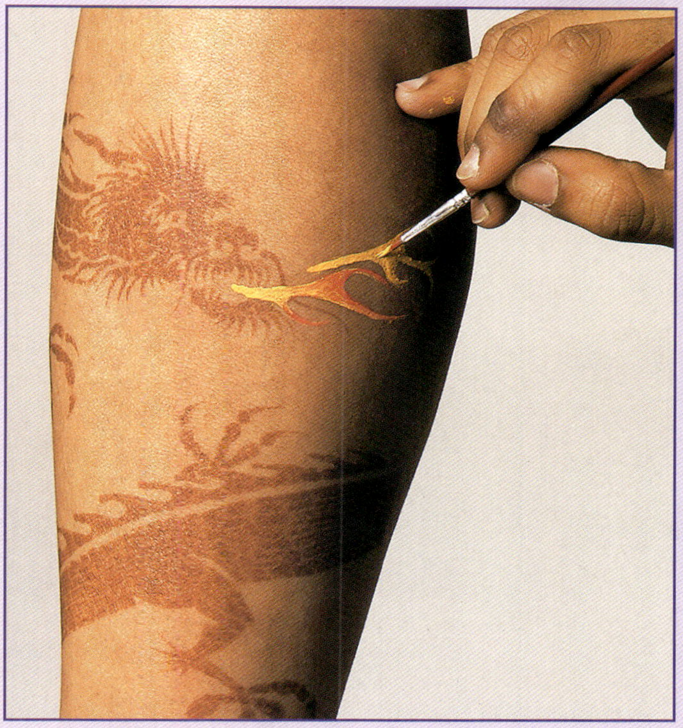

9 Now you can begin using the body paints to add detail.

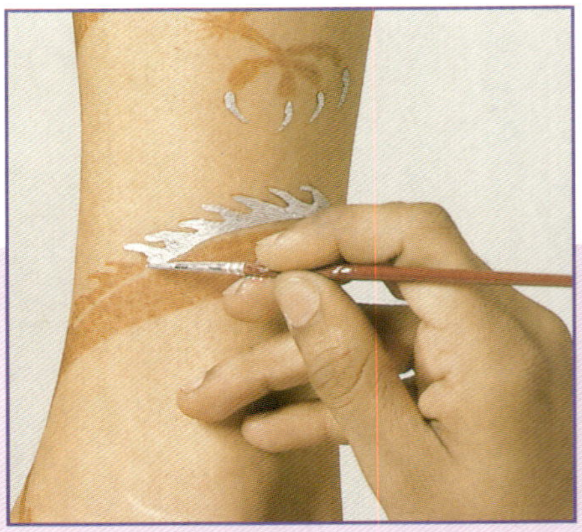

10 Add as much or as little embellishment as you wish.

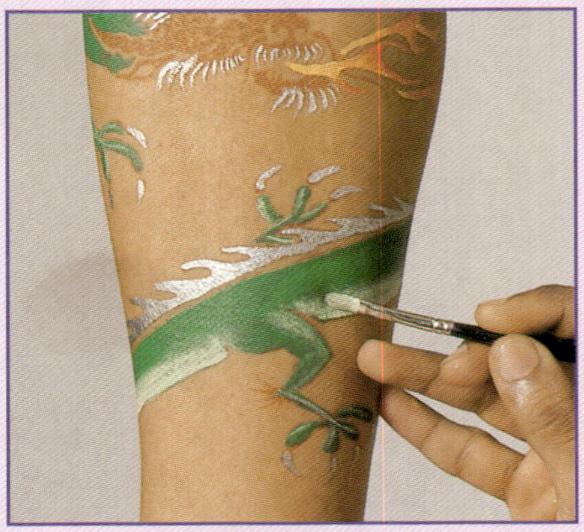

11 Here you can already see how stunning this design is.

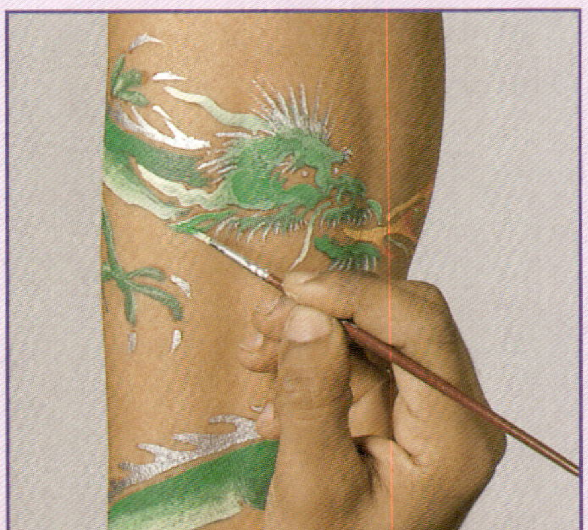

12 Add a few finishing touches.

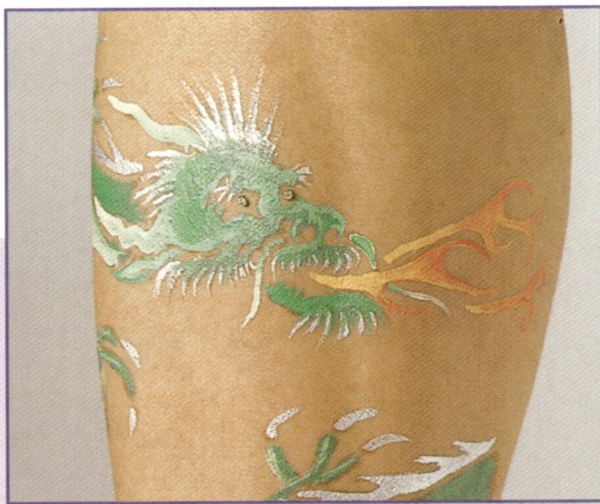

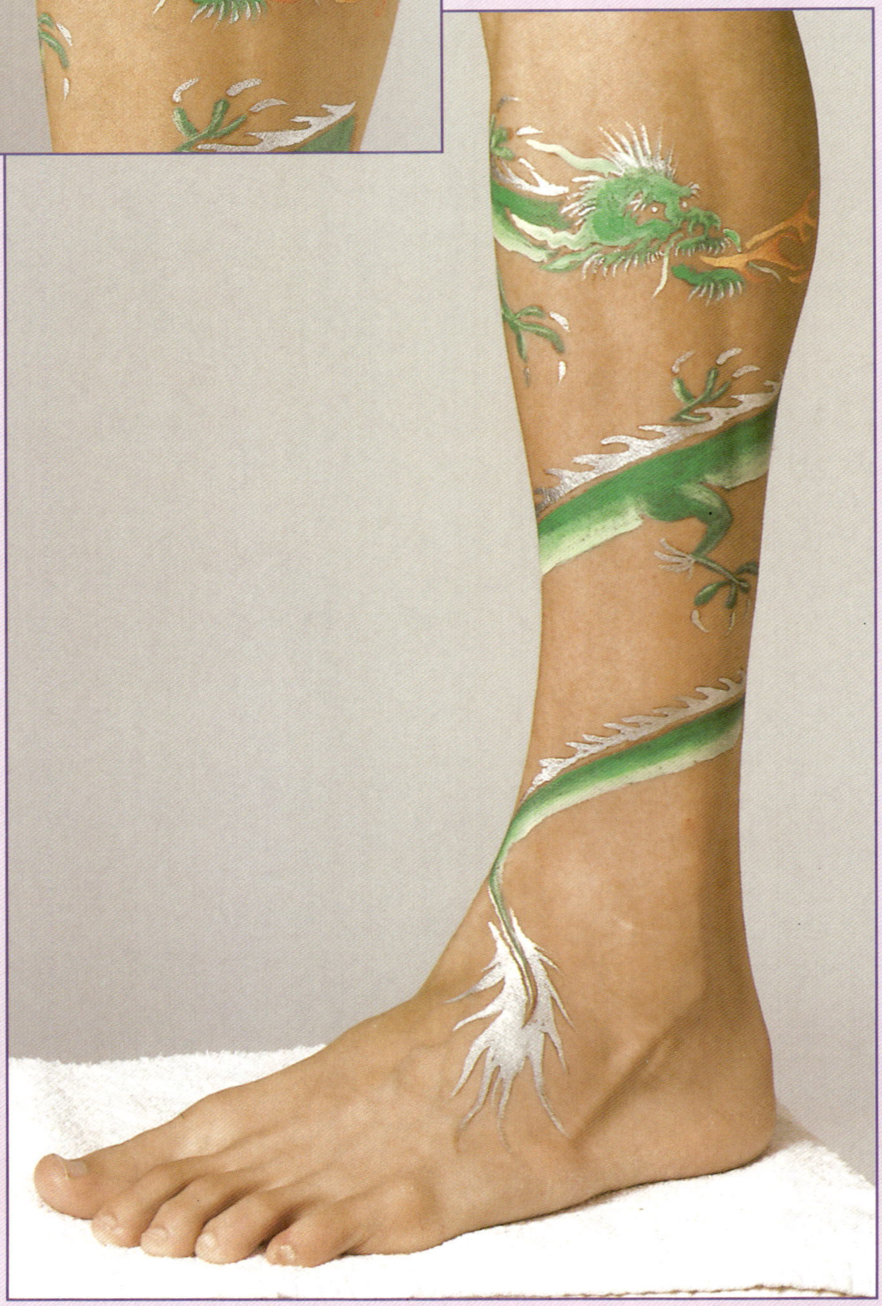

Random pattern

Freehand henna designs can be as simple or as detailed as you wish. Try combining different shapes and strokes. A large area such as the thigh is ideal for trying out your designs. This pattern is stunning, and very masculine.

YOU WILL NEED

- Cotton pads
- Alcohol solution (witch hazel)
- Henna (eucalyptus) oil
- Henna and applicator
- Sealant

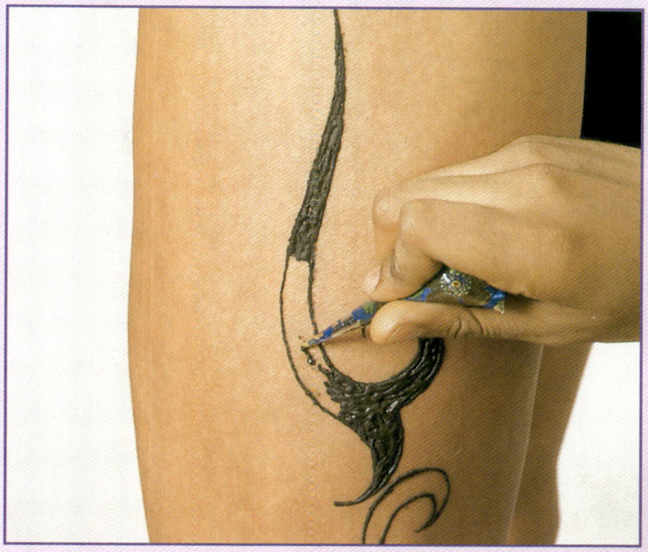

1 First outline your design, then fill in the central areas.

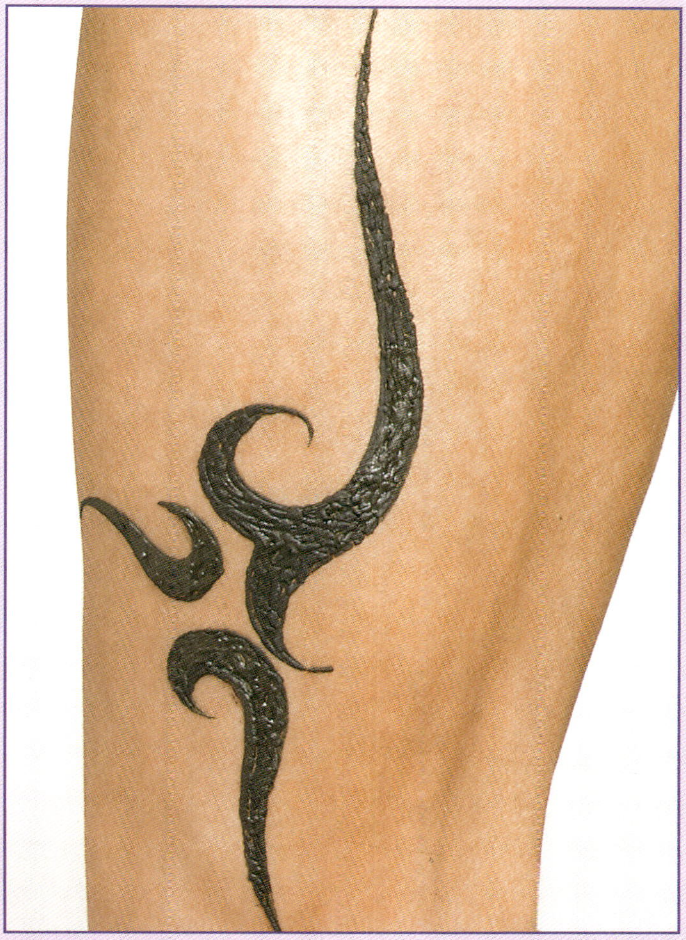

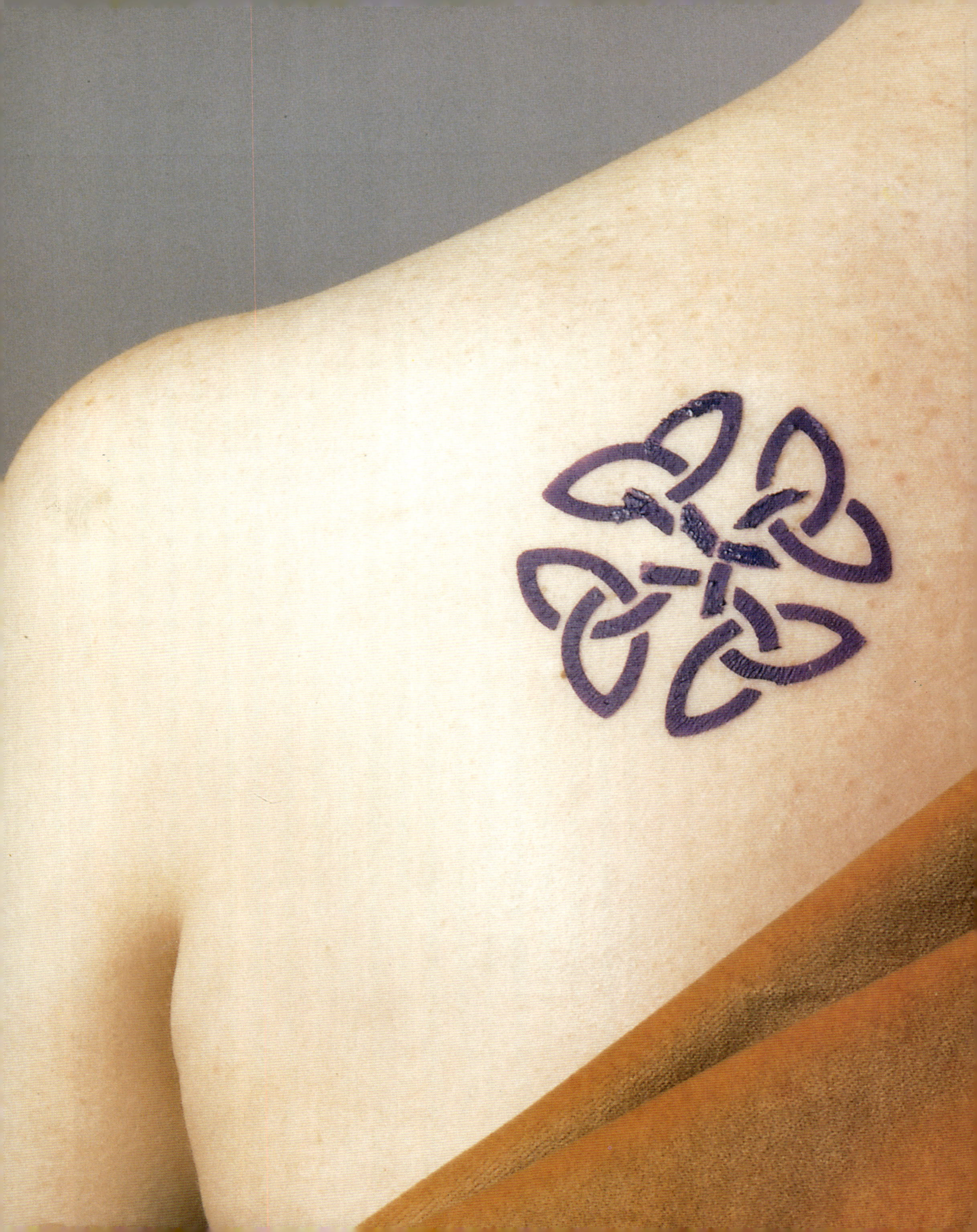

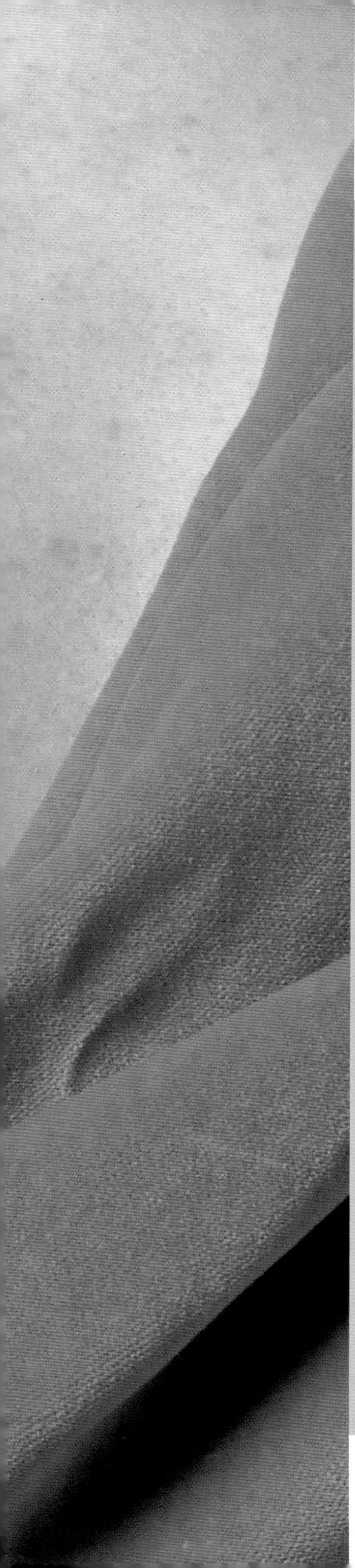

PAINT designs

Water-based body paints can enliven semi-permanent or henna tattoos by making them brighter and more colourful, as well as creating a different texture. They are usually sold in kits containing a dozen or more colours. Remember that because they are water-based, designs created with these paints will only last for a day or less and will dissolve if they come into contact with water.

There are different ways of applying body paints. They can be applied with brushes, pens, ink pads or even spray paints or airbrushing.

Stencils will make sure your design is clean and even, but once you gain confidence you can draw freehand designs – either copying from a pattern book, or creating your own designs.

Floral armband

This is a pretty and simple design which can be enlivened by using two or more colours. It is very feminine, and will look lovely on hot summer days.

YOU WILL NEED
- Cotton pads
- Alcohol solution (witch hazel)
- Stencil
- Art pens

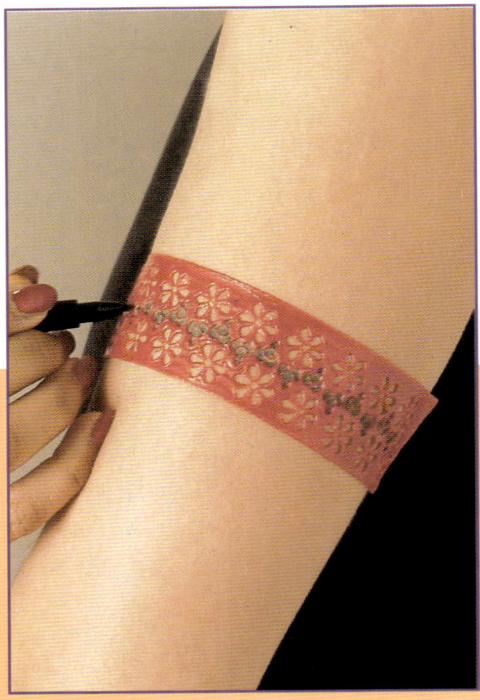

1 After cleansing the skin, apply the stencil and begin to fill in using the pens.

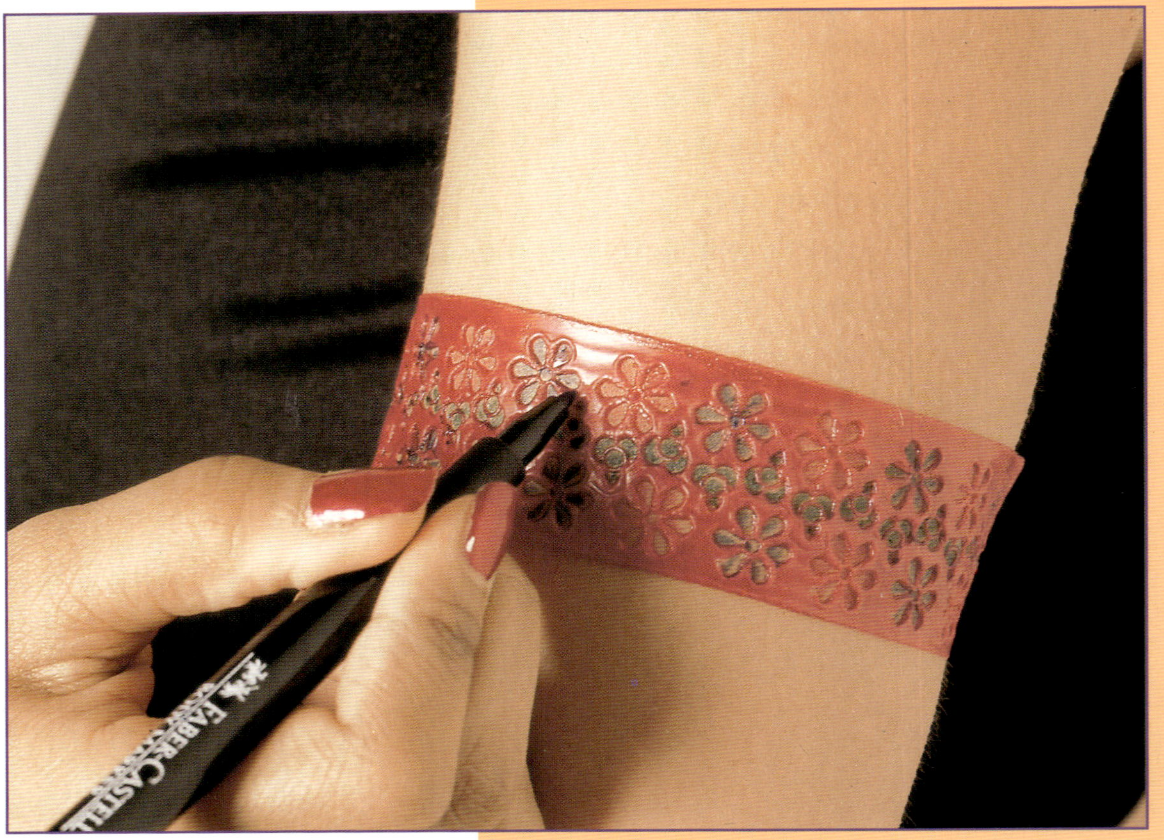

2 Fill in some more using the first colour.

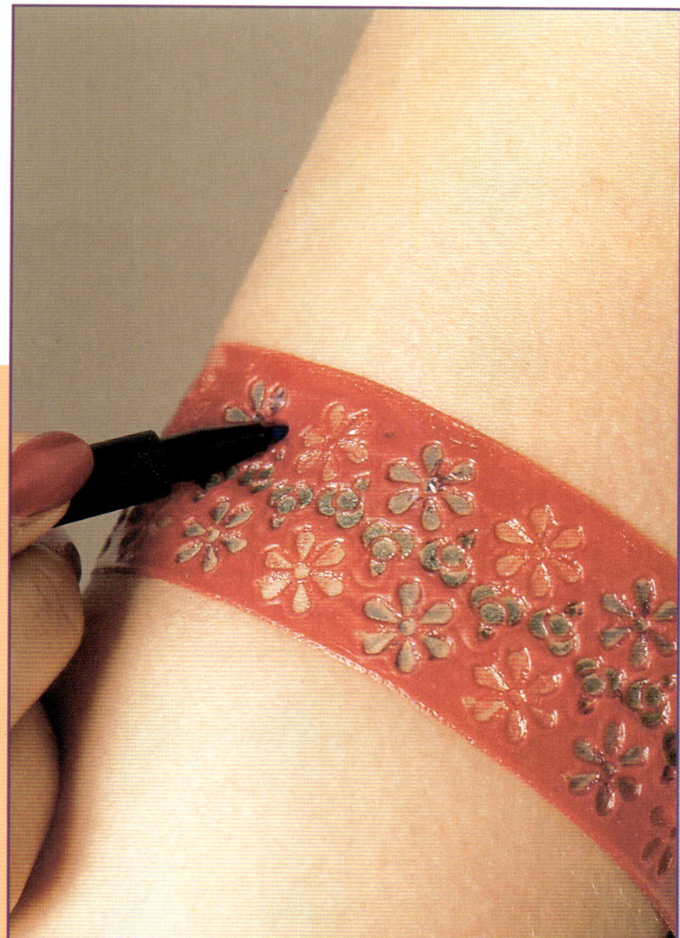

3 Complete the stencil using a different colour (or colours).

4 When the ink is dry, gently peel back the stencil.

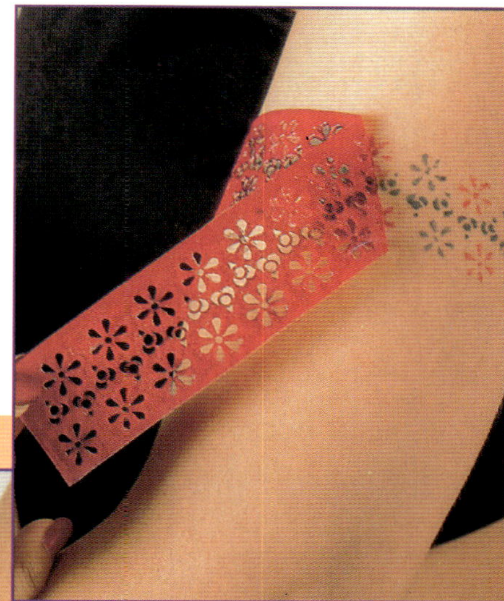

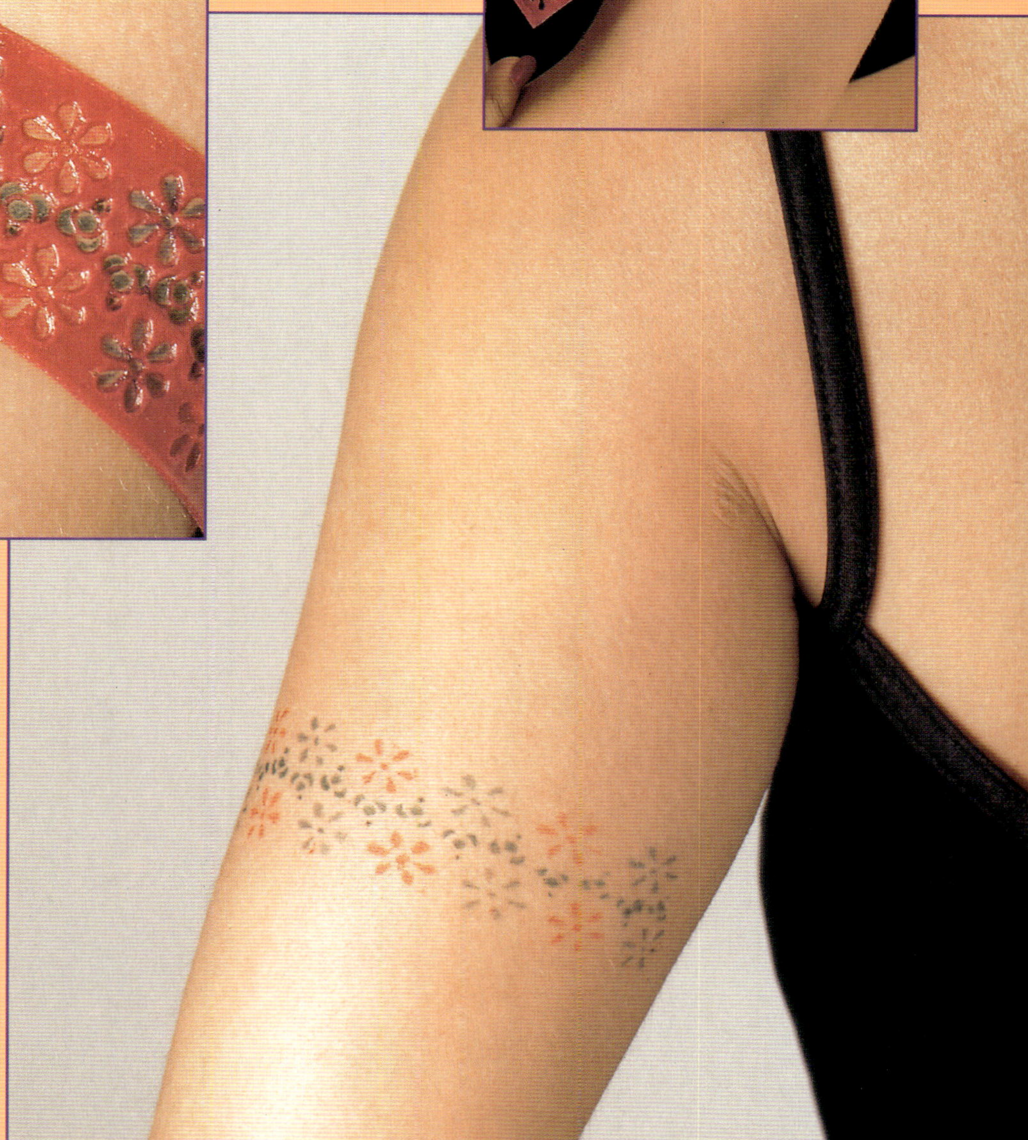

Kanji symbols

Some of the most popular Kanji characters mean 'peace', 'beauty', 'truth' and 'love', or, as shown here, 'happiness'. The stencils can be used in many ways – with inkpad colours or even with airbrushes.

YOU WILL NEED

- Cotton wool
- Alcohol solution (witch hazel)
- Paper towel
- Stencil
- Thimble & ink pad
- Coloured inks

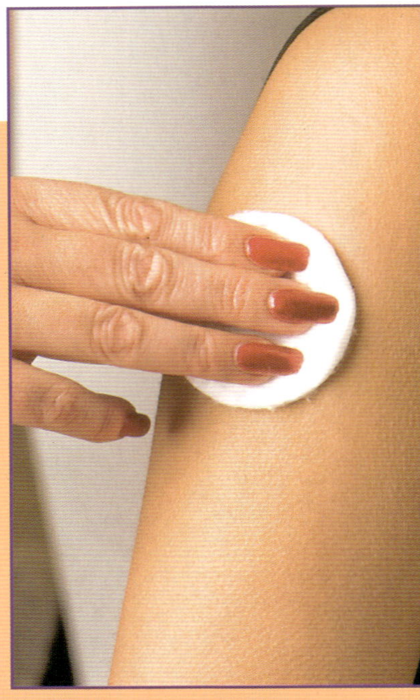

1 First cleanse the skin.

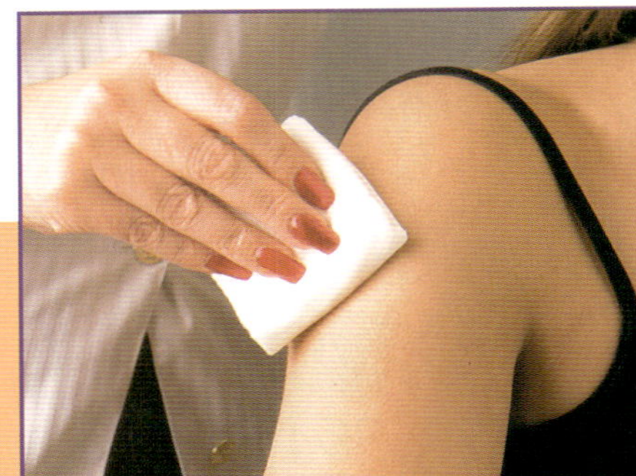

2 Then pat skin dry with a paper towel.

3 Next apply the stencil in the required position.

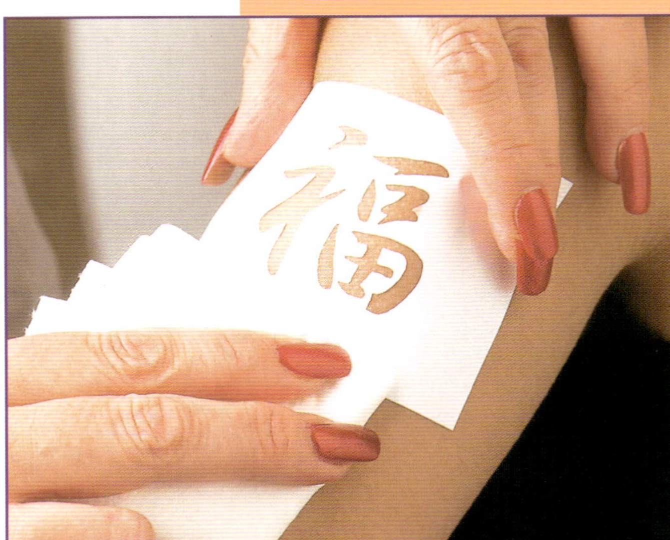

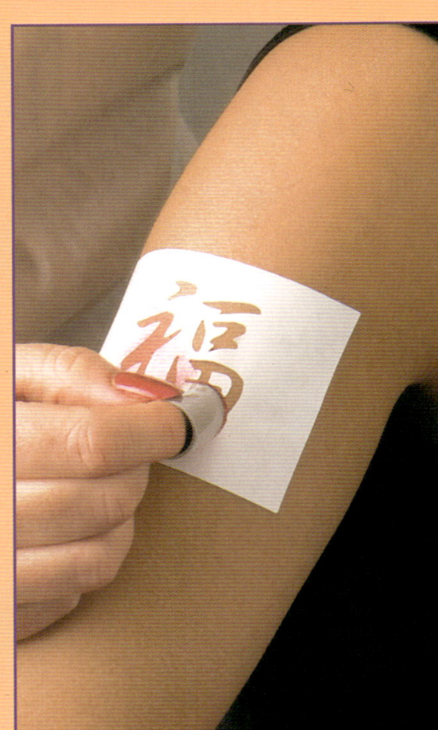

4 Use the thimble and ink pad to apply ink to the stencil.

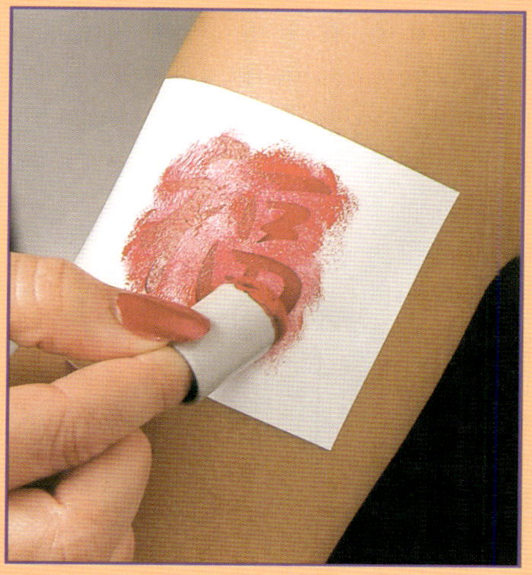

5 Add more ink until the stencil is completely filled.

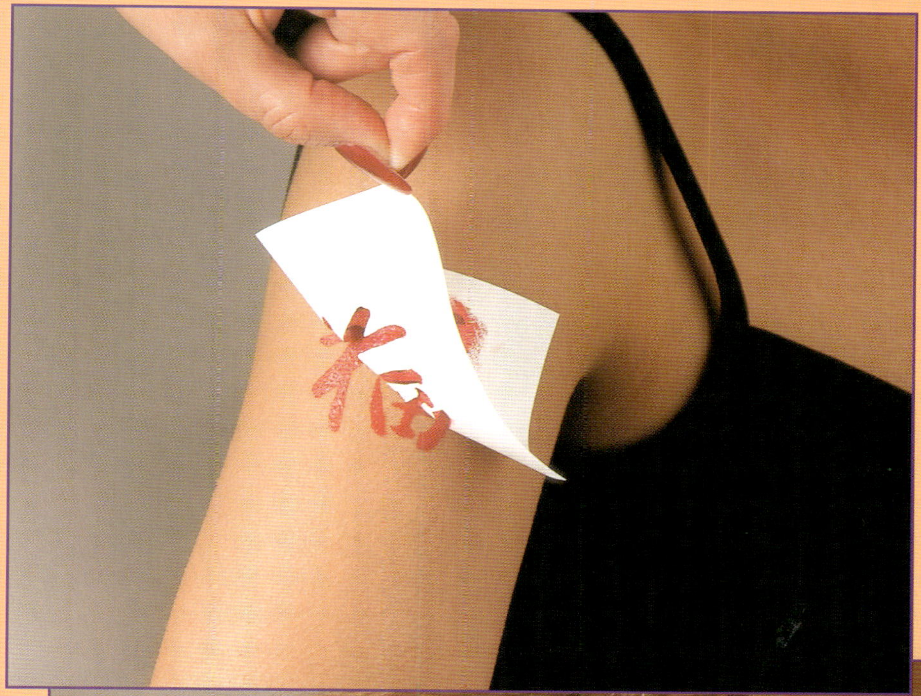

6 Peel off the stencil.

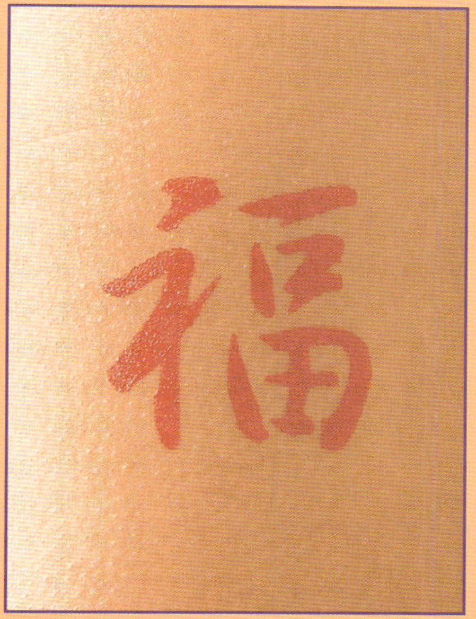

7 The finished design.

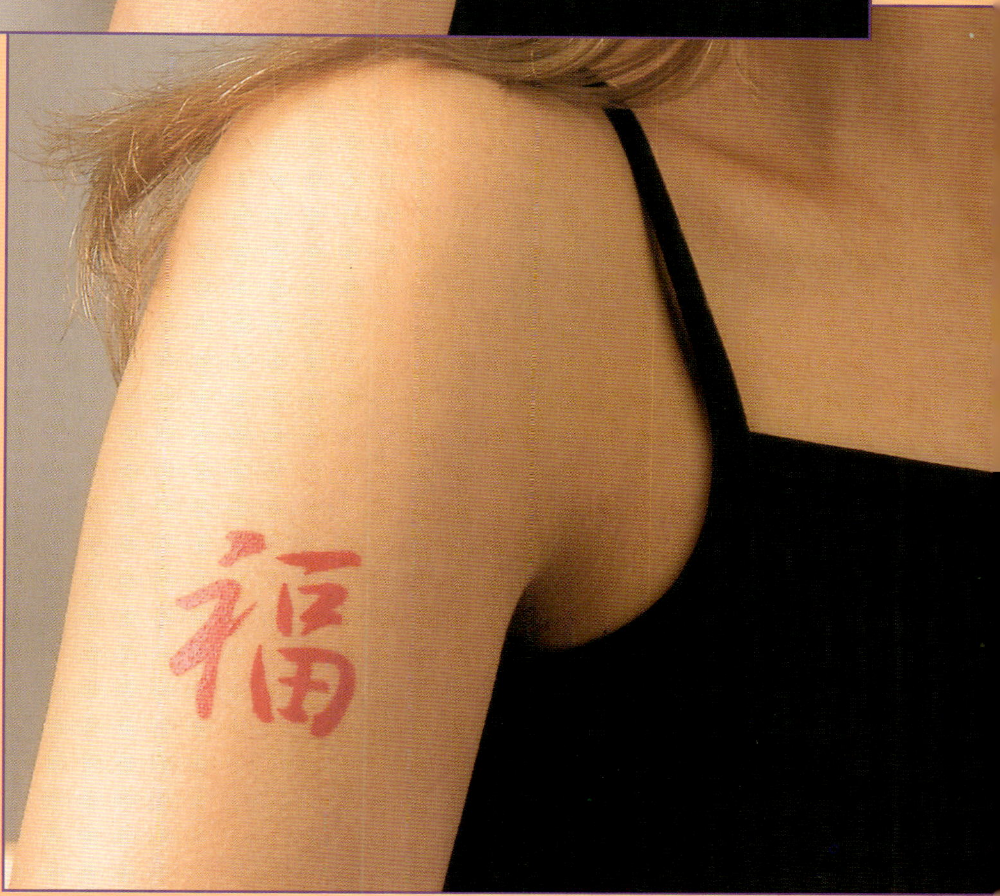

Sunrise

Stencilled designs are a good way to try out different styles without having to take the plunge of having a permanent tattoo. They can be placed anywhere on the body. This fun flower design works wonderfully at the base of the spine.

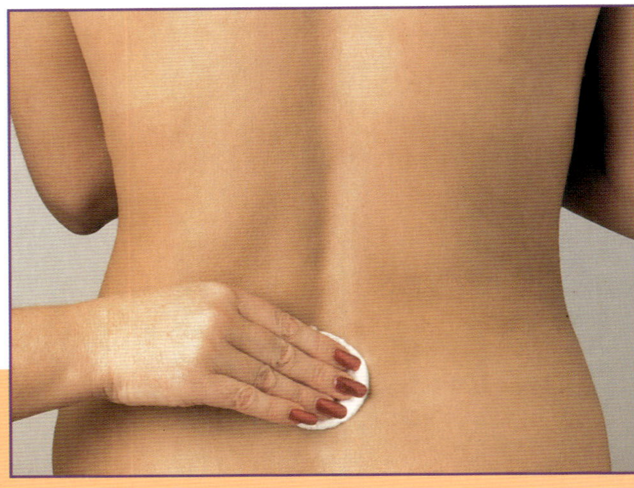

1 First cleanse the skin.

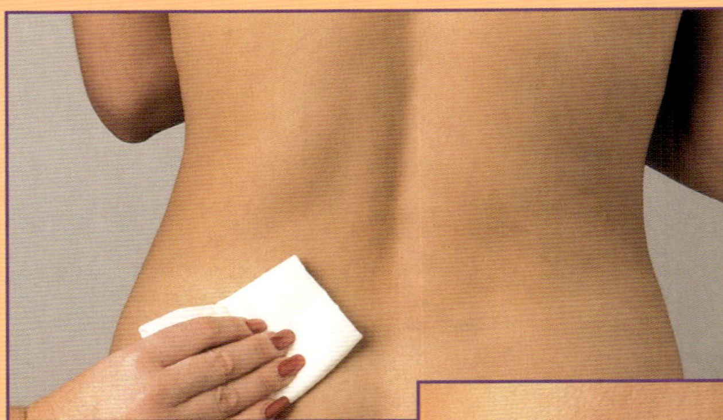

2 Then pat the skin dry with a paper towel.

YOU WILL NEED

- Cotton pads
- Alcohol solution (witch hazel)
- Stencil
- Thimble and ink pad

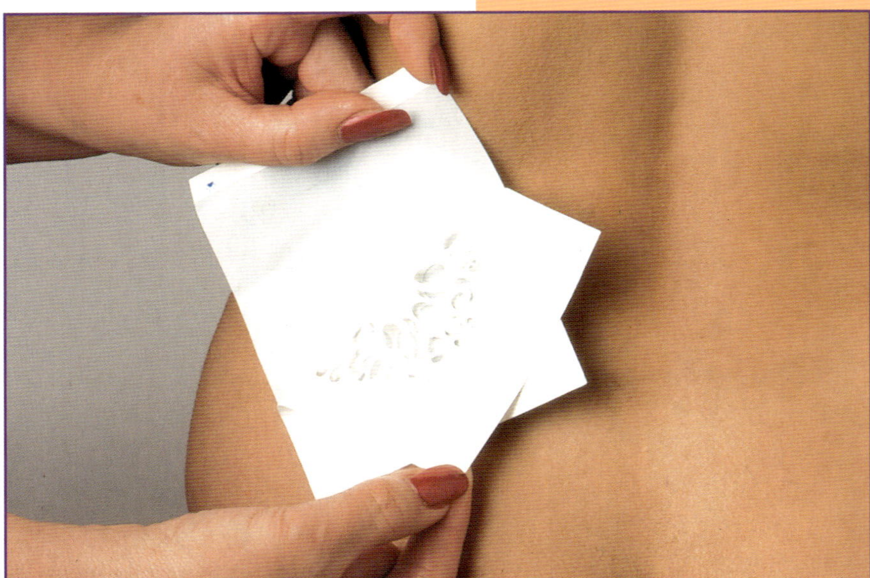

3 Peel off the stencil from its backing paper.

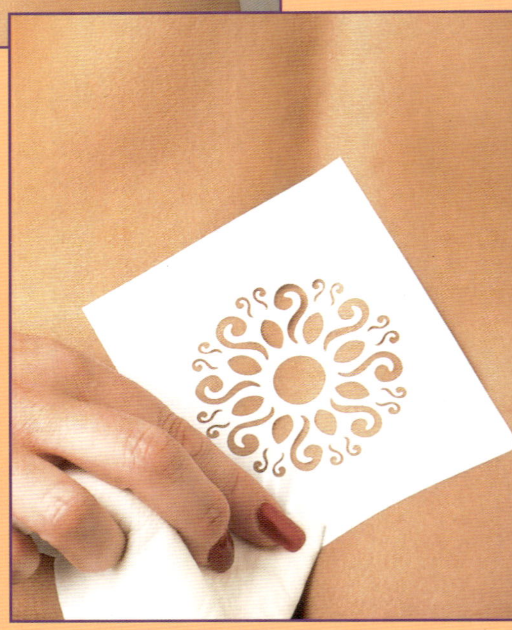

4 Apply the stencil and secure into position.

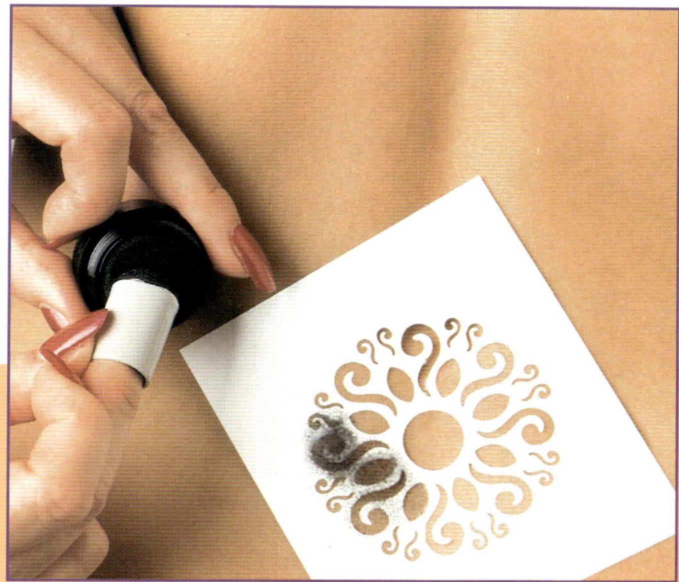

5 Using the thimble and ink pad, gently apply ink to the stencil.

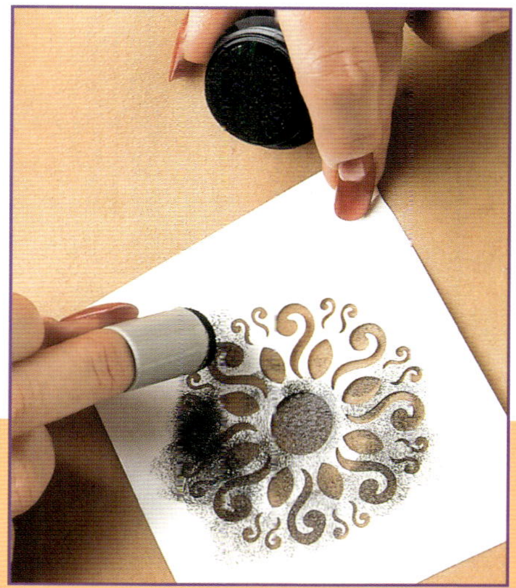

6 Apply more ink until stencil is filled.

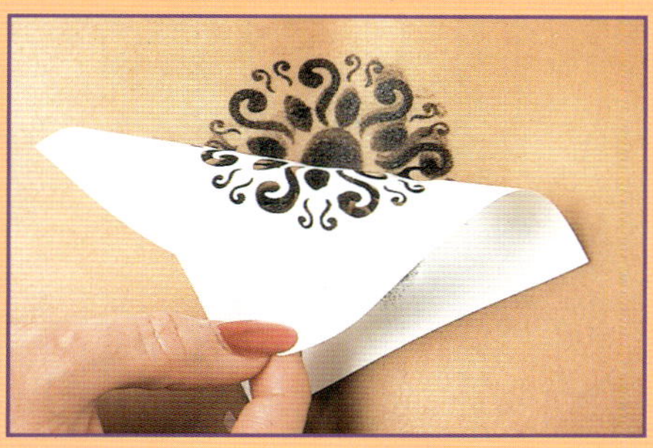

7 When the design is finished, peel away the stencil.

8 Here you can see the finished design.

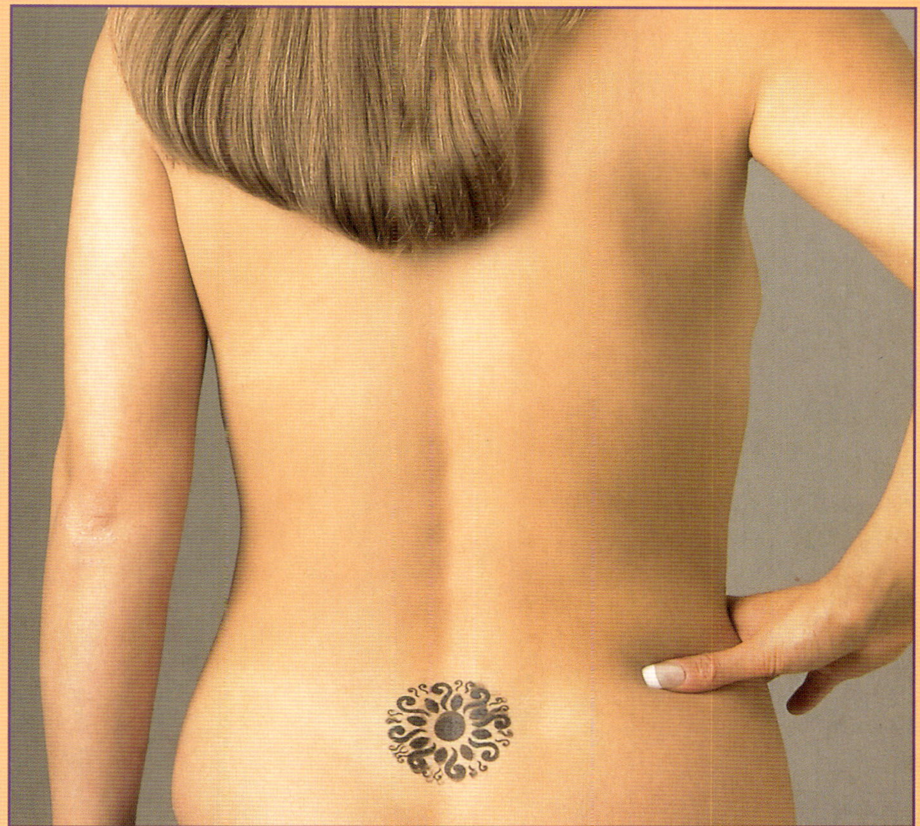

Freehand sun

This is a quick and easy way to create a pretty, delicate design. More embellishment can be added, as described in other chapters, but the gold and blue colours make this simple design stand out well.

YOU WILL NEED
- Cotton pads
- Alcohol solution (witch hazel)
- Body paints
- Fine art brushes

1 After cleansing and drying the skin, begin the design using the yellow paint.

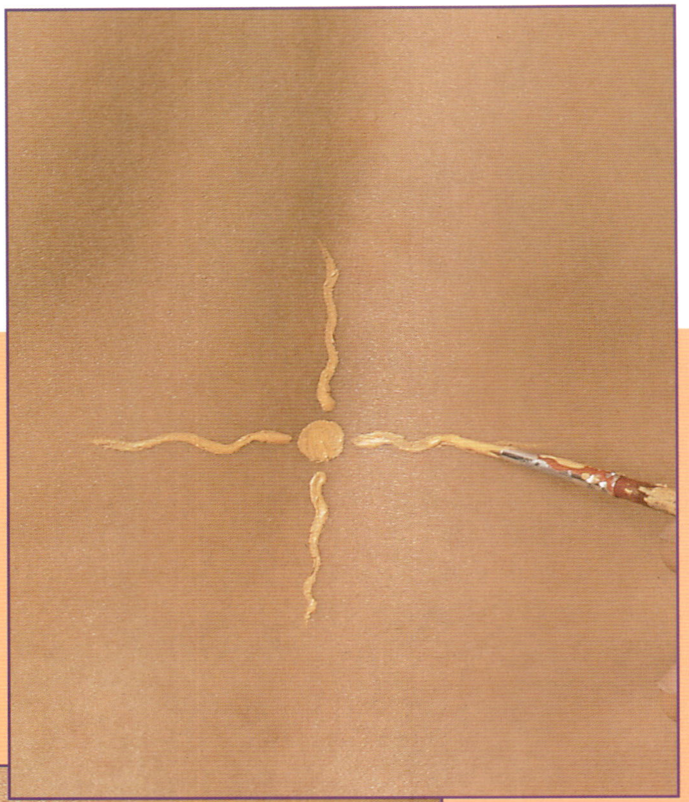

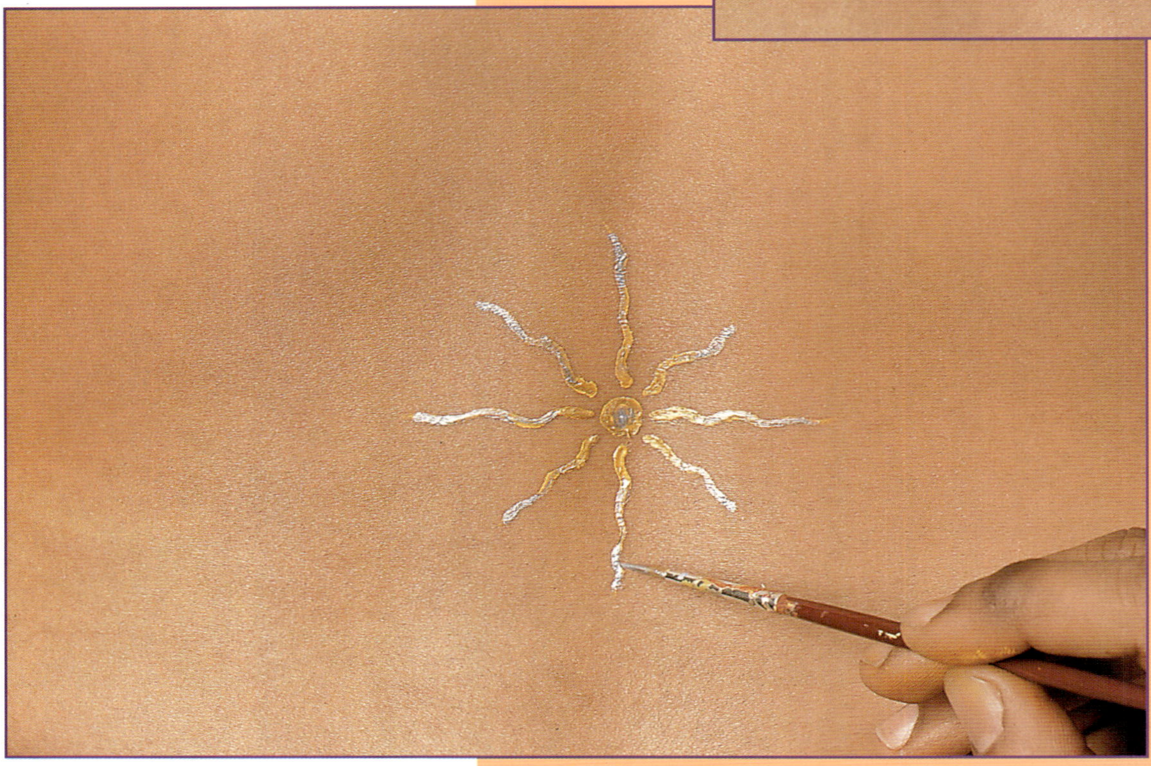

2 Continue the design, finishing off with blue tips.

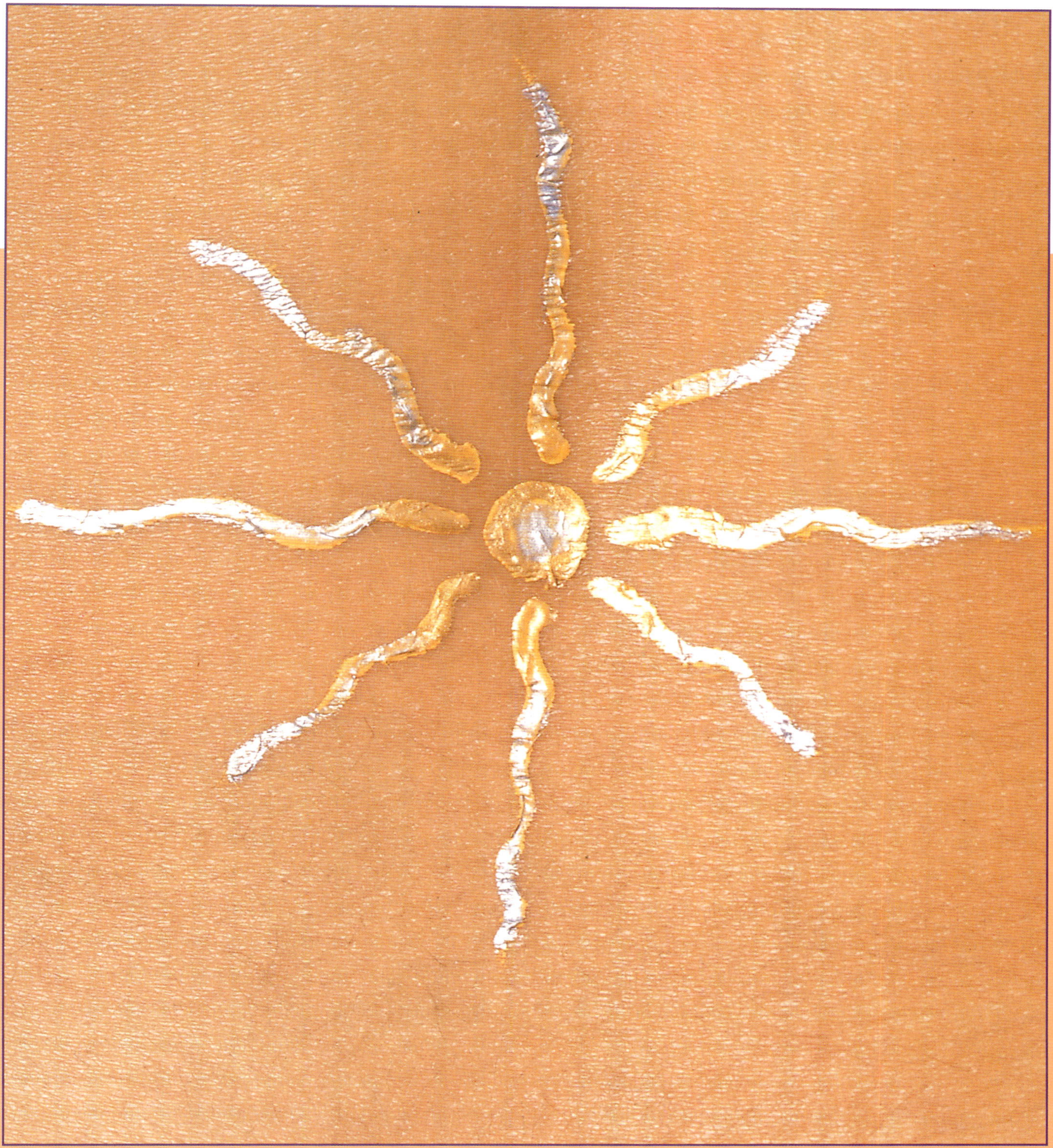

Face-painting

Face-painting can be done simply for fun or to add a touch of drama to eveningwear. It can be as simple or as detailed as you like. This is a simple freehand design.

YOU WILL NEED

- Cotton pads
- Alcohol solution (witch hazel)
- Body paints
- Fine art brushes

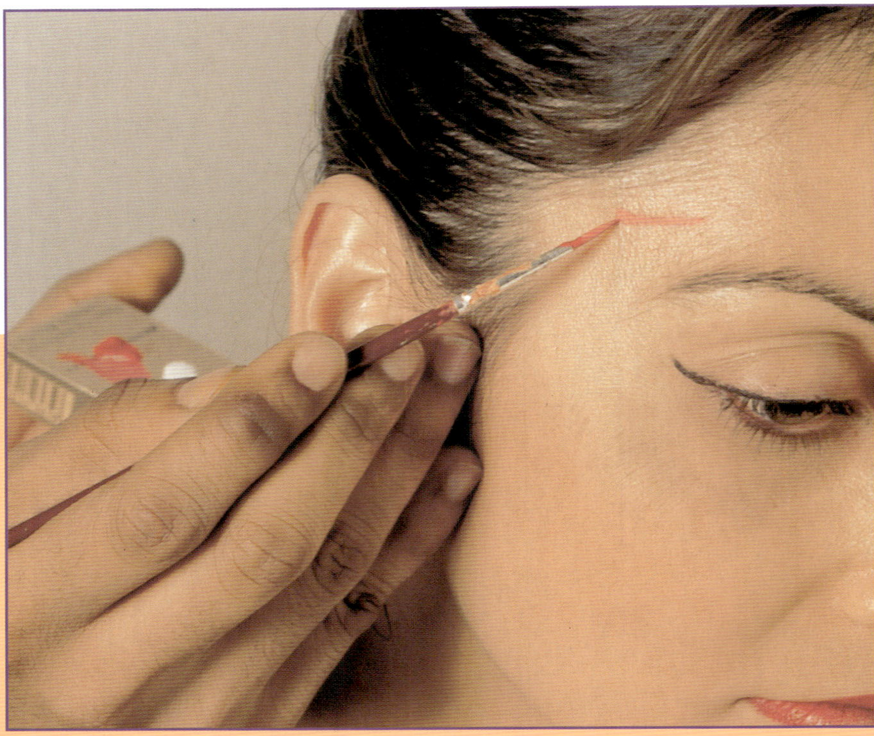

1 Cleanse the part of your face that you are going to paint by wiping it with a cotton pad dipped in alcohol solution and then let it dry thoroughly before beginning your design.

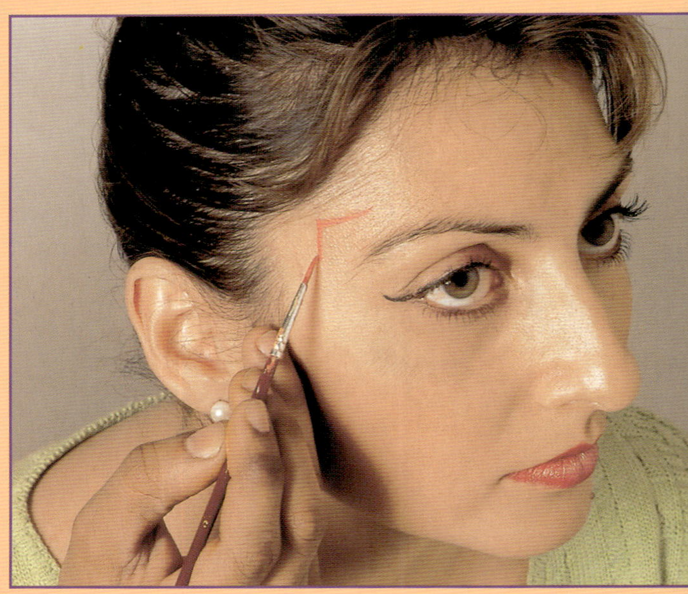

2 Continue the design. You will need to use a fine art brush. Correct any mistakes with a dampened cotton bud.

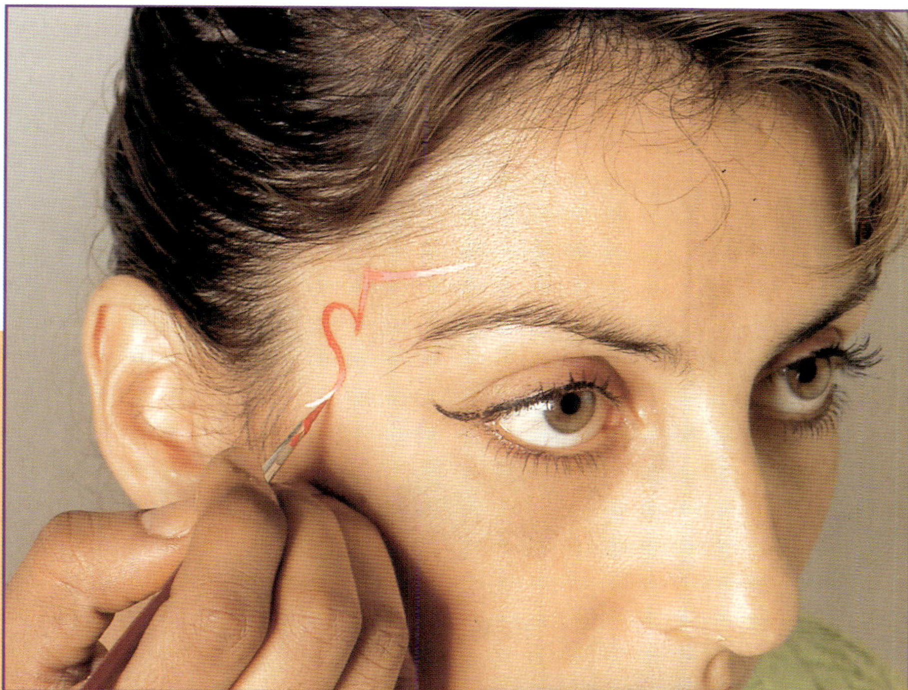

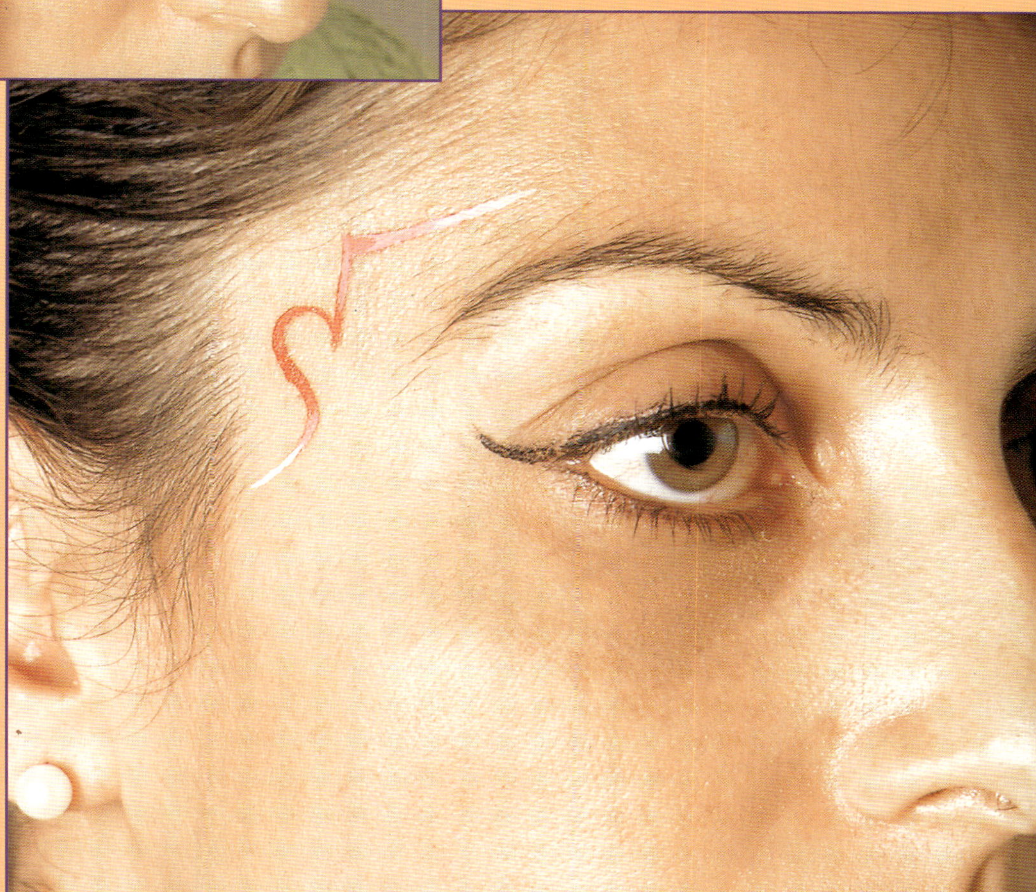

3 Add a different colour to create a toned effect, and complete with a swirl.

Tribal markings

This design is based upon traditional Maori tribal markings. As you can see it is not something you'd choose for everyday wear, but it will certainly add a dramatic effect for a party!

YOU WILL NEED
- Cotton pad
- Alcohol solution (witch hazel)
- Black body paint
- Fine art brush

1 Begin the design.

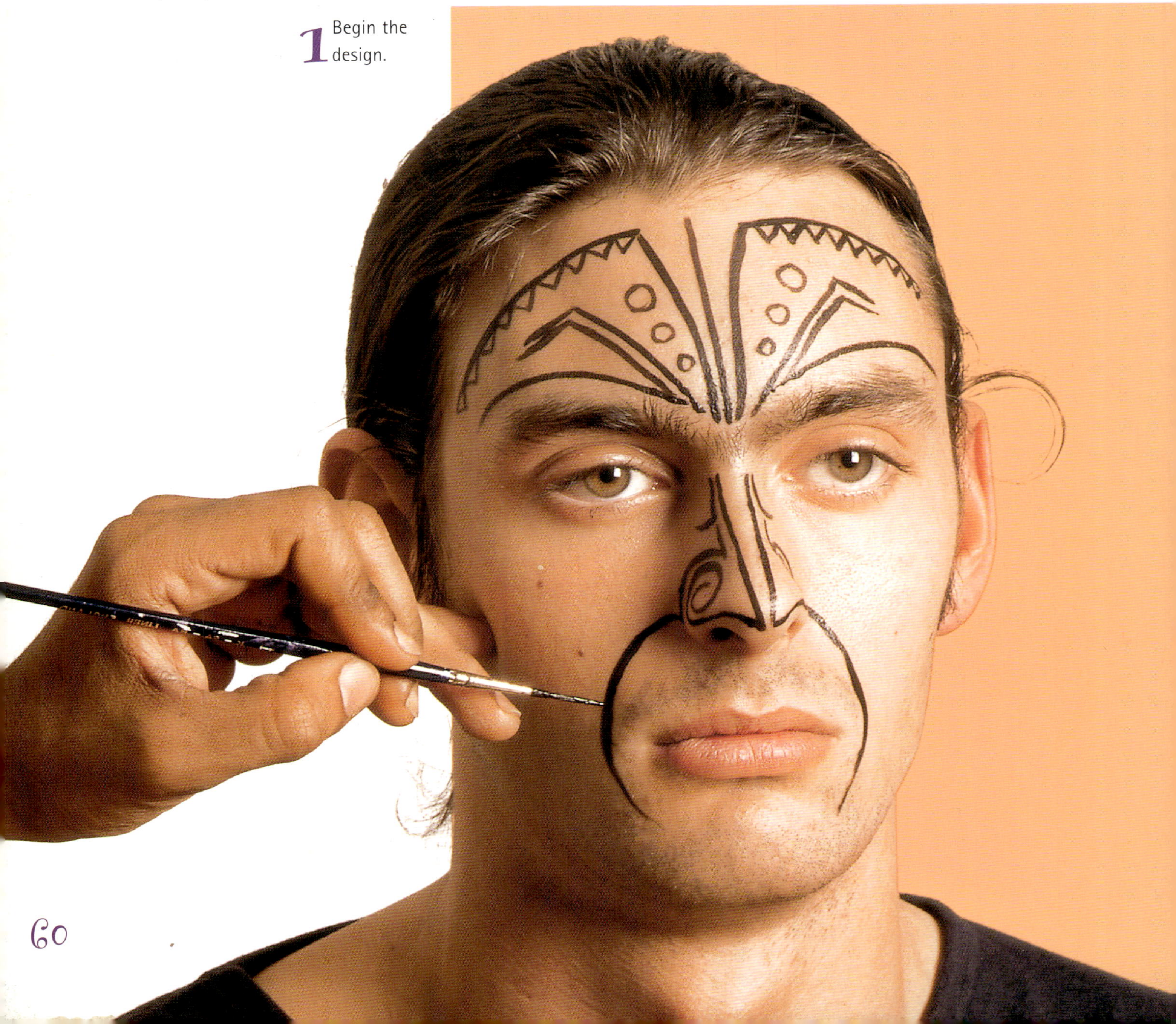

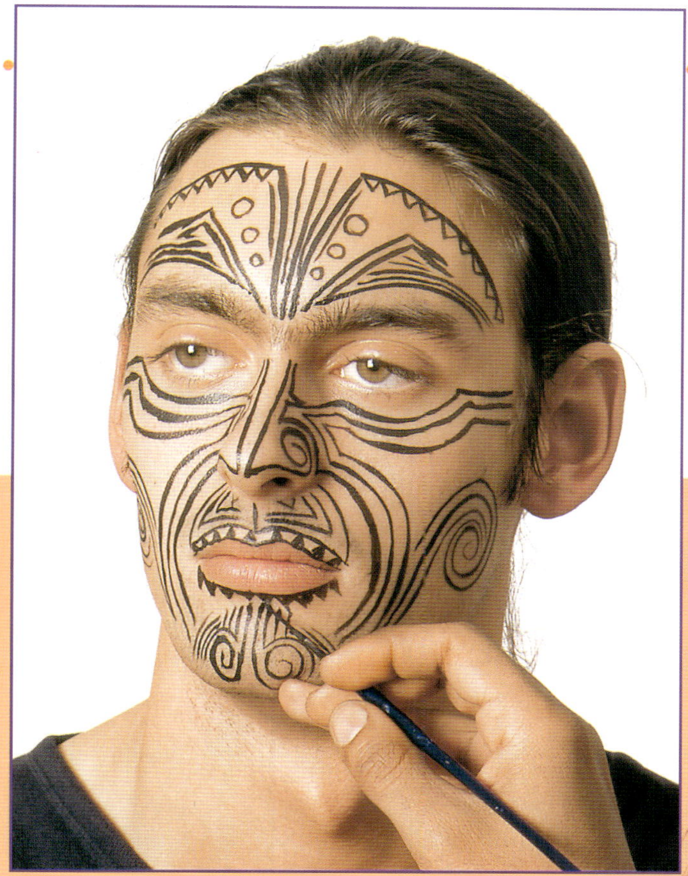

2 Finish the design. If you do not want to cover the whole face, you can use sections of the design in different areas.

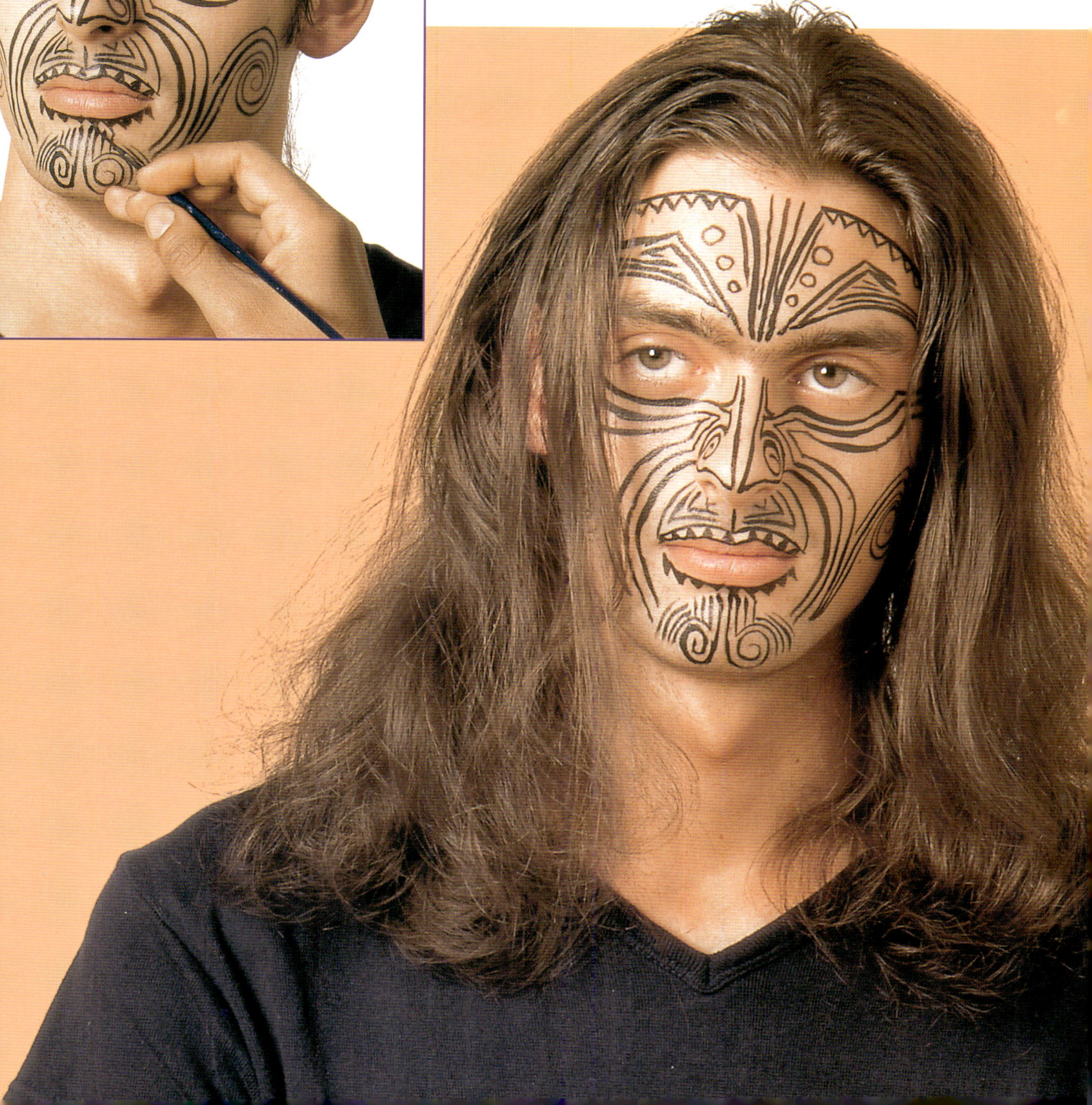

Aztec design

Some dramatic body-art designs can be created with body paints and jewellery. You can use a particular piece of clothing or jewellery to inspire your design, as we have done with this Peruvian beaded anklet.

YOU WILL NEED
- Cotton pad
- Alcohol solution (witch hazel)
- Body paints
- Fine art brushes

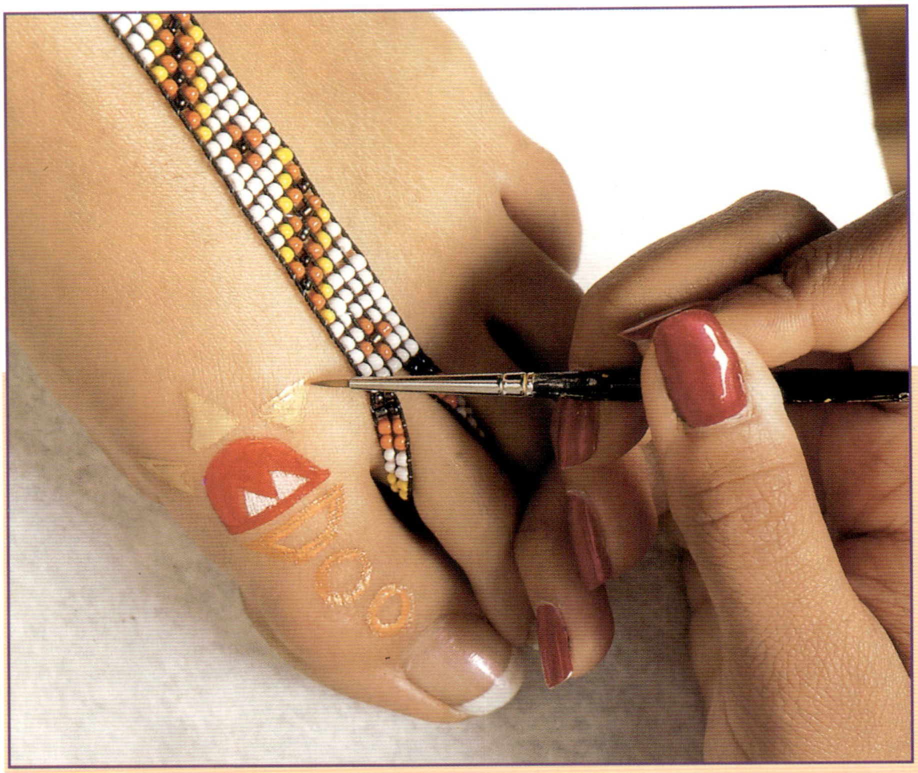

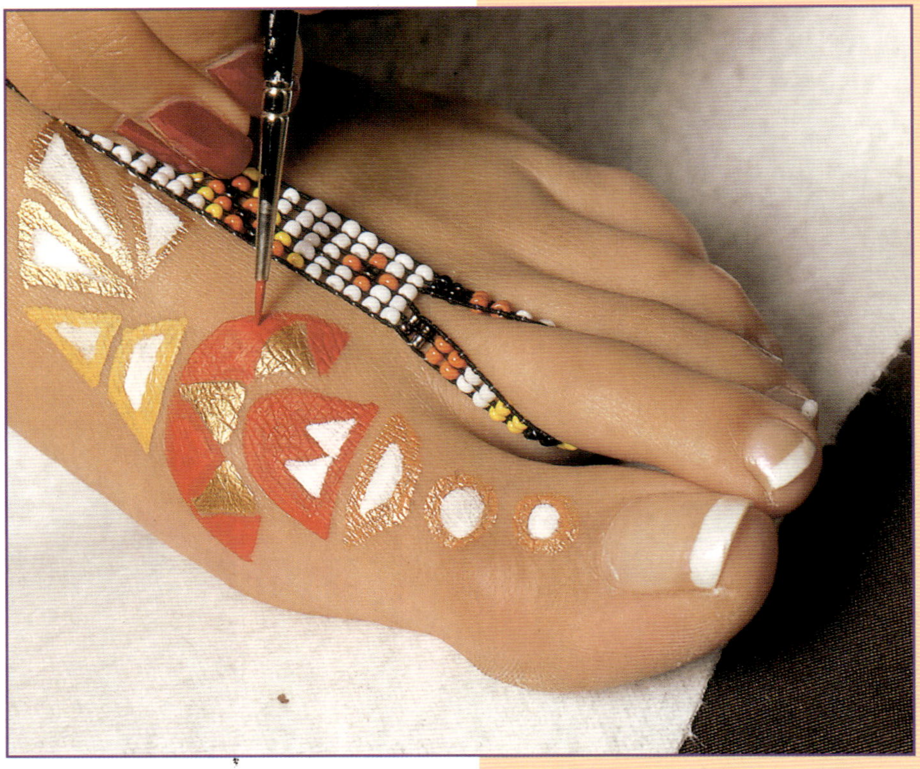

1 Cleanse the area on which you are going to paint your design by wiping it with a cotton pad dipped in alcohol solution and then let it dry thoroughly before beginning your design.

2 It can be helpful to make a sketch or picture of the design that you can then follow. Gradually fill in the design.

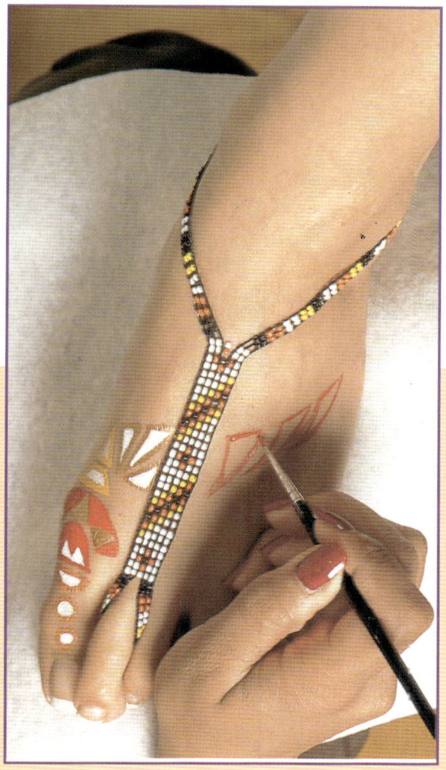

3 For a balanced effect, continue the design across the other side of the foot.

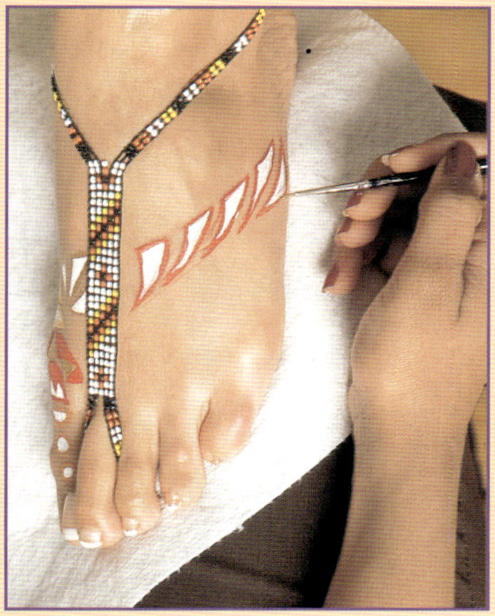

4 Fill in the pattern.

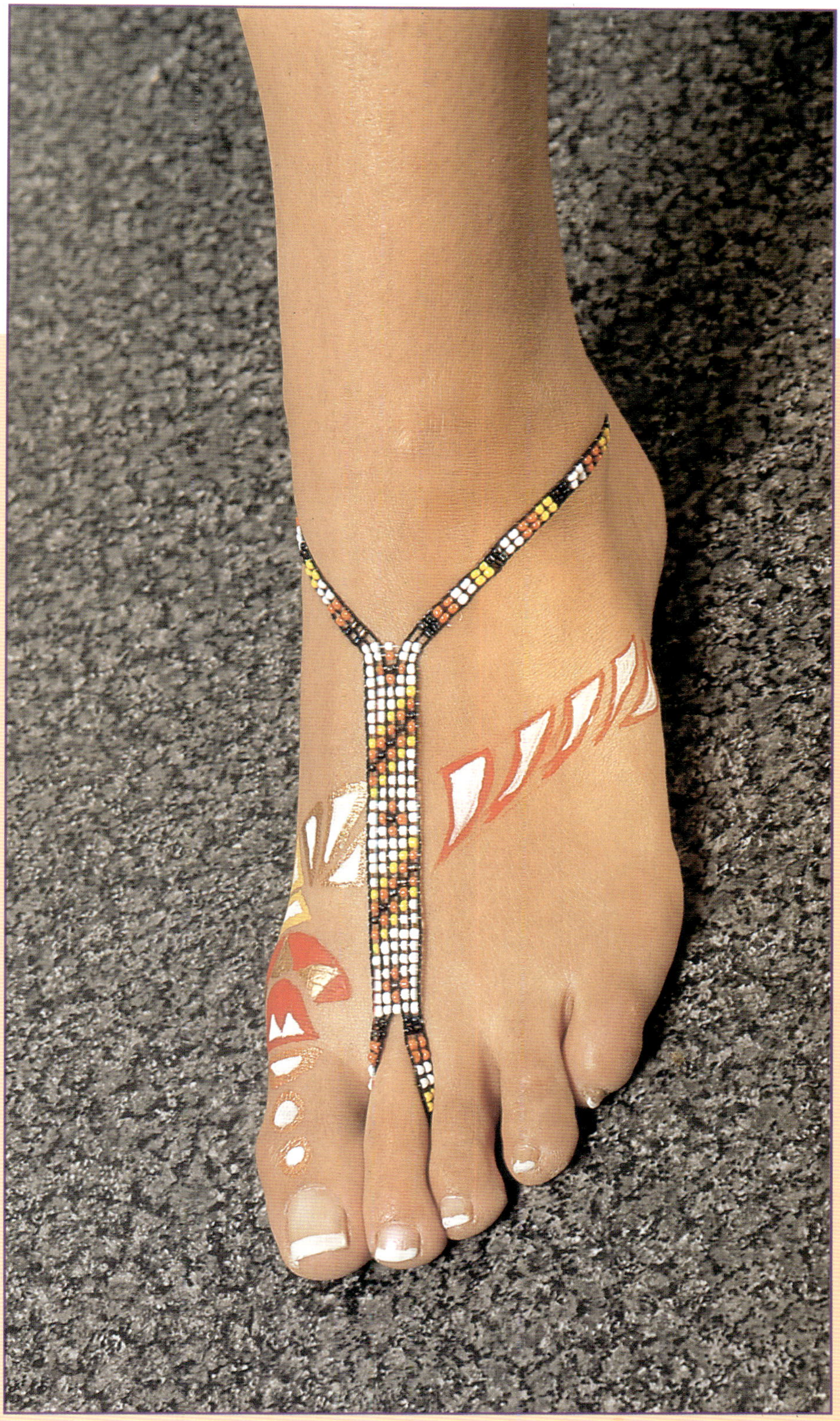

Tranquillity and Happiness

Japanese characters are particularly popular in all forms of body art, and designs are available with characters that mean a variety of different things. These characters, Tranquillity and Happiness, are particularly charming.

YOU WILL NEED
- Cotton pads
- Alcohol solution (witch hazel)
- Body paints
- Fine art brushes
- Body glitter

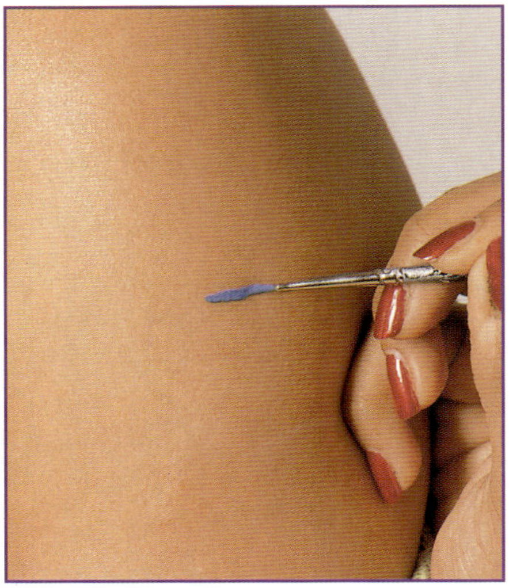

1 After cleansing the skin, decide where you want to begin your character.

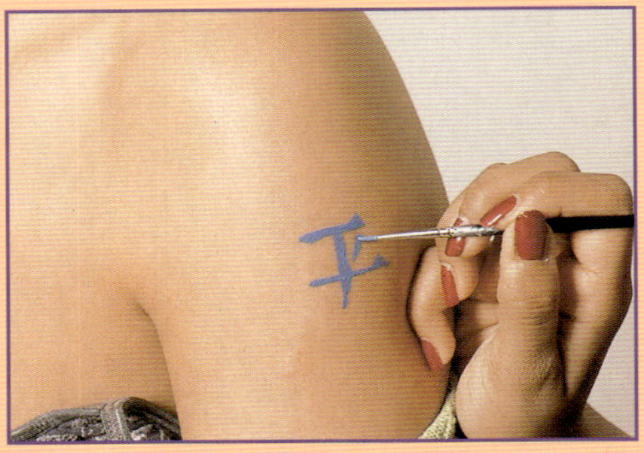

2 Carefully paint in the first strokes.

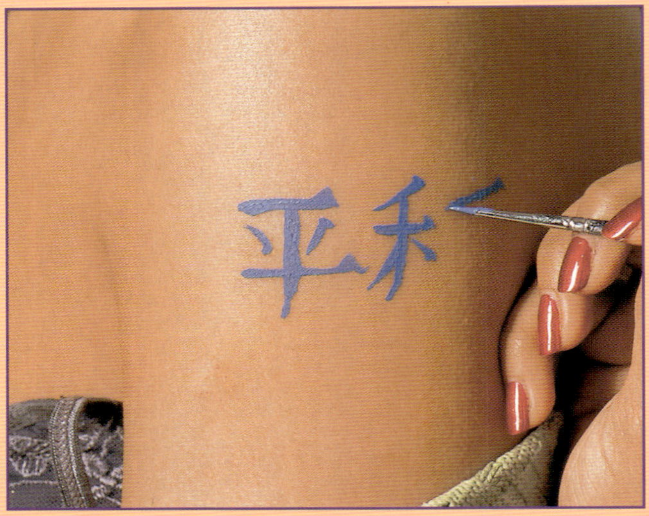

3 Keep the characters well spaced and distinct.

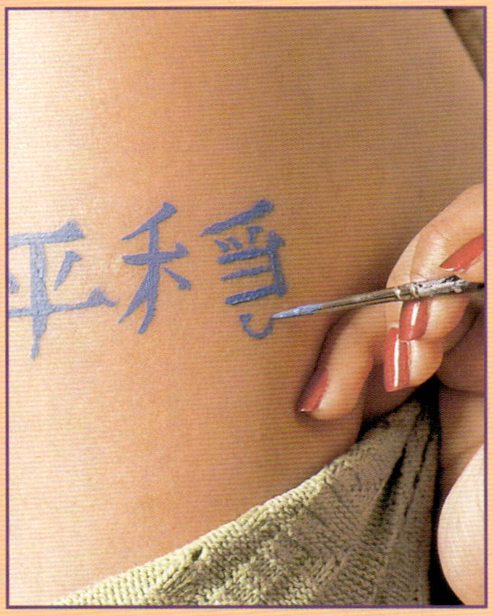

4 Keep your hand steady so that the characters are clear.

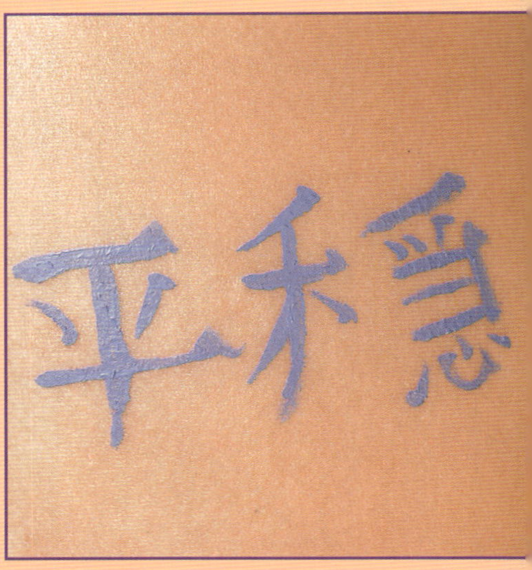

5 The finished Japanese word.

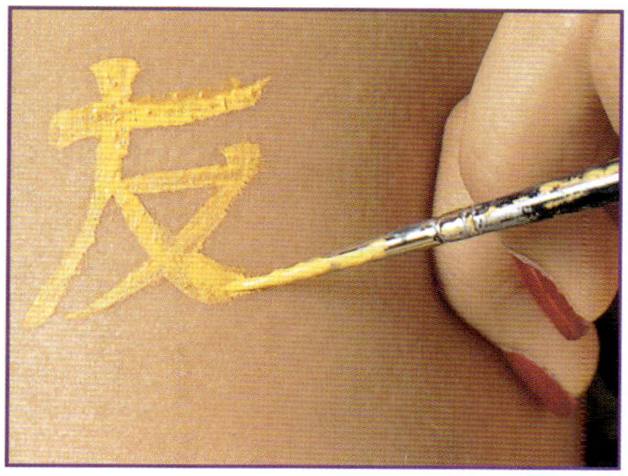

6 You can leave the design here, but a second word underneath can be even more effective.

7 Again, keep the characters well spaced.

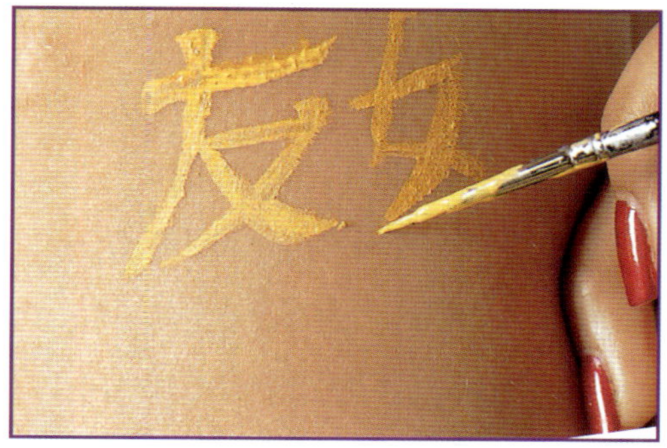

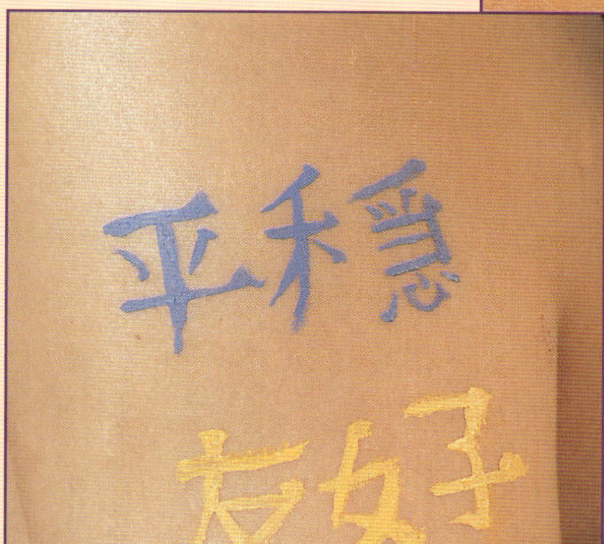

8 Here is the finished design.

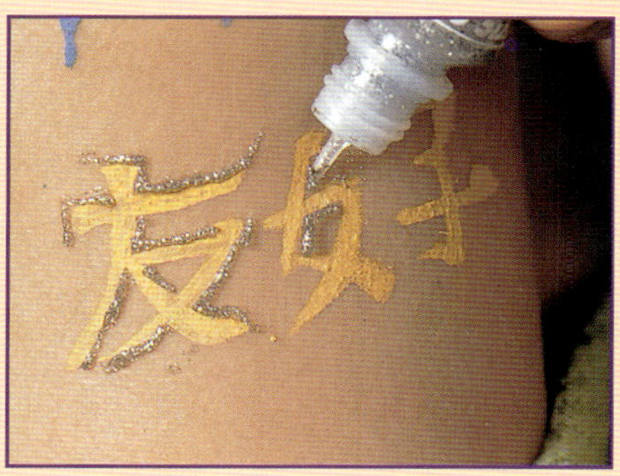

9 As a further embellishment you can add glitter to one or both of the words.

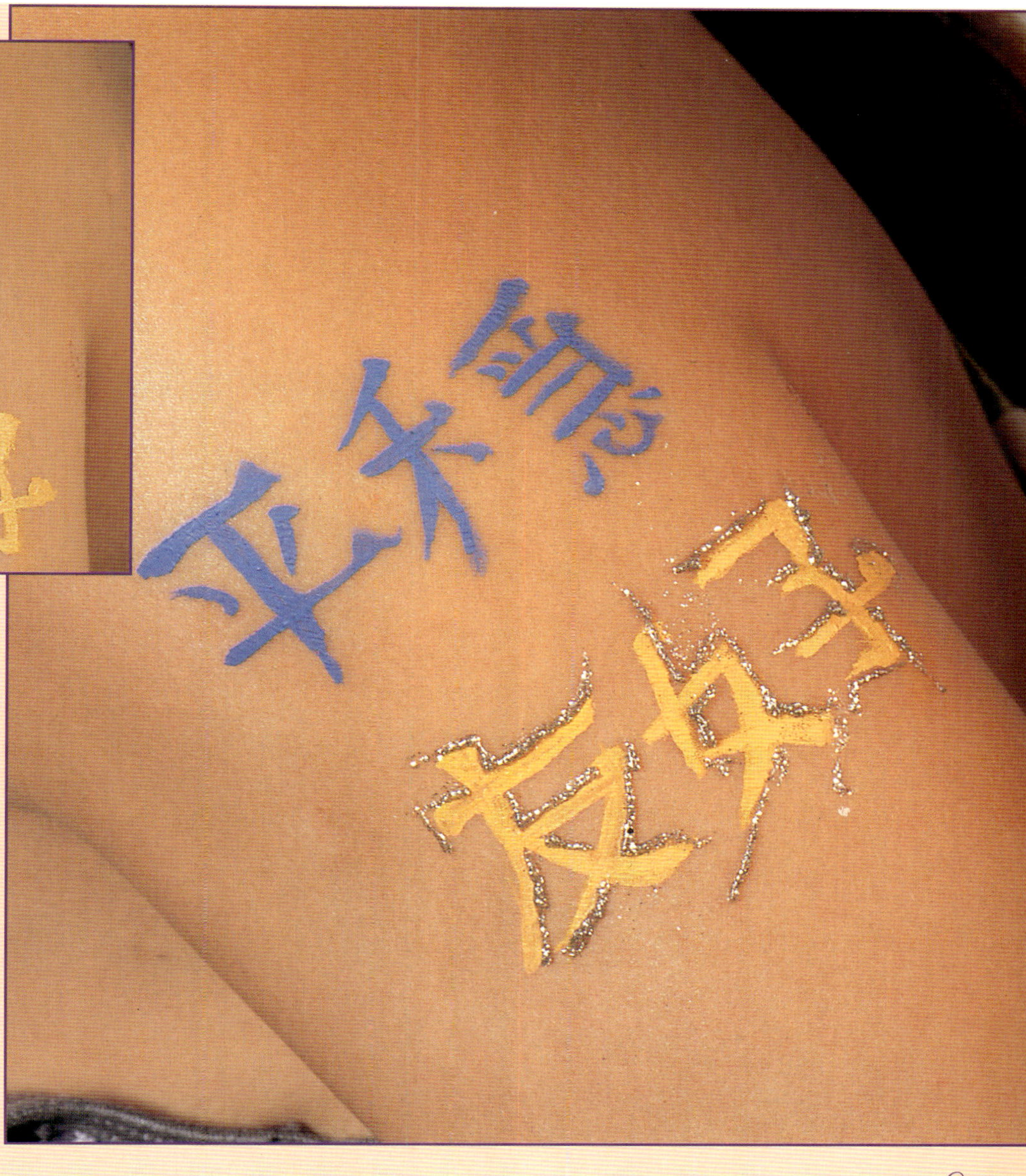

Metal twist

Airbrushing stencil designs come in all types and patterns, and are ideal for both men and women. Metal Twist is an excellent design for men – very masculine, but not at all aggressive.

YOU WILL NEED

- Alcohol-free wipes
- Tissues
- Self-adhesive stencil
- Airbrushing kit
- Water-based paint
- Cotton bud
- Water
- Soft powder brush
- Talcum powder (unscented)

1 Prepare the skin by cleaning it with alcohol-free wipes and then dry it thoroughly with tissues.

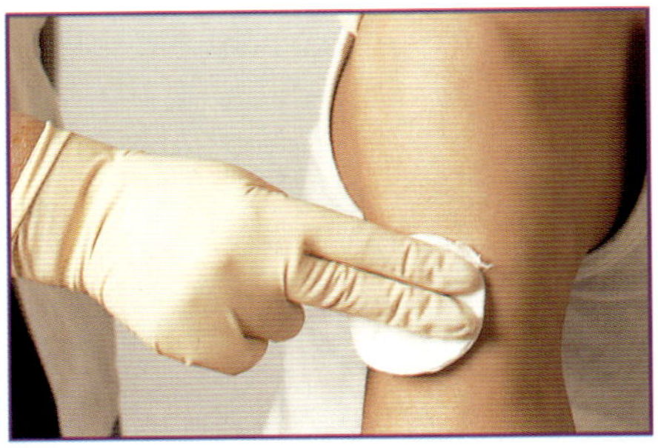

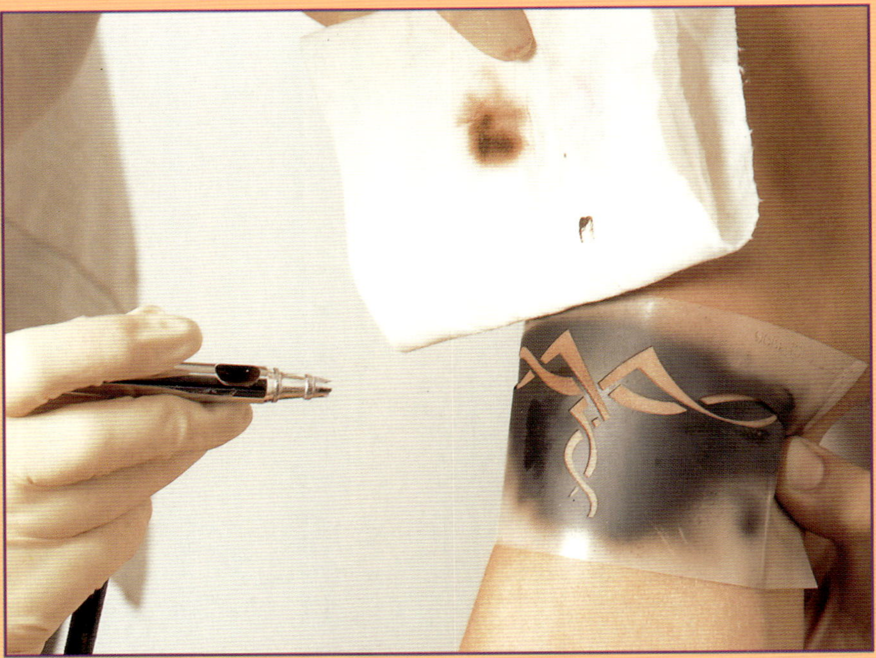

2 Peel off the self-adhesive backing and place the stencil in the desired position. Using the airbrush, build up a light, consistent airflow and spray your chosen colour of paint over the stencil.

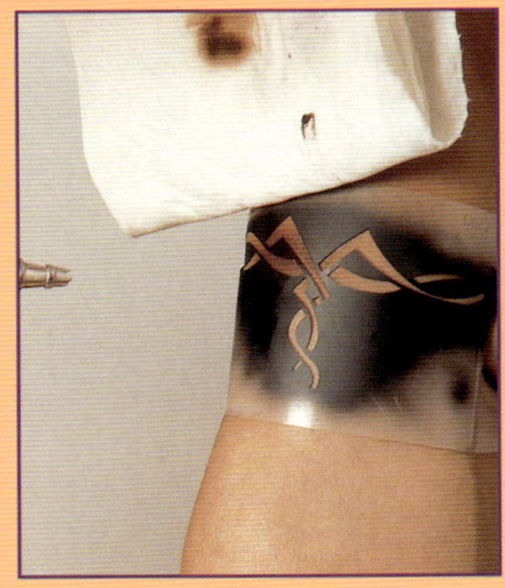

3 Build up the colour and depth gradually.

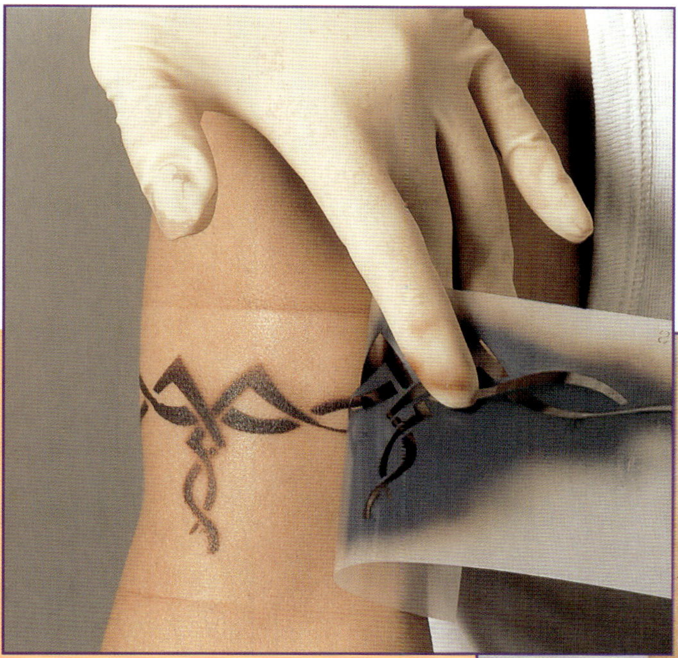

4 When the paint is completely dry, carefully remove the stencil.

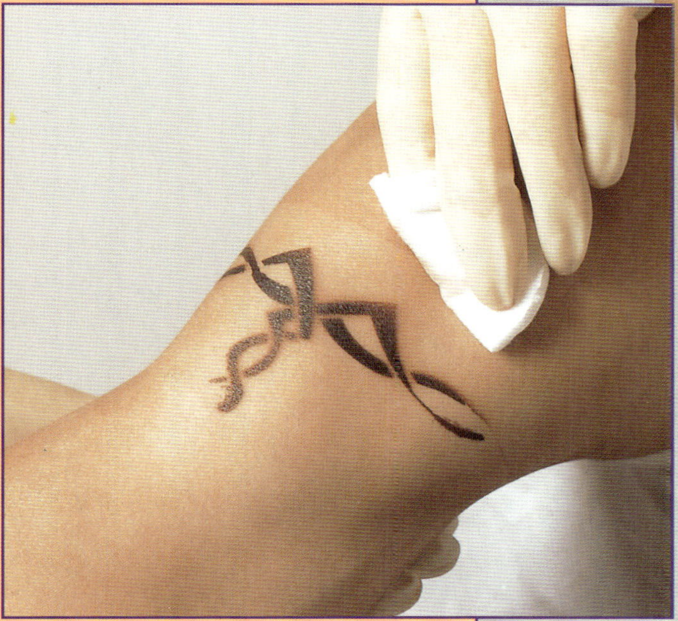

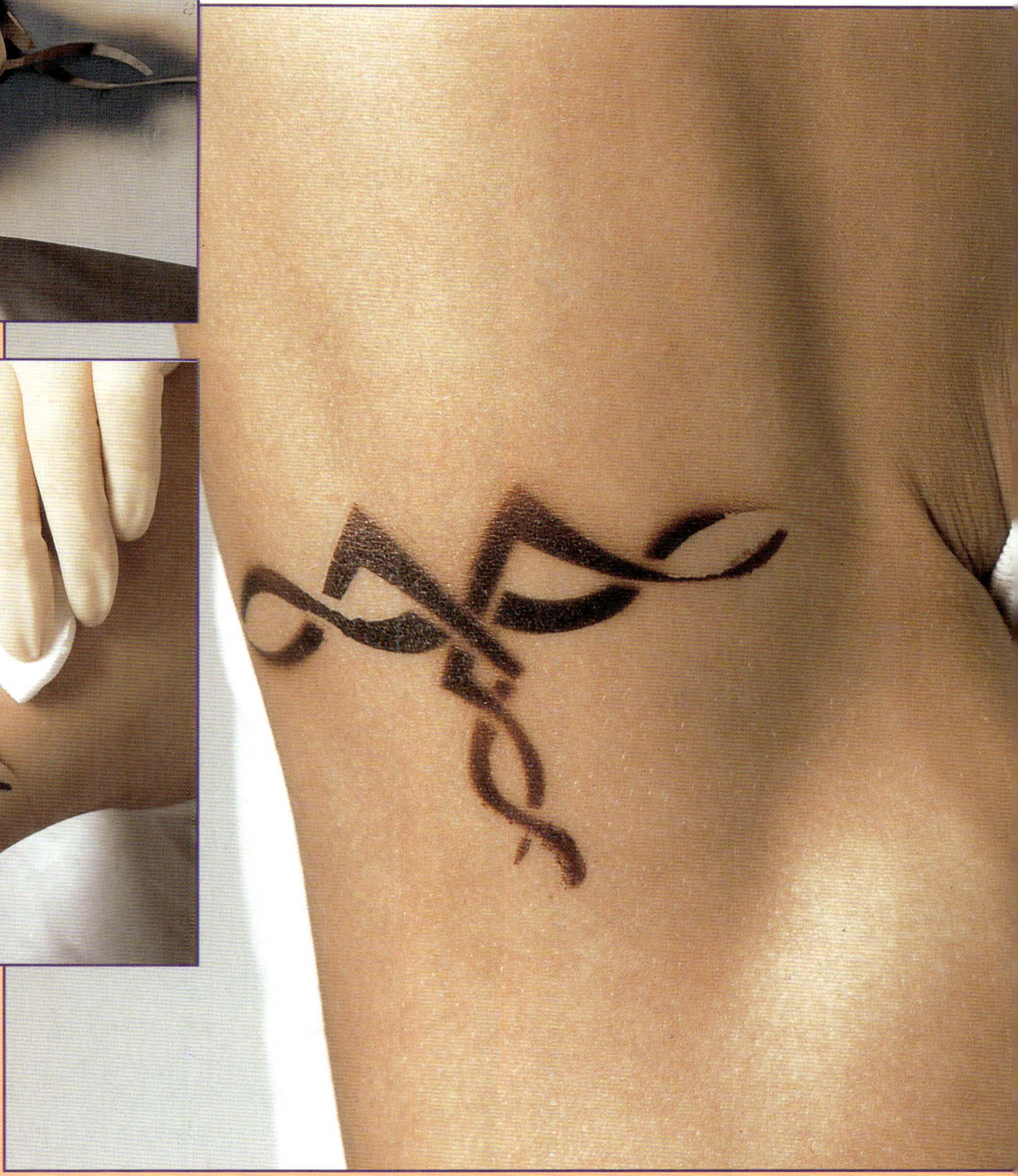

5 If necessary, you can wipe off any stray paint with a paper towel or damp cotton bud. Using a soft powder brush, lightly dust some talcum powder over the design to seal it and then lightly brush it away.

Celtic knotwork

These stencils are ideal for people who are not naturally artistic. In a wide range of reusable designs, they can be placed almost anywhere on the body. Celtic designs are always popular, and the shoulder is an excellent place for such designs.

YOU WILL NEED
- Alcohol-free wipes
- Tissues
- Self-adhesive stencil
- Airbrushing kit
- Water-based paint
- Cotton bud
- Water
- Soft powder brush
- Talcum powder (unscented)

1 Prepare your skin by cleaning it with alcohol-free wipes and then dry it thoroughly with tissues. Peel off the self-adhesive backing and place the stencil in the desired position.

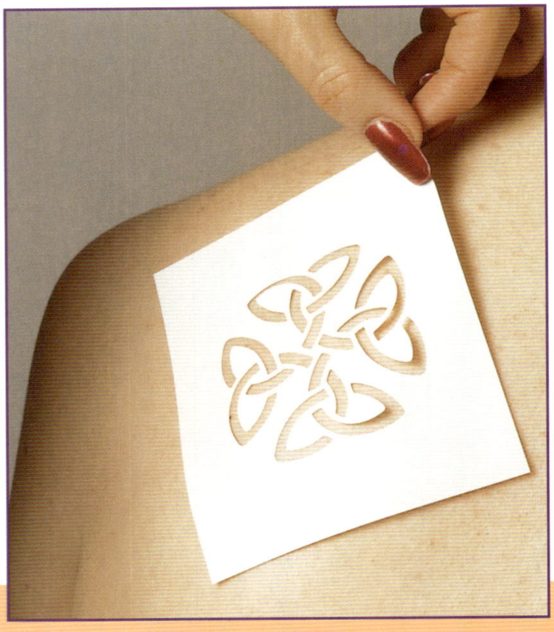

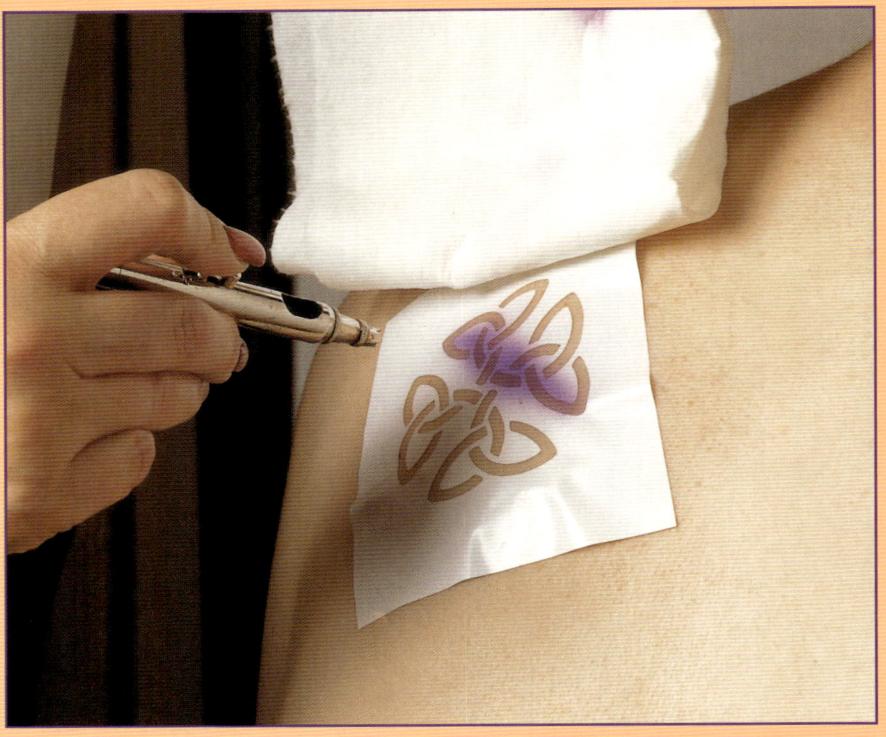

2 Using the airbrush, build up a consistent airflow and lightly spray your chosen colour of paint over the stencil. Build up the colour and depth gradually.

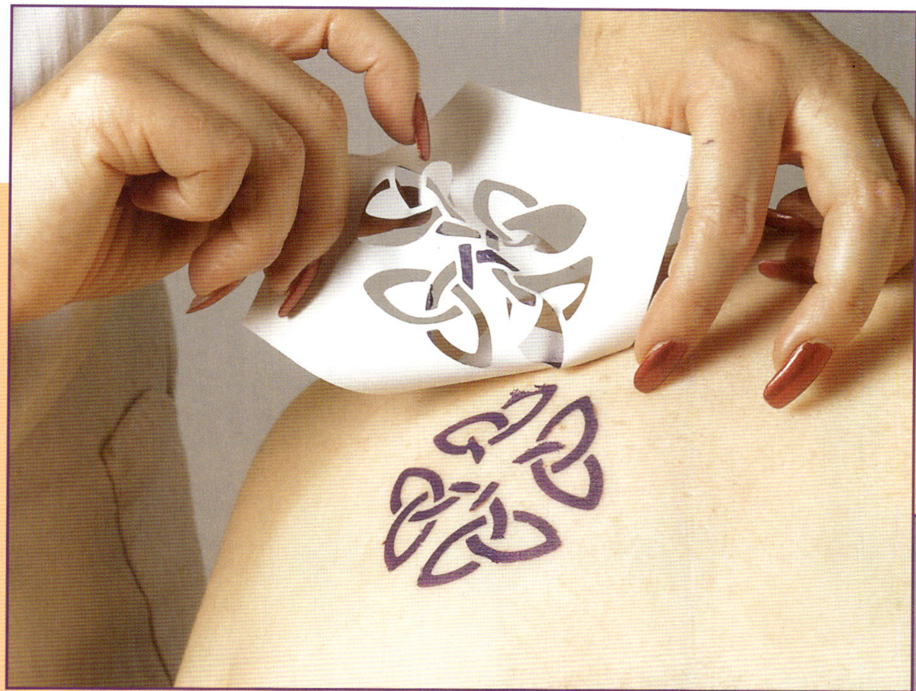

3 When the paint is completely dry, carefully remove the stencil. If necessary, you can wipe off any stray paint with a damp cotton bud or paper towel.

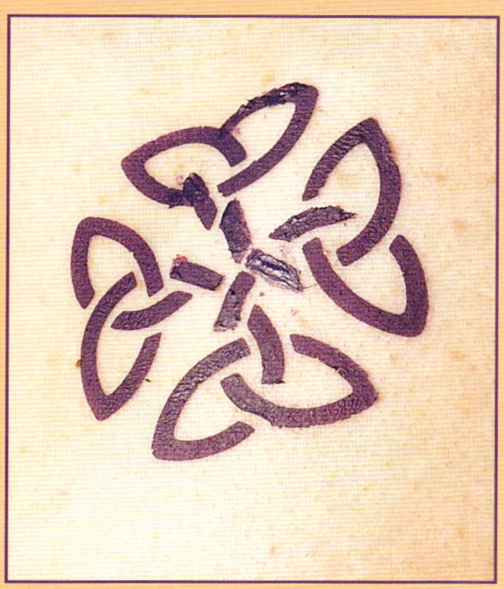

4 Using a soft powder brush, lightly dust some talcum powder over the design to seal it and then lightly brush it away.

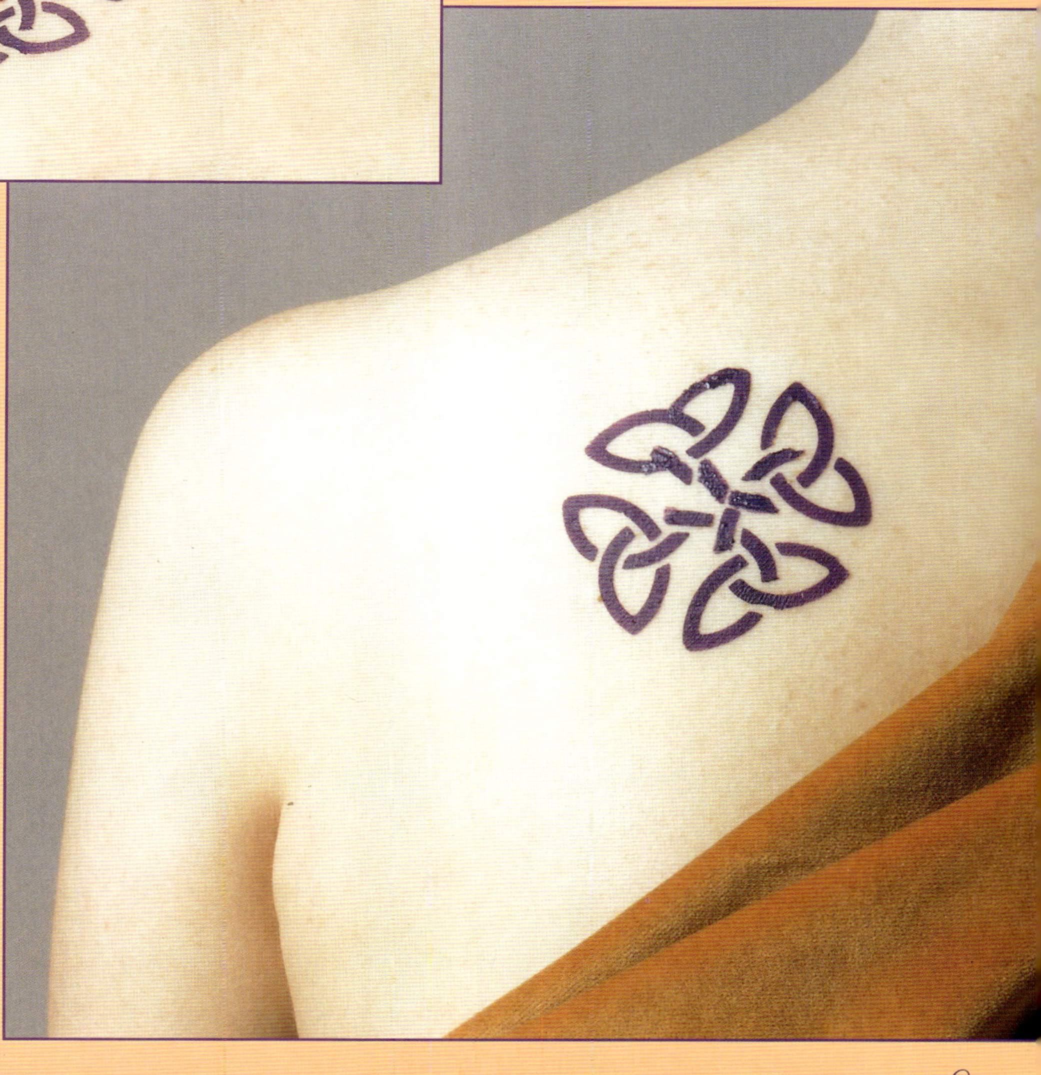

Airbrushed barbed-wire

Not only can airbrushed designs be created on almost any part of the body, but you can mix and match all sorts of colours and designs – from the sweetly feminine to the dramatically gothic. The same effect can also be created using body spray paints.

YOU WILL NEED
- Alcohol-free wipes
- Tissues
- Self-adhesive stencil
- Airbrushing kit
- Water-based paint
- Soft powder brush
- Talcum powder (unscented)

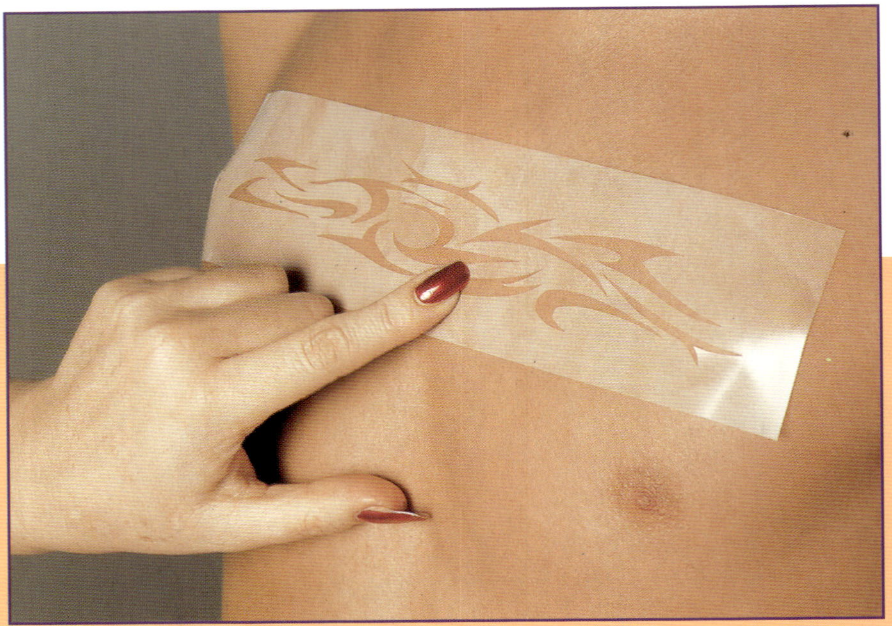

1 Prepare your skin by cleaning it with alcohol-free wipes and then dry it thoroughly with tissues. Peel off the self-adhesive backing and carefully place the stencil in the desired position.

2 Using the airbrush, lightly spray your chosen colour of paint over it.

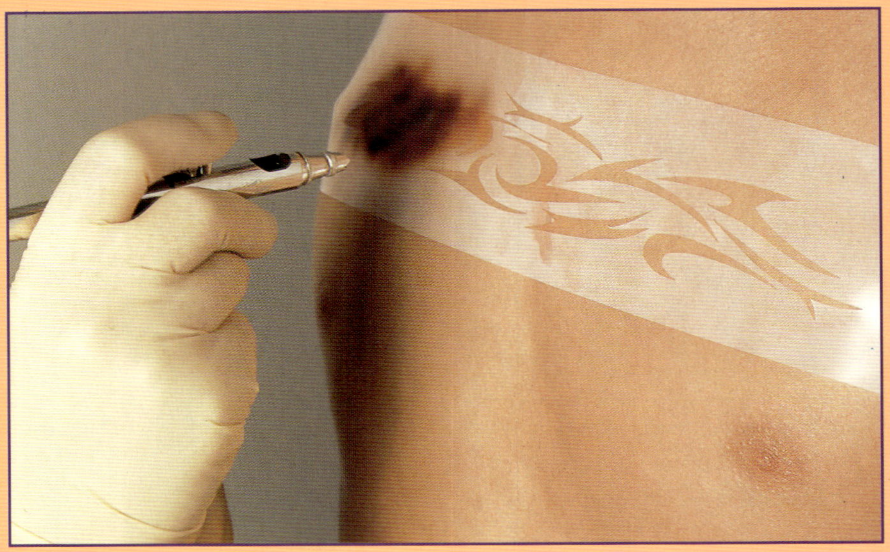

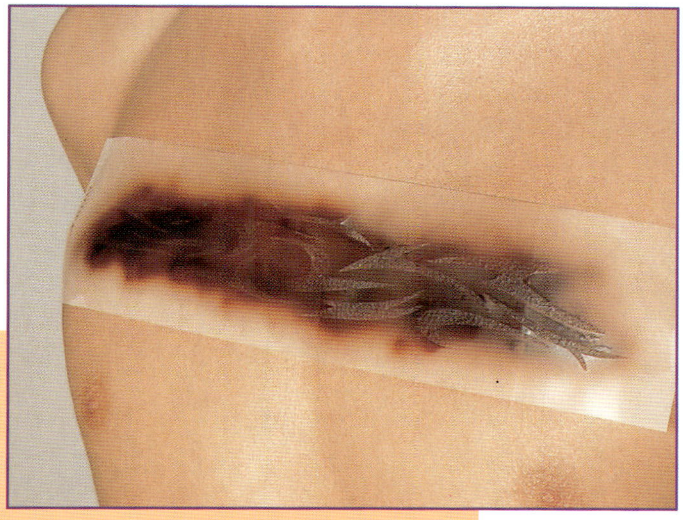

3 Build up the colour and depth of the paint gradually to avoid flooding the stencil.

4 When the paint is completely dry, carefully remove the stencil.

5 Use a cloth or paper towel to clean the edges. Then using a soft powder brush, lightly dust some talcum powder over the design to seal it and then gently brush it away.

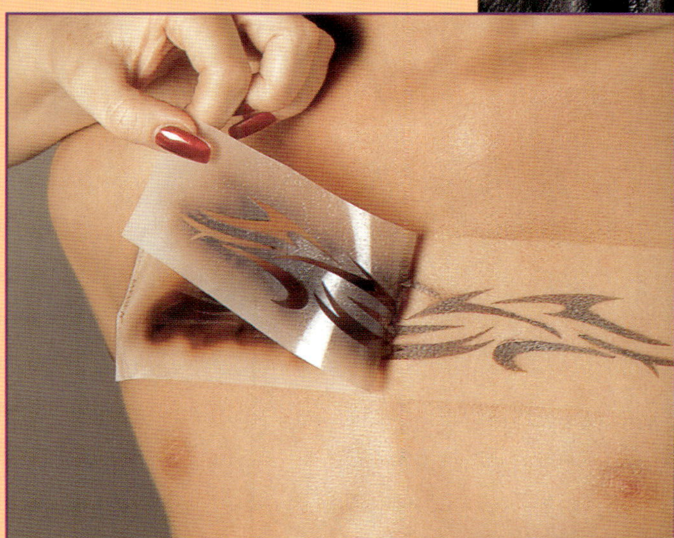

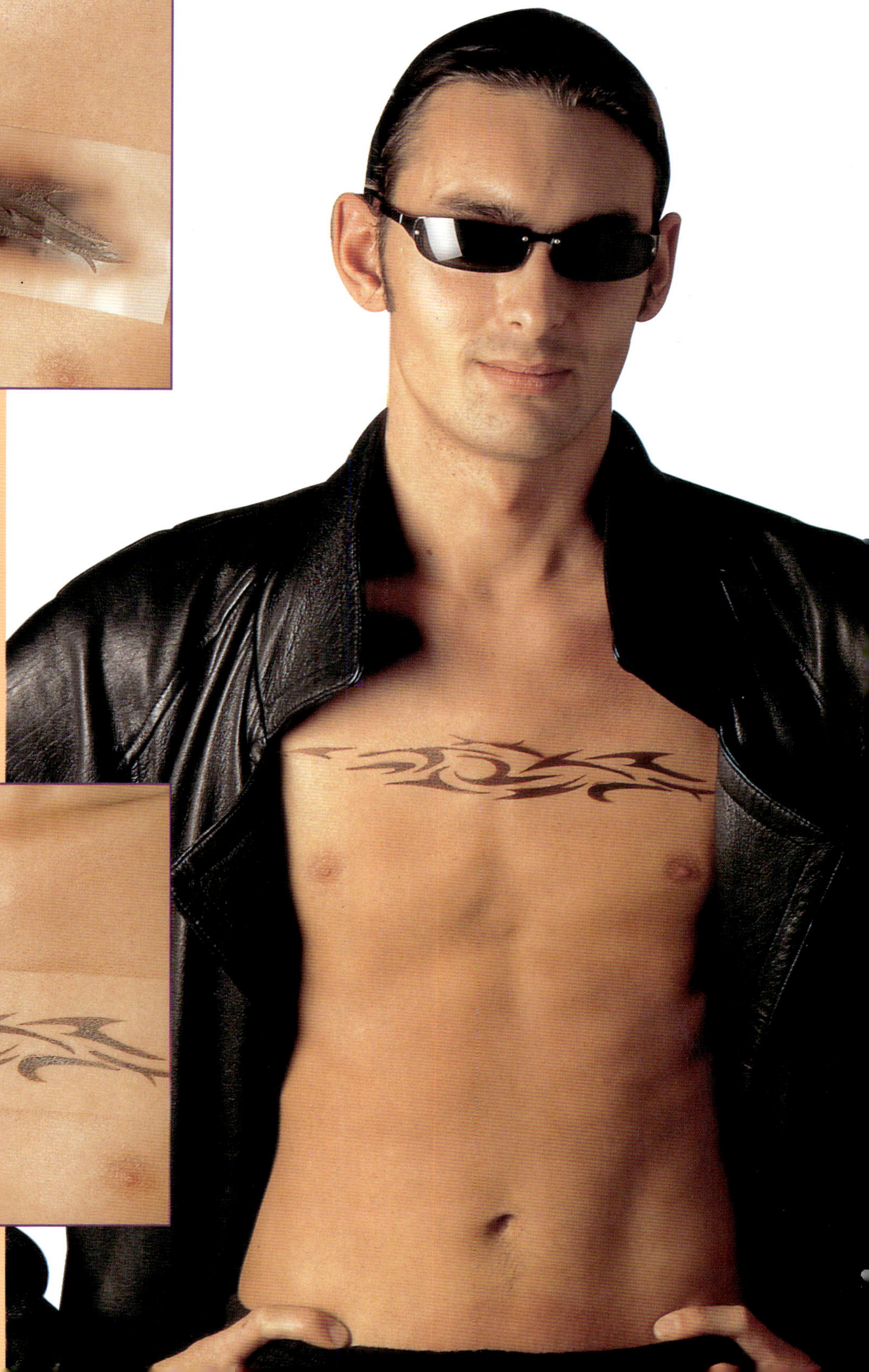

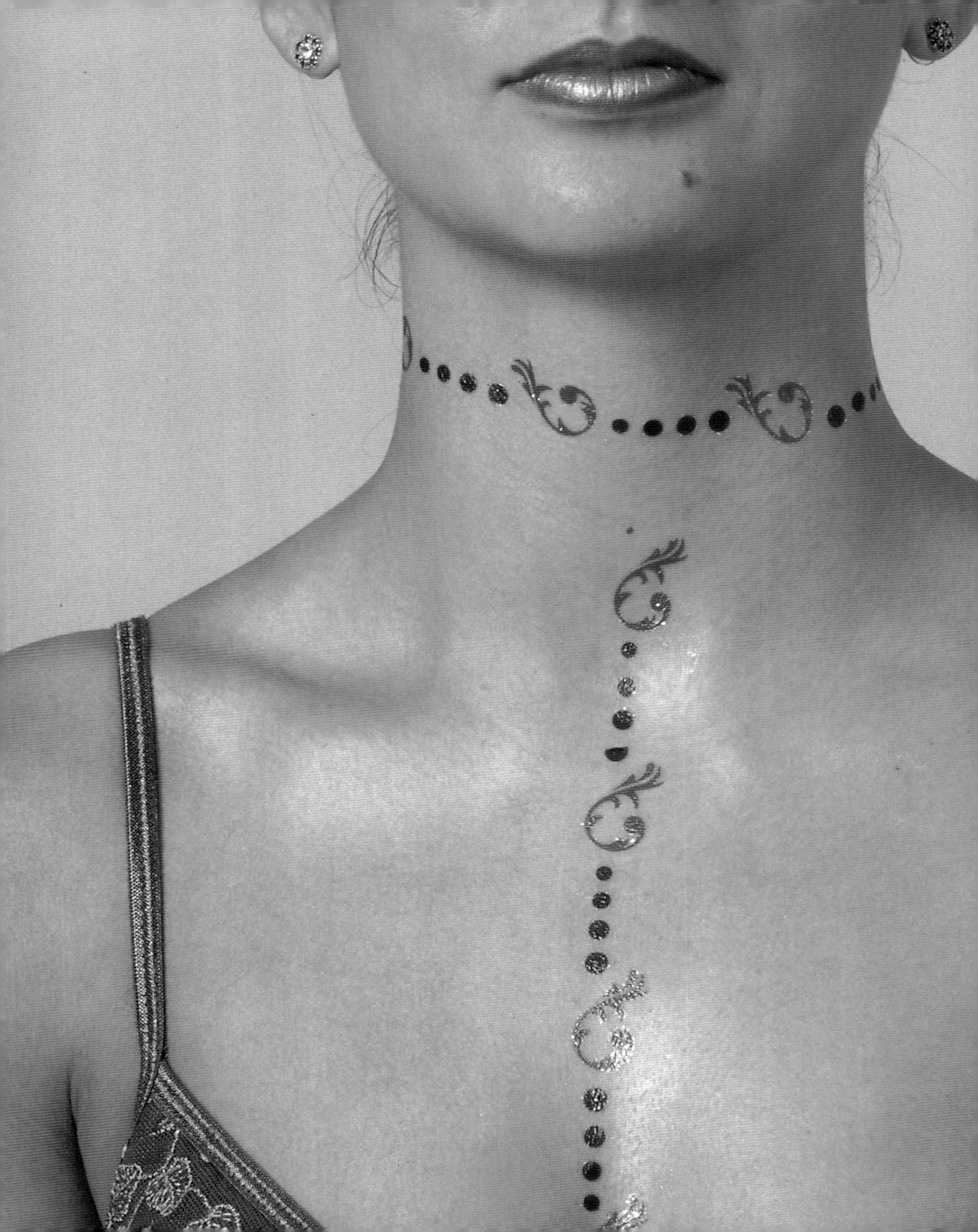

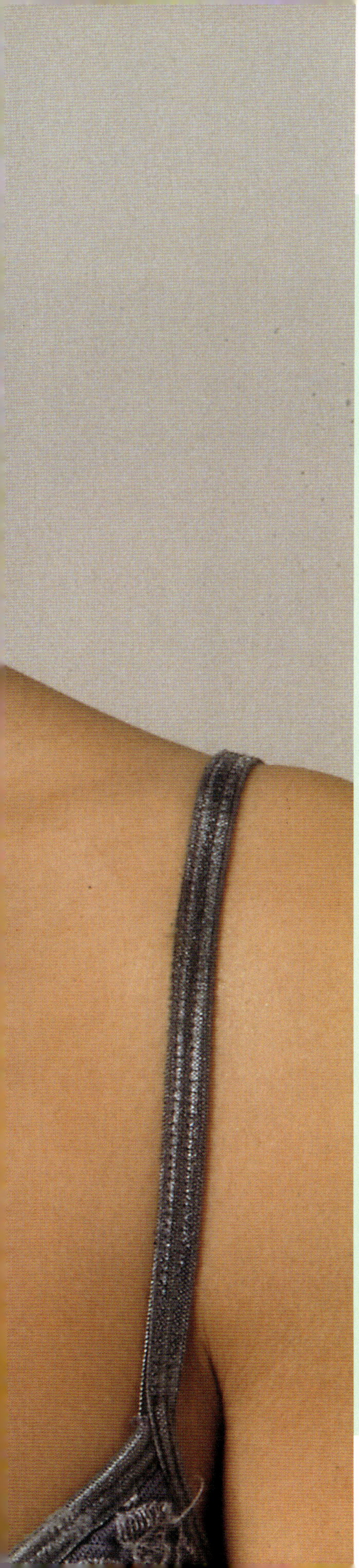

TEMPORARY TATTOO designs

Temporary tattoos are a great way to create quick and easy designs to suit every occasion. They are simple to apply, relatively hard-wearing and easy to remove. They come in a huge variety of styles, sizes, colours and types, ranging from feminine flowers and butterflies to abstract patterns, barbed wire and ornate armbands.

They can be placed anywhere on the body, so are ideal for accessorising specific outfits and occasions.

Barbed-wire bracelet and ring

This is a fun design that will be ideal for creating a spiky, harder-edged look for a party – or simply for livening up a dull day!

YOU WILL NEED

- Cotton pads
- Alcohol solution (witch hazel)
- Semi-permanent barbed-wire tattoos
- Scissors
- Warm water
- Paper towel or tissue

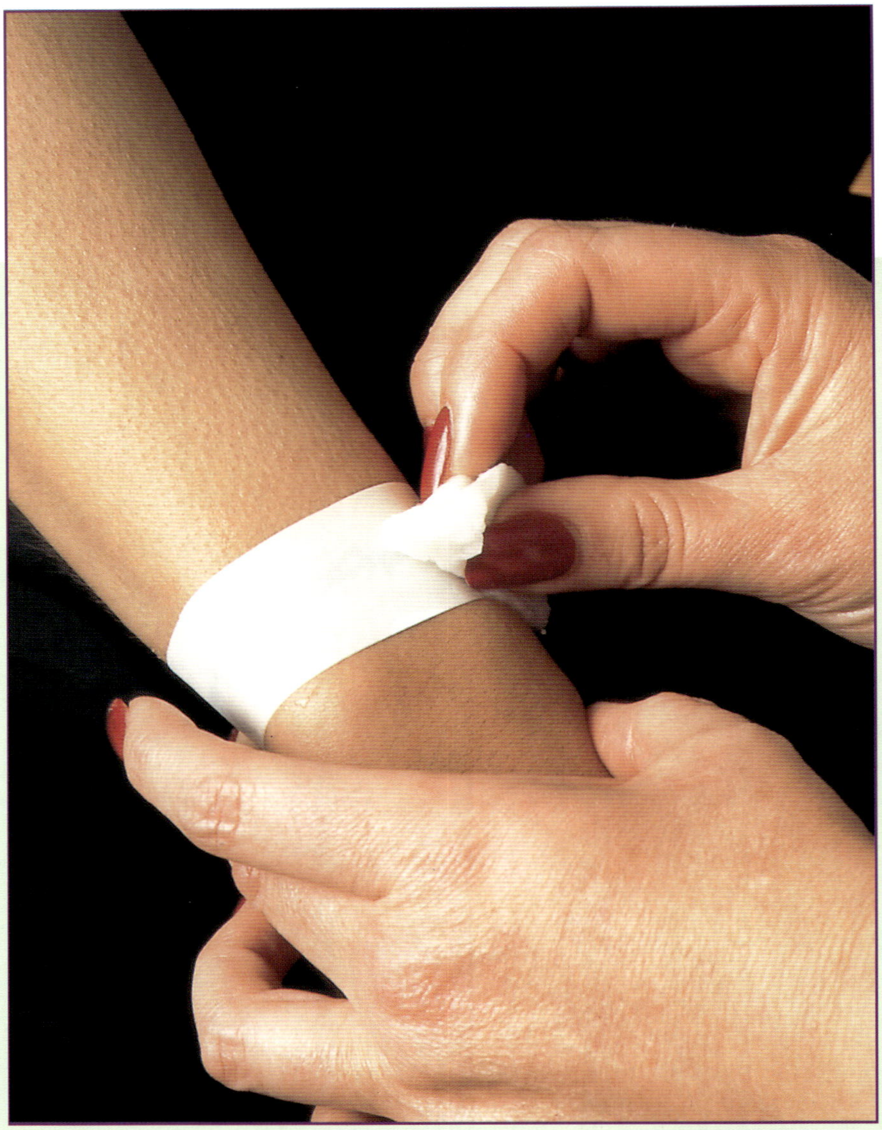

1 Cleanse the areas on which you are going to place your designs by wiping them with a cotton pad dipped in alcohol solution and then letting them dry thoroughly. Cut out the first tattoo design with a pair of scissors. Remove the clear plastic covering over the top of the design. Position the tattoo face downwards on your skin.

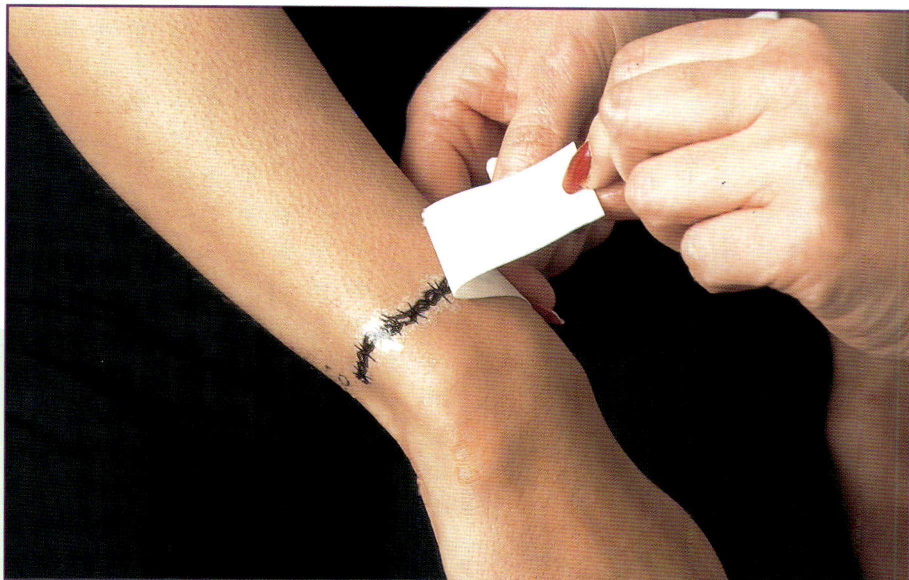

2 Press a cotton pad dipped in warm water over the tattoo and hold it there for thirty seconds to allow the water to penetrate the tattoo. Carefully slide off the tattoo's backing paper and then rinse the design with water before gently patting it dry with a paper towel or tissue.

3 Repeat the process for the second tattoo.

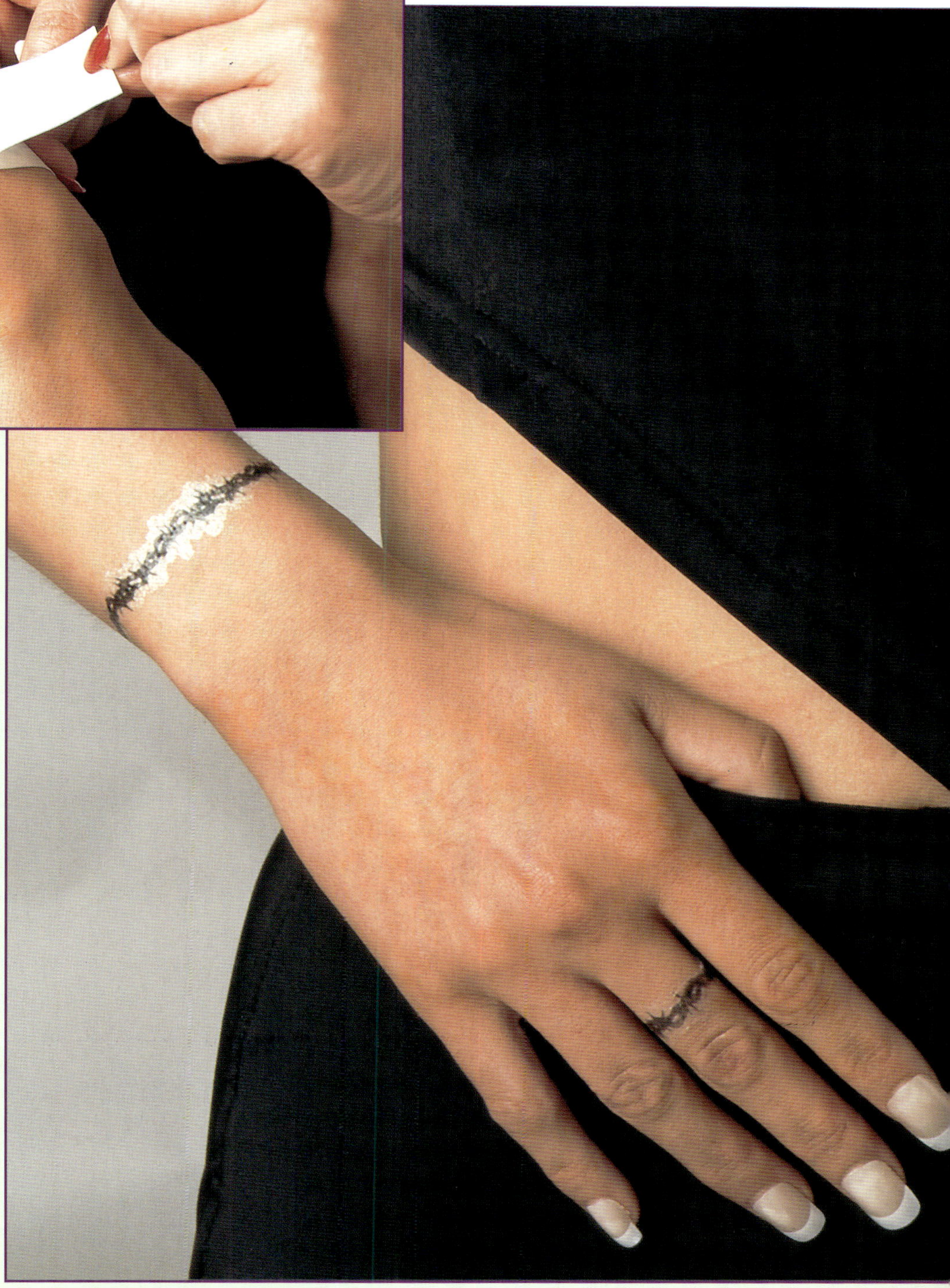

Aztec armband

Aztec designs are very popular, and work well with bold colours and patterns. As well as the armband shown here, why not complement the design with a ring or wristband?

YOU WILL NEED

- Cotton pads
- Alcohol solution (witch hazel)
- Semi-permanent
- Aztec-style tattoo
- Scissors
- Warm water
- Paper towel or tissue

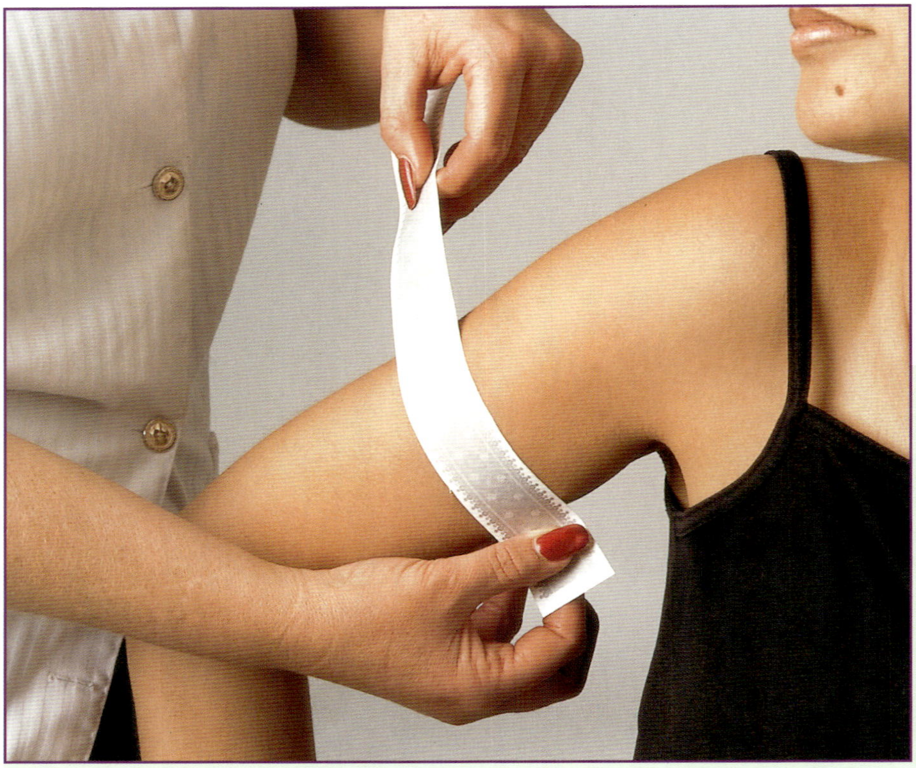

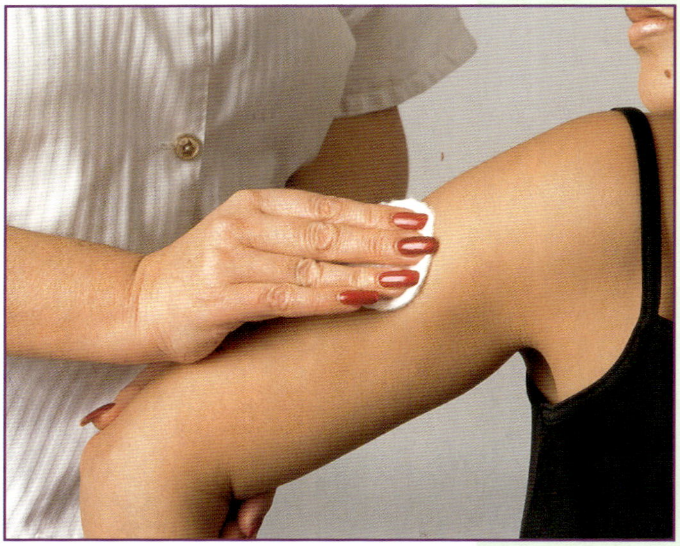

1 Cleanse the area on which you are going to place your design by wiping it with a cotton pad dipped in alcohol solution and then letting it dry thoroughly.

2 Cut out the tattoo design with a pair of scissors. Remove the clear plastic covering over the top of the design. Position the tattoo face downwards on your skin.

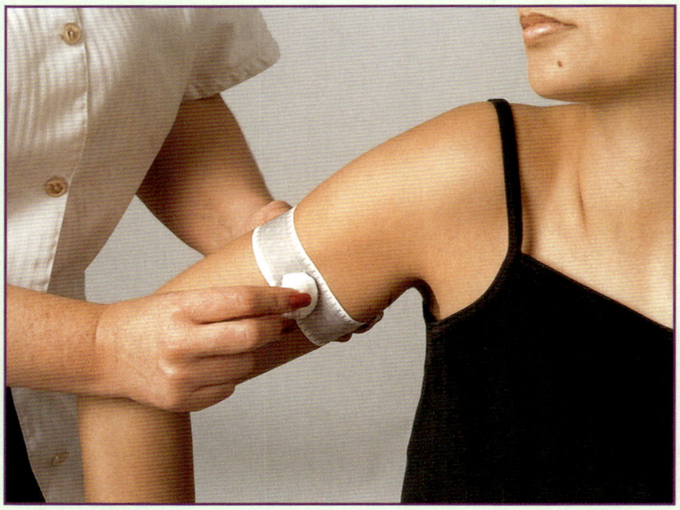

3 Press a cotton pad dipped in warm water over the tattoo and hold it there for thirty seconds to allow the water to penetrate the tattoo.

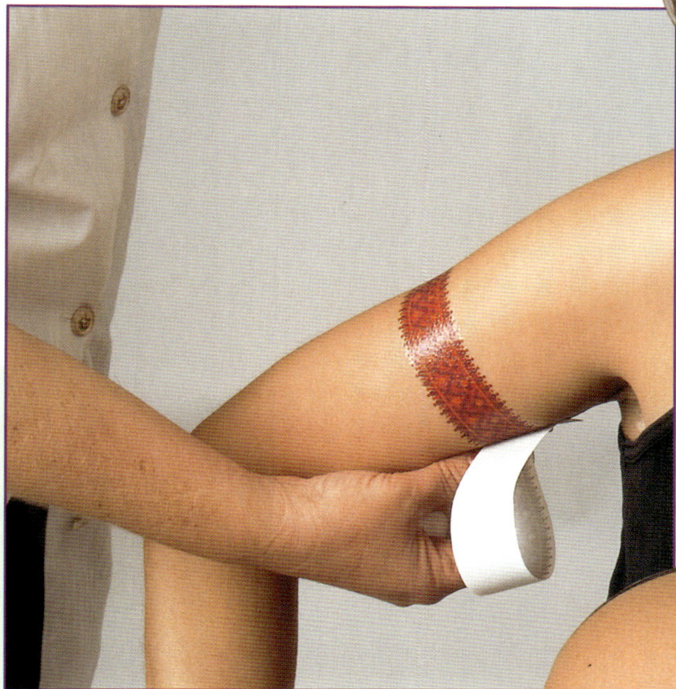

4 Carefully slide off the tattoo's backing paper and then rinse the design with water.

5 Gently pat it dry with a paper towel or tissue and you are ready to go.

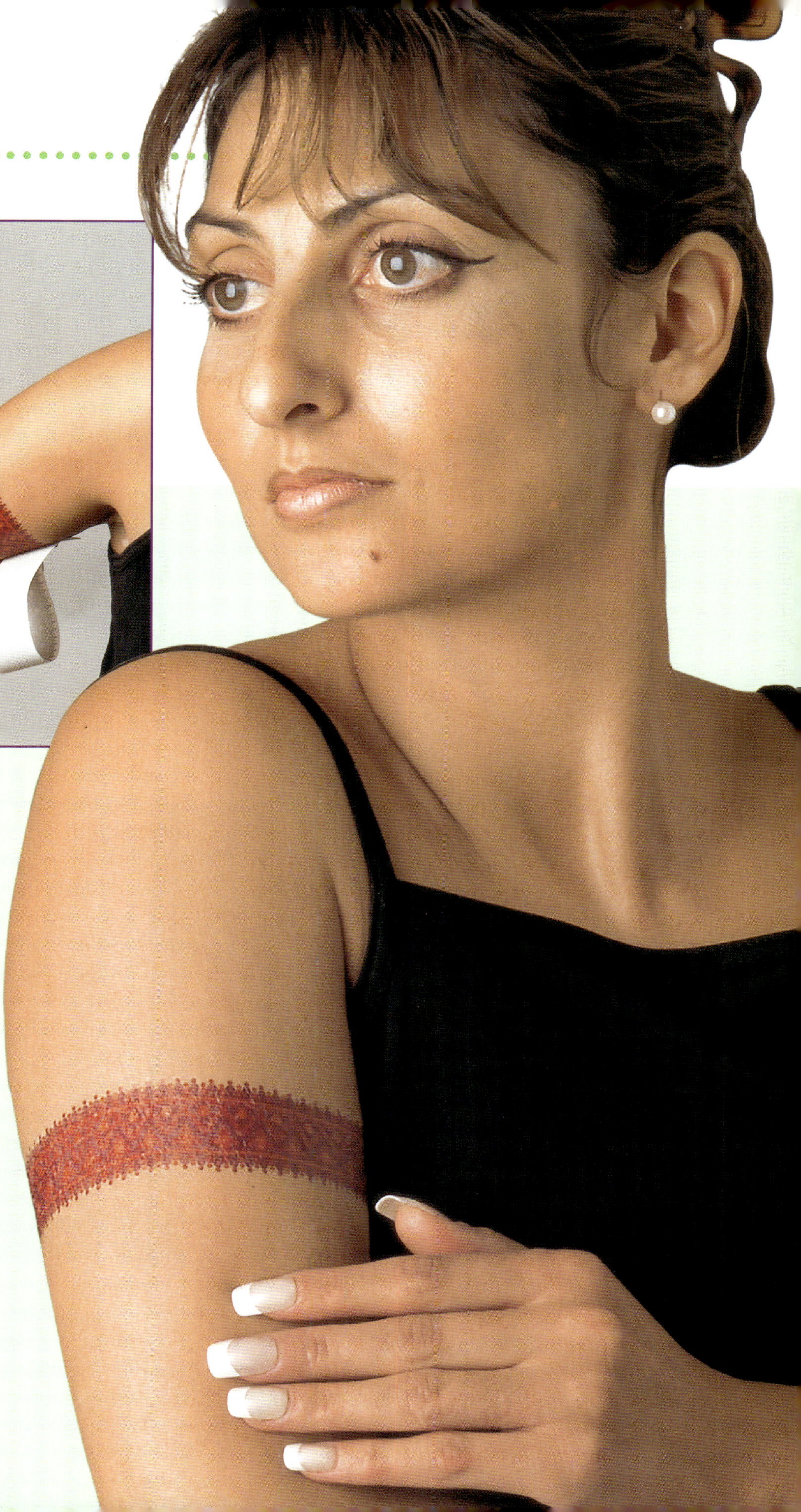

Neck choker

This design was created by joining two tattoos together to give a chained effect that looks stunning with eveningwear.

YOU WILL NEED
- Cotton pads
- Alcohol solution (witch hazel)
- Semi-permanent choker tattoo
- Scissors
- Warm water
- Paper towel or tissue

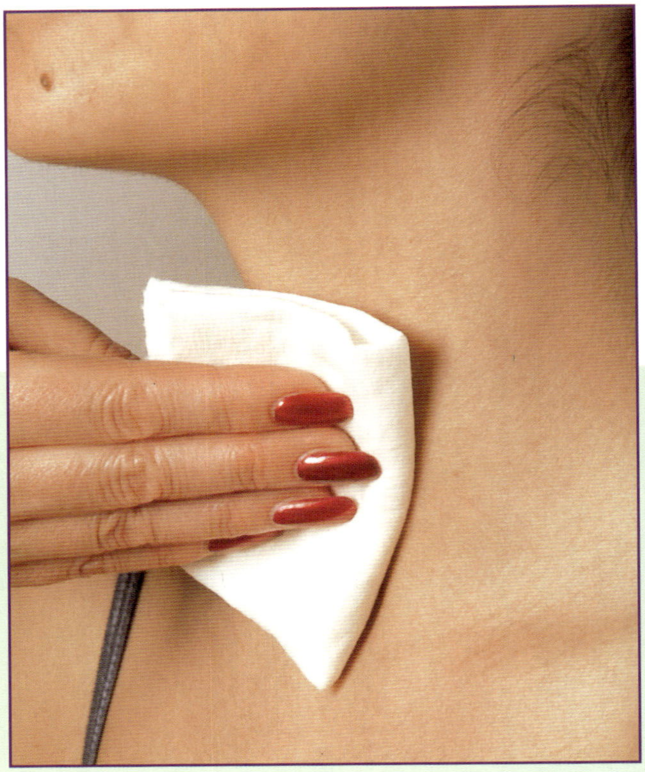

2 Let your skin dry thoroughly before applying the tattoo.

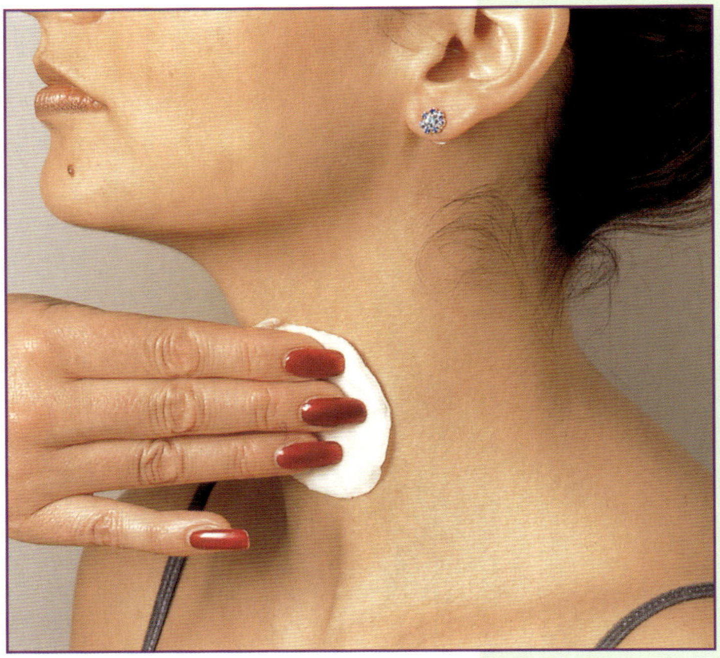

1 Cleanse your neck by wiping it with a cotton pad dipped in alcohol solution.

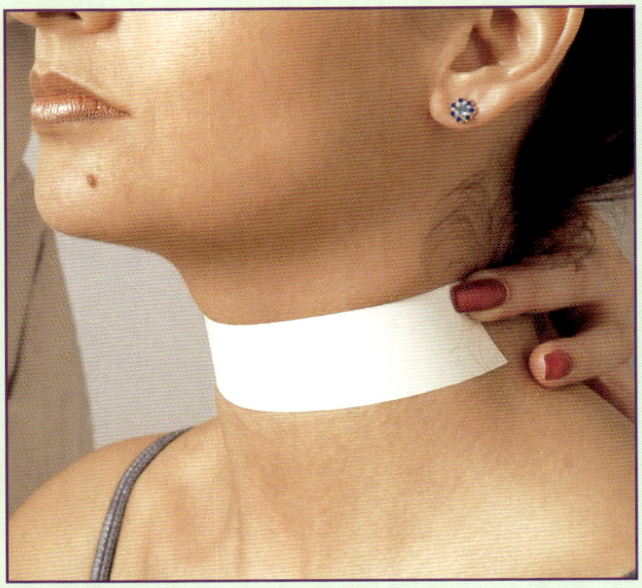

3 Cut out the tattoo to the desired length with a pair of scissors. Remove the clear plastic covering over the top of the design. Position the tattoo face downwards on your neck.

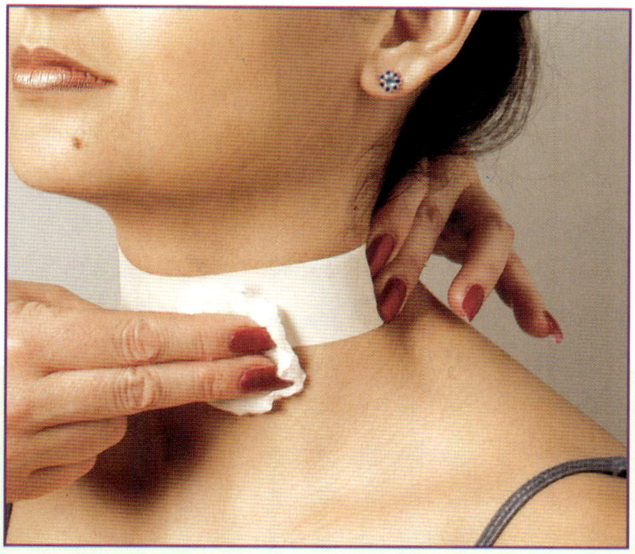

4 Press a cotton pad dipped in warm water over the tattoo and hold it there for fifteen to twenty seconds to allow the water to penetrate the tattoo.

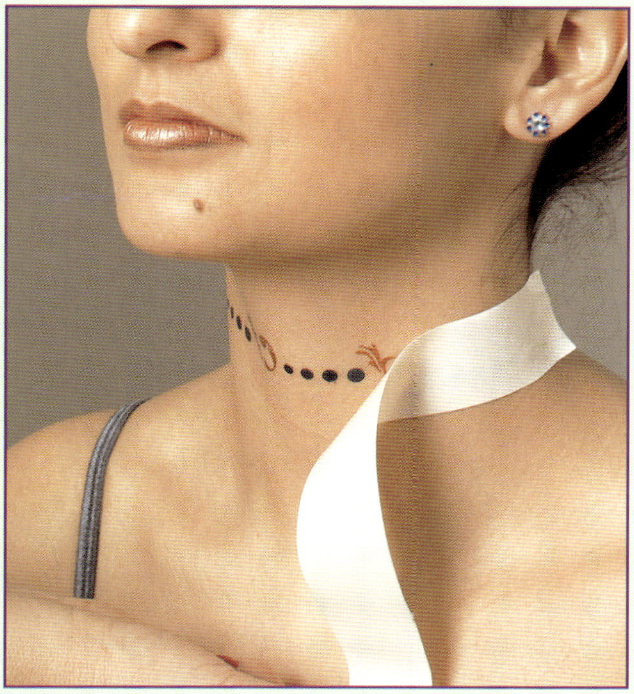

5 Carefully slide off the tattoo's backing paper and then rinse the design with water before gently patting it dry with a paper towel or tissue.

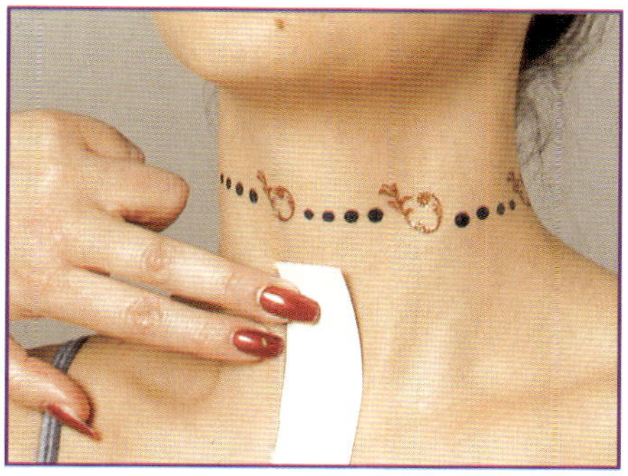

6 Apply a further transfer down the chest to complete the design.

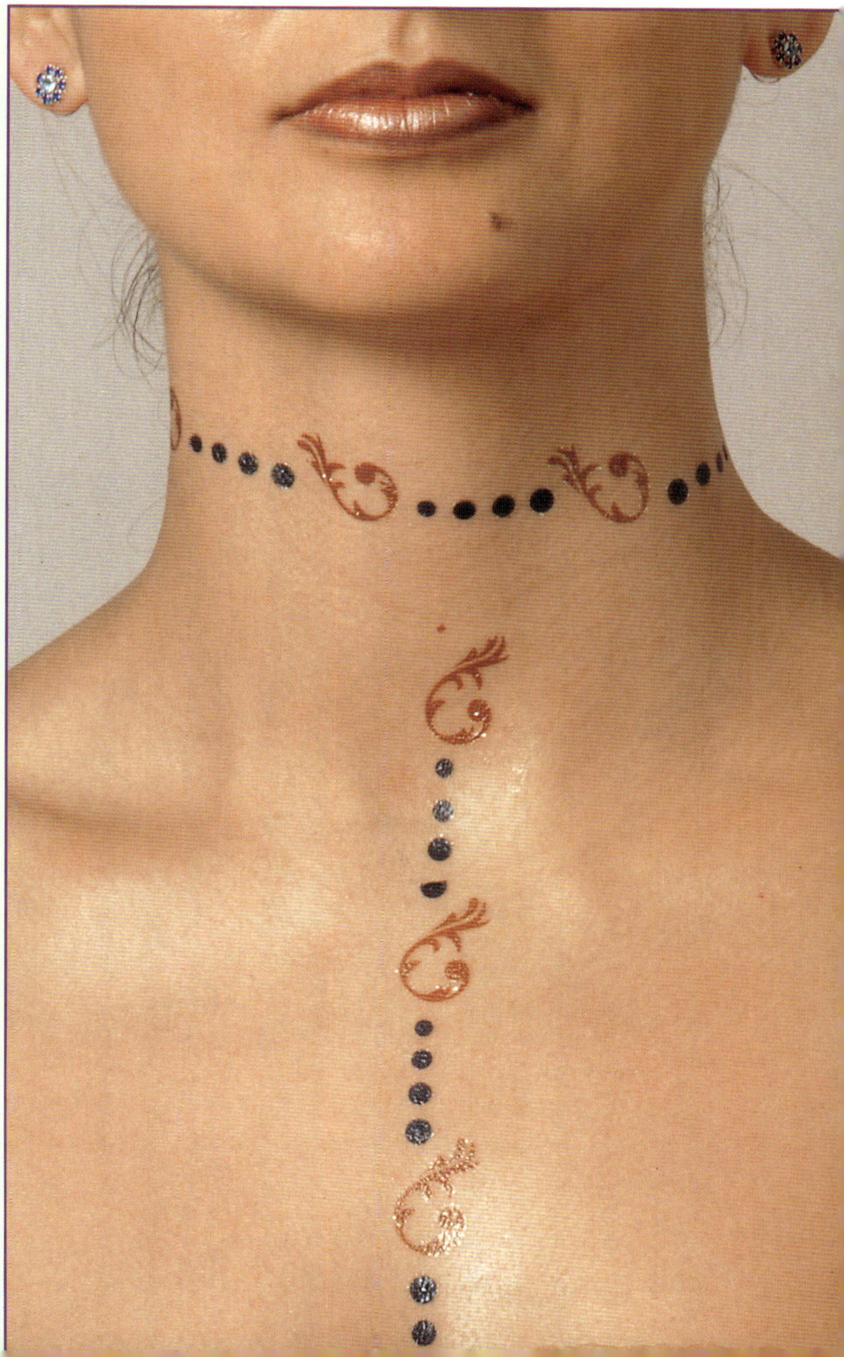

Butterfly magic

This project combines a pretty semi-permanent tattoo with some sparkling gems for a glittering, and very feminine, effect.

YOU WILL NEED
- Cotton pads
- Alcohol solution (witch hazel)
- Butterfly tattoo
- Scissors
- Warm water
- Paper towel or tissue
- Body gems
- Tweezers

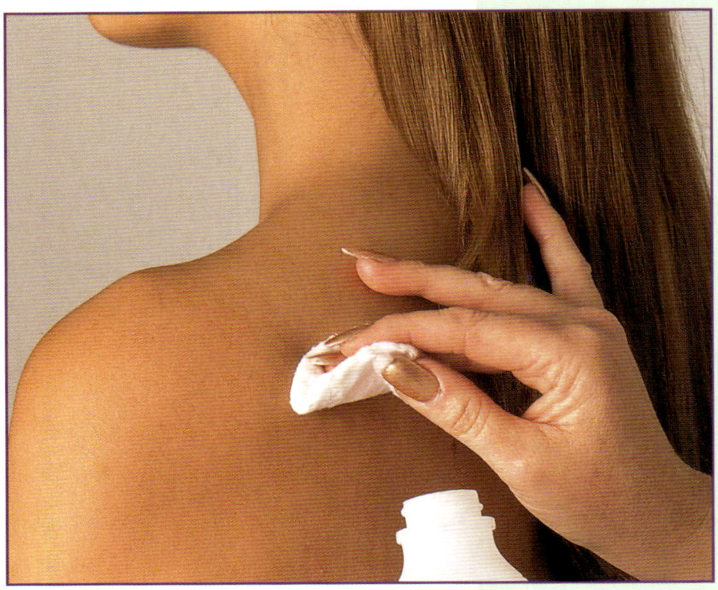

1 Cleanse the area on which you are going to place your design by wiping it with a cotton pad dipped in alcohol solution

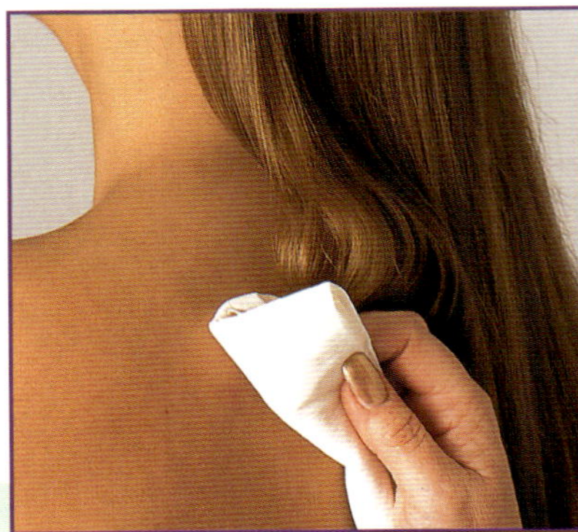

2 Pat the skin dry with a paper towel.

3 Cut out the two butterfly designs with a pair of scissors. Remove the clear plastic covering over the top of the first tattoo.

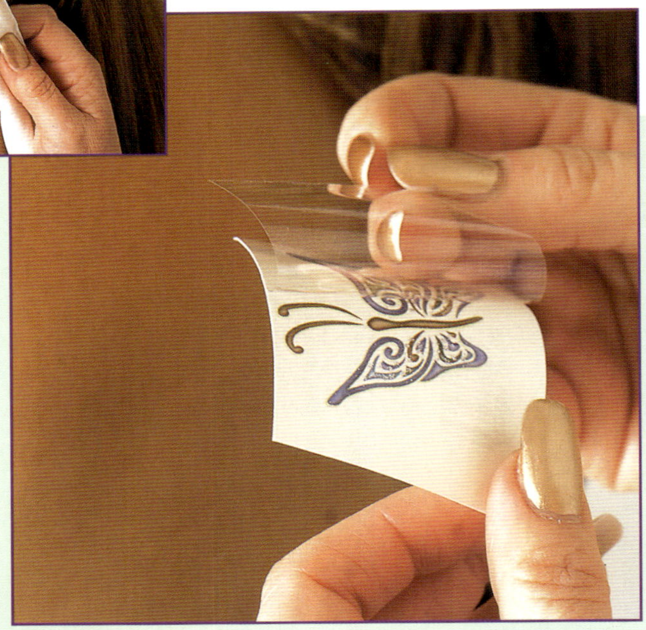

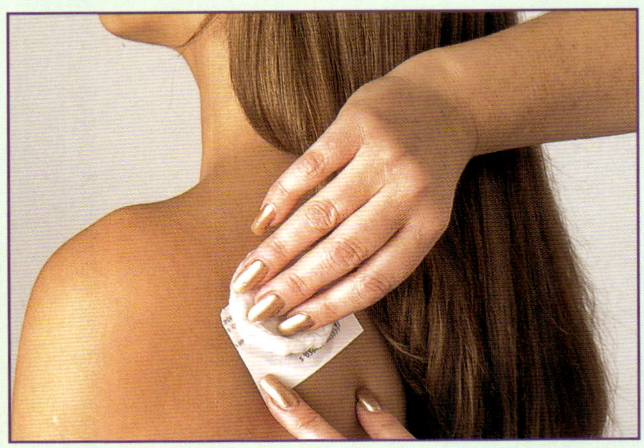

4 Position the tattoo face downwards on your shoulder. Press a cotton pad dipped in warm water over the tattoo and hold it there for forty to fifty seconds to allow the water to penetrate the tattoo.

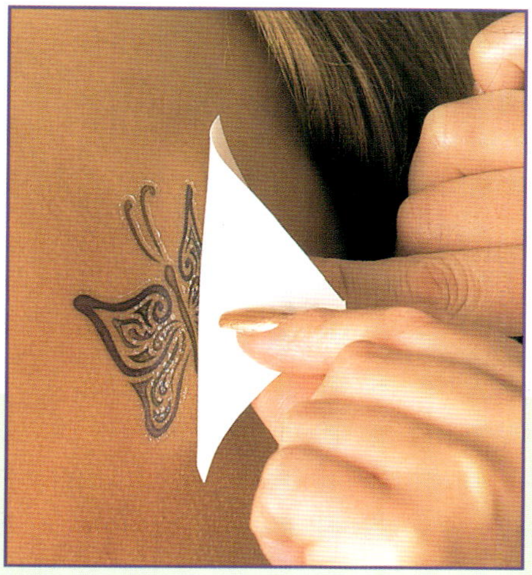

5 Carefully slide off the tattoo's backing paper and then rinse the design with water.

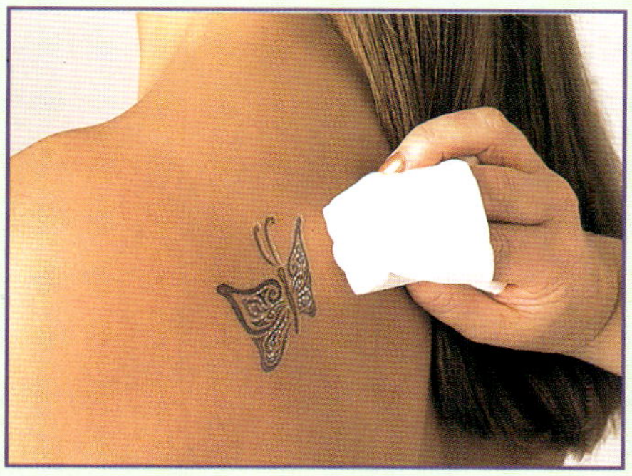

6 Then gently pat the tattoo dry with a paper towel or tissue.

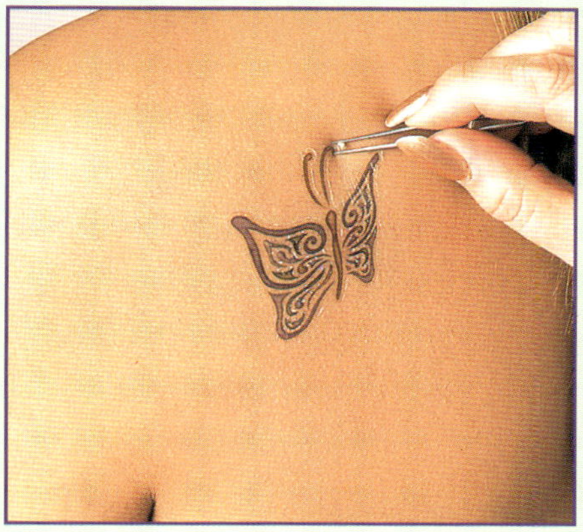

7 Using tweezers, place a gem on one of the butterfly's antennae.

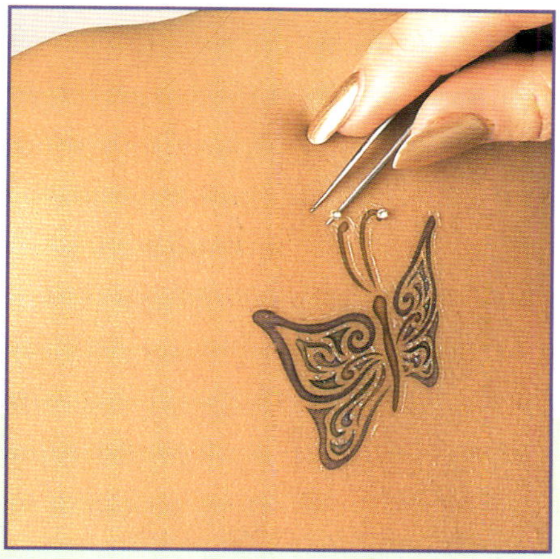

8 Then apply a second gem. You will have to press the gem quite firmly into the skin to ensure it adheres.

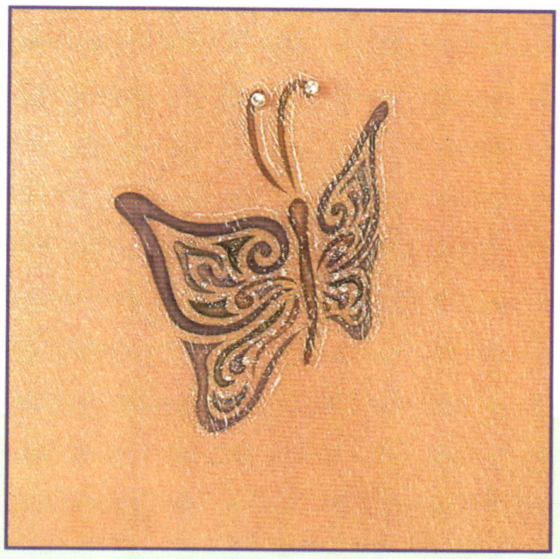

9 The finished result will be ideal for a summer party.

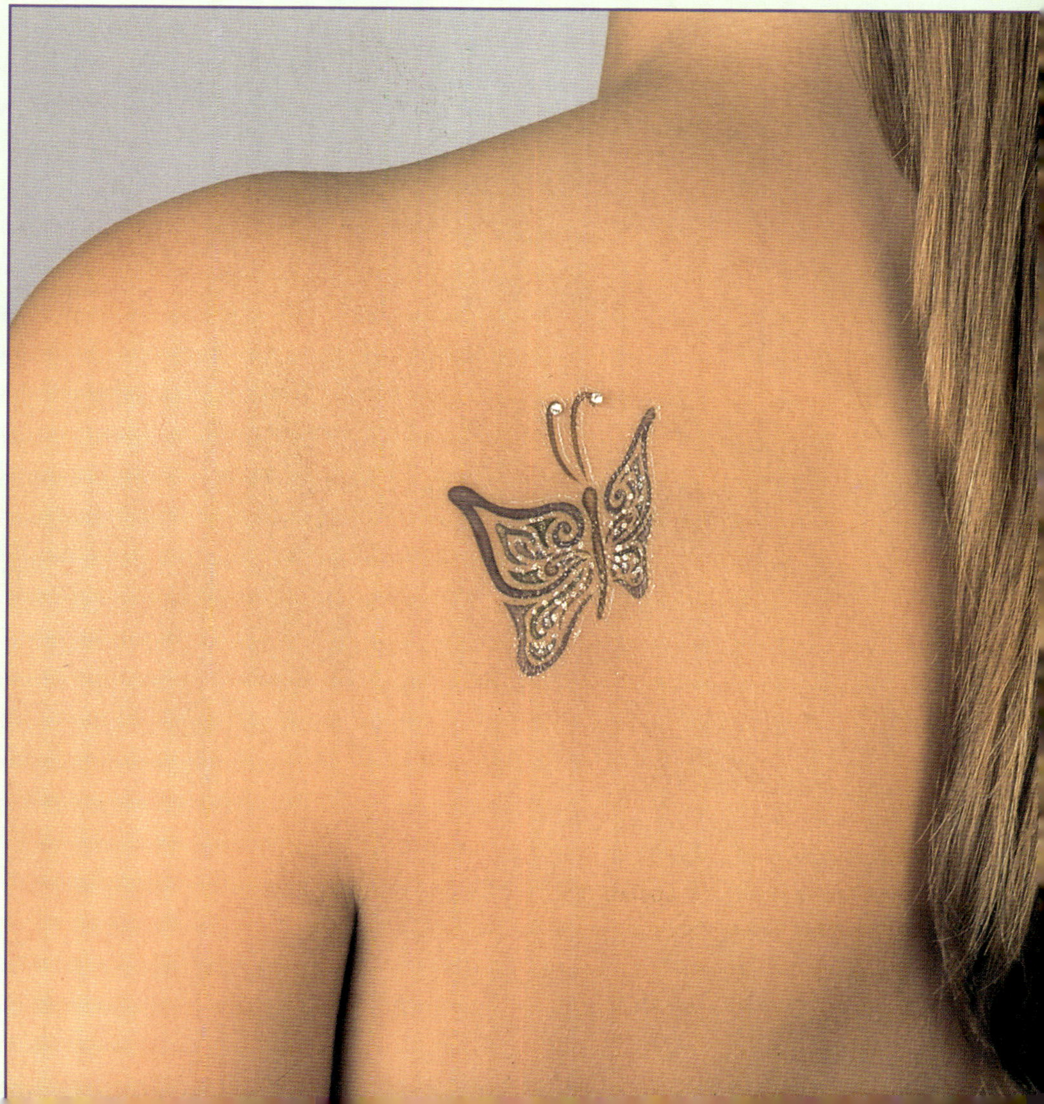

Temporary hand tattoos

Hand tattoos are available in many colours and designs, from very simple, minimalist patterns to quite ornate designs. Position them either on the back of your hand or on your palm. Many are sold with extra tattoos that you can place on your wrist or arm to complement your hand tattoo.

YOU WILL NEED

- Cotton pads
- Alcohol solution (witch hazel)
- Hand tattoo
- Scissors
- Warm water
- Tissue

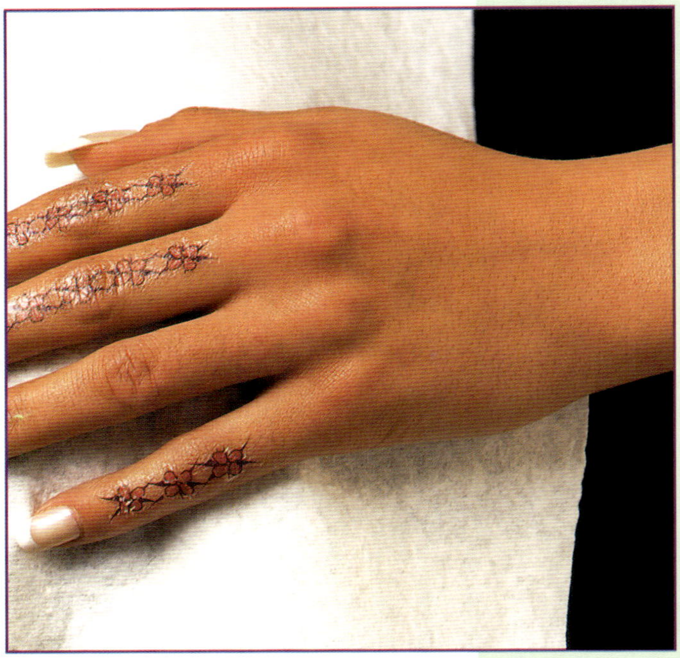

1 Ensure that your skin is oil-free by wiping it with a cotton pad dipped in alcohol solution and then let it dry thoroughly. Cut out the hand tattoo with a pair of scissors. Here we have already applied the first part of the tattoo.

2 Place the tattoo face downwards on your hand and gently press it into place.

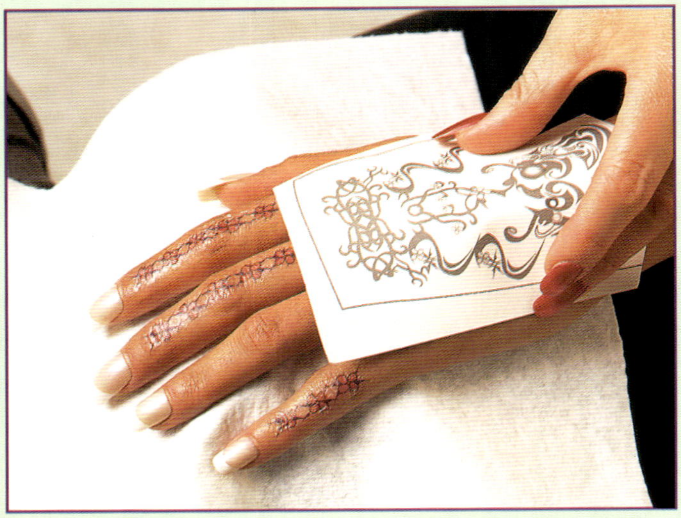

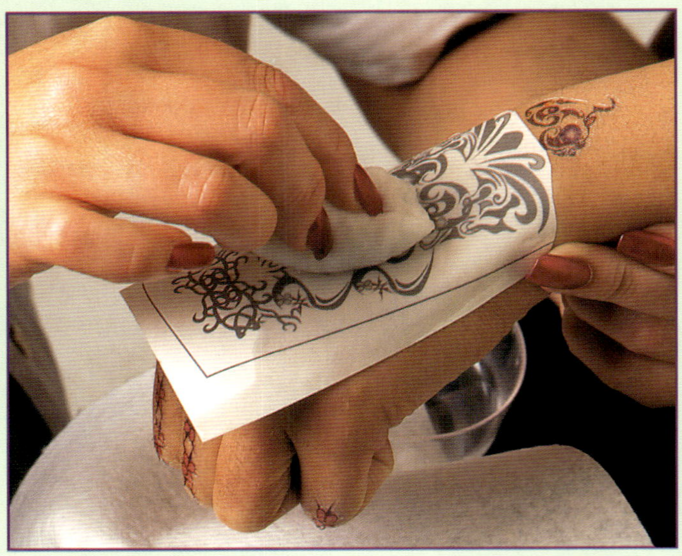

3 Moisten a cotton pad with warm water and, using even pressure, gently pat it over the tattoo to secure it.

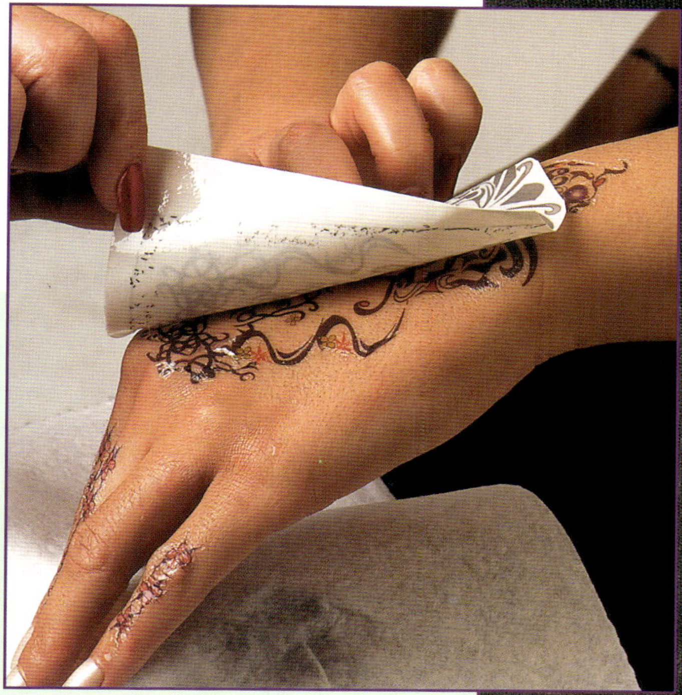

4 Wait for about forty to fifty seconds and then carefully peel away the backing paper.

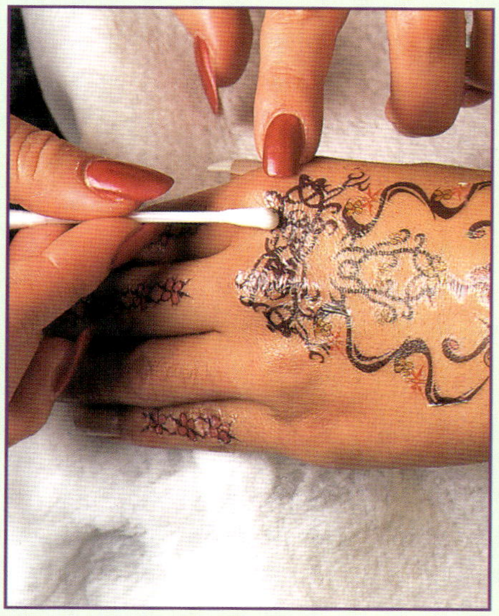

5 Press a cotton bud over the tattoo to make sure that it is completely secure. Now carefully pat it dry with a tissue.

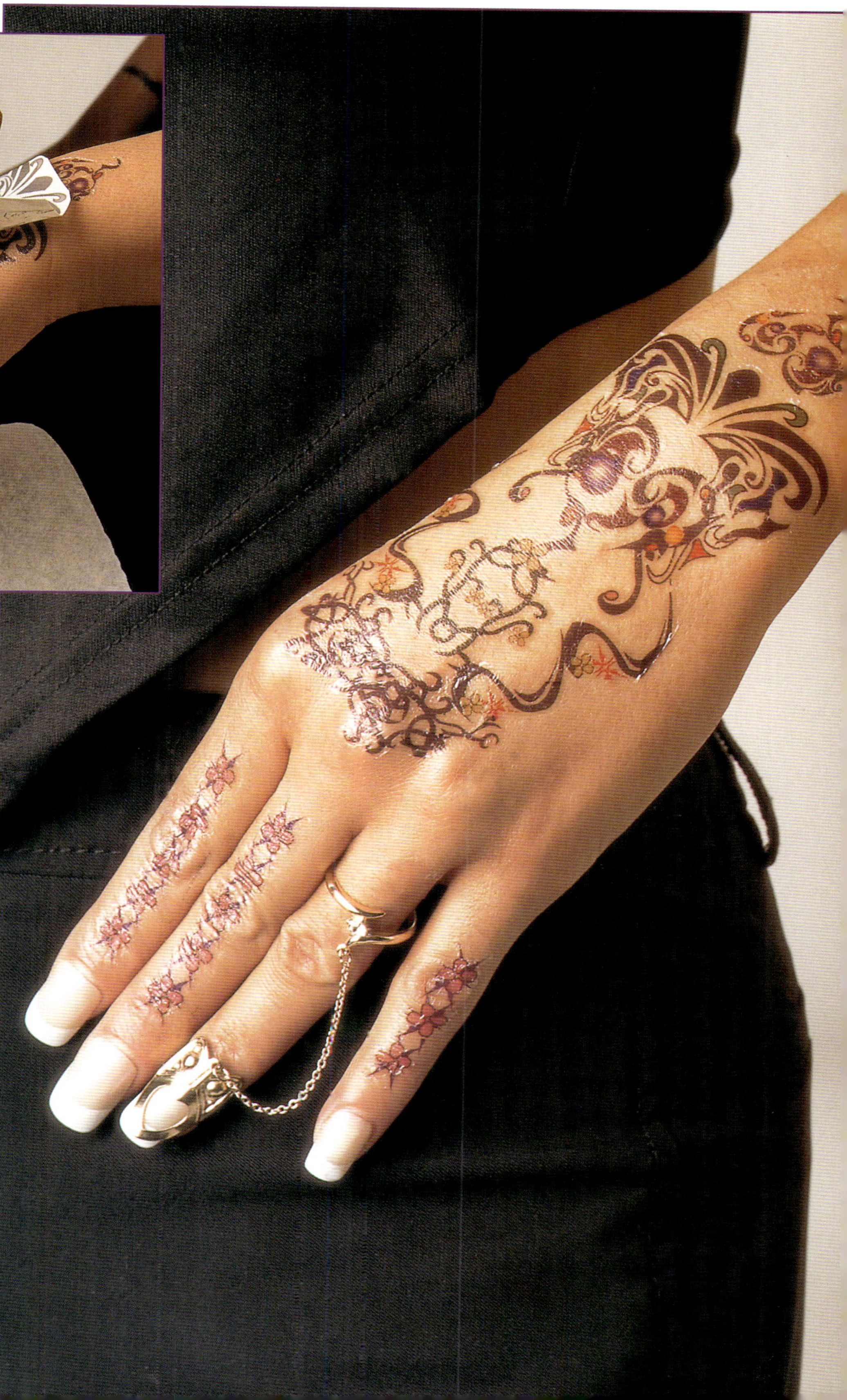

Neon eagle

For added effect, you can highlight or embellish a simple tattoo by using body paints. You do not have to go wild – a few freehand strokes can create a highly individual look. Here we're using a one-colour neon tattoo.

YOU WILL NEED

- Cotton pads
- Alcohol solution (witch hazel)
- Semi-permanent eagle tattoo
- Scissors
- Warm water
- Paper towel or tissue
- Body paints (optional)

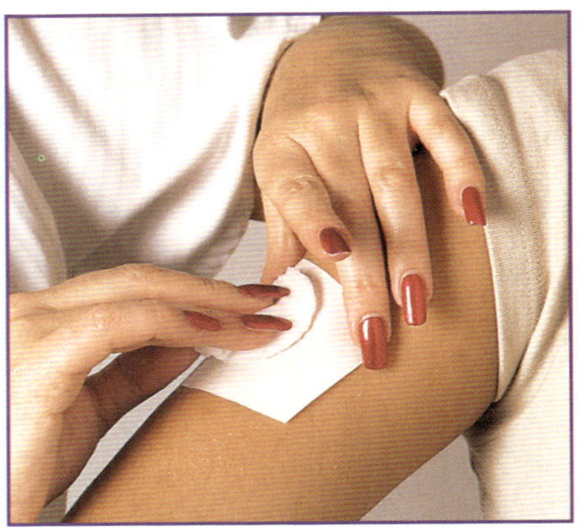

1 Cleanse the area on which you are going to place your design by wiping it with a cotton pad dipped in alcohol solution and then let it dry thoroughly. Cut out the tattoo and remove the clear plastic covering. Position the tattoo face downwards on your skin. Press a cotton pad dipped in warm water over the tattoo and hold it there for fifteen to twenty seconds to allow the water to penetrate the tattoo.

2 Carefully slide off the tattoo's backing paper and then rinse the design with water before gently patting it dry with a paper towel or tissue.

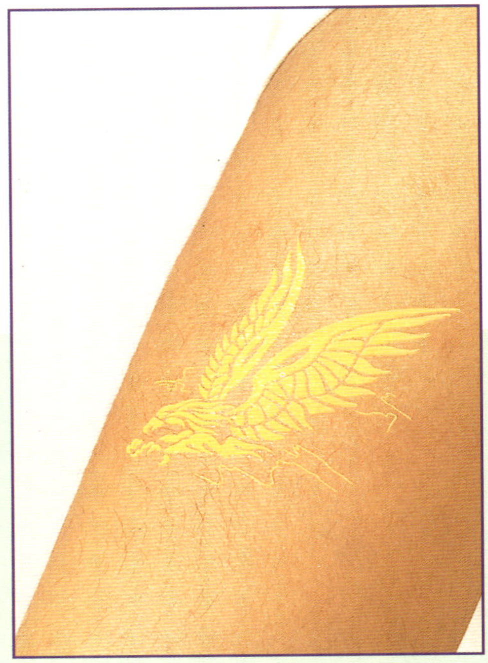

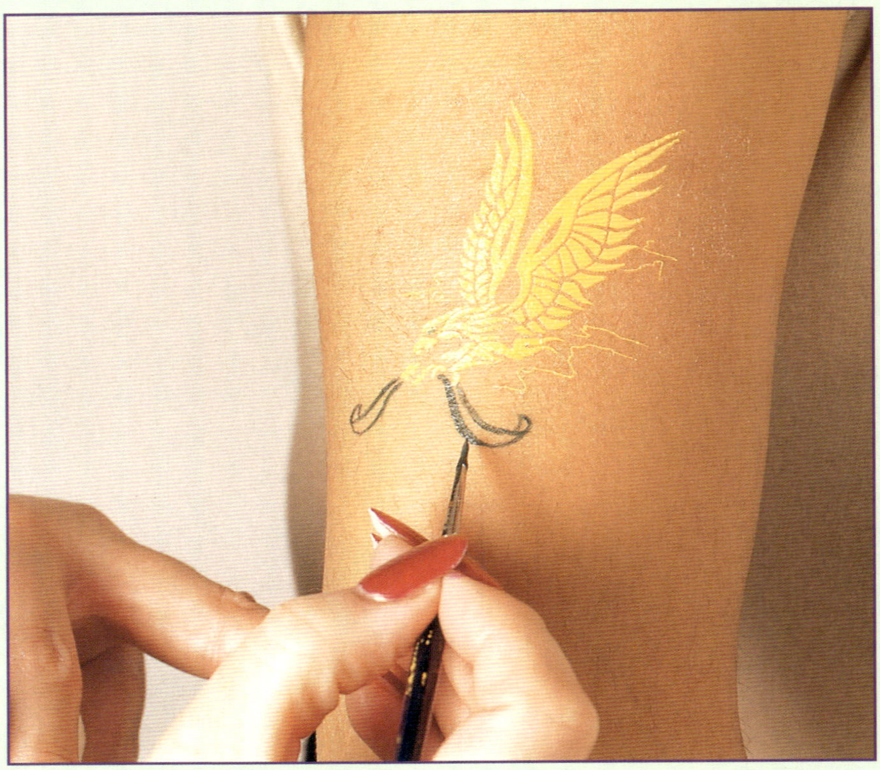

3 Now add a few freehand strokes in one of more colours of body paint.

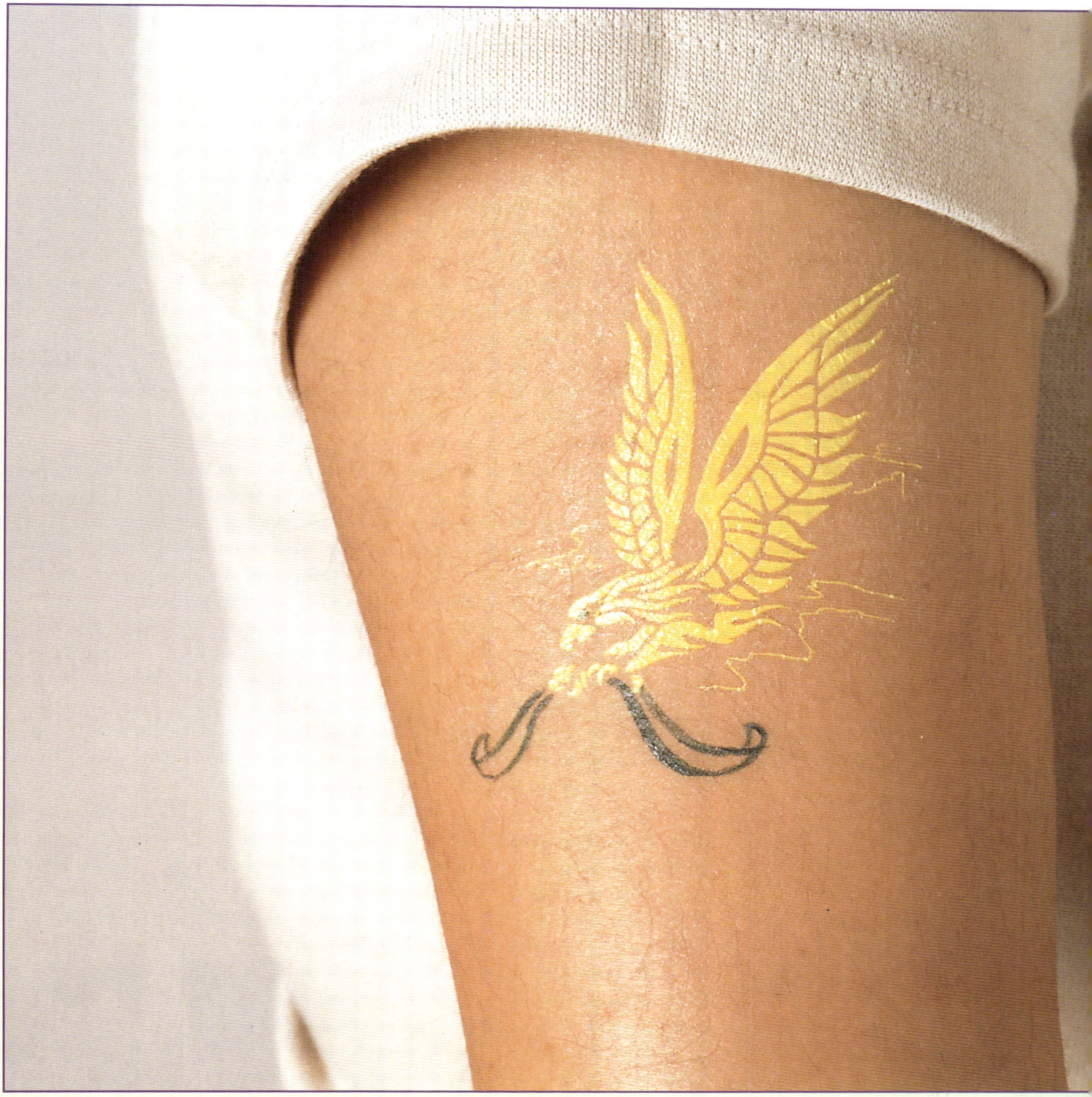

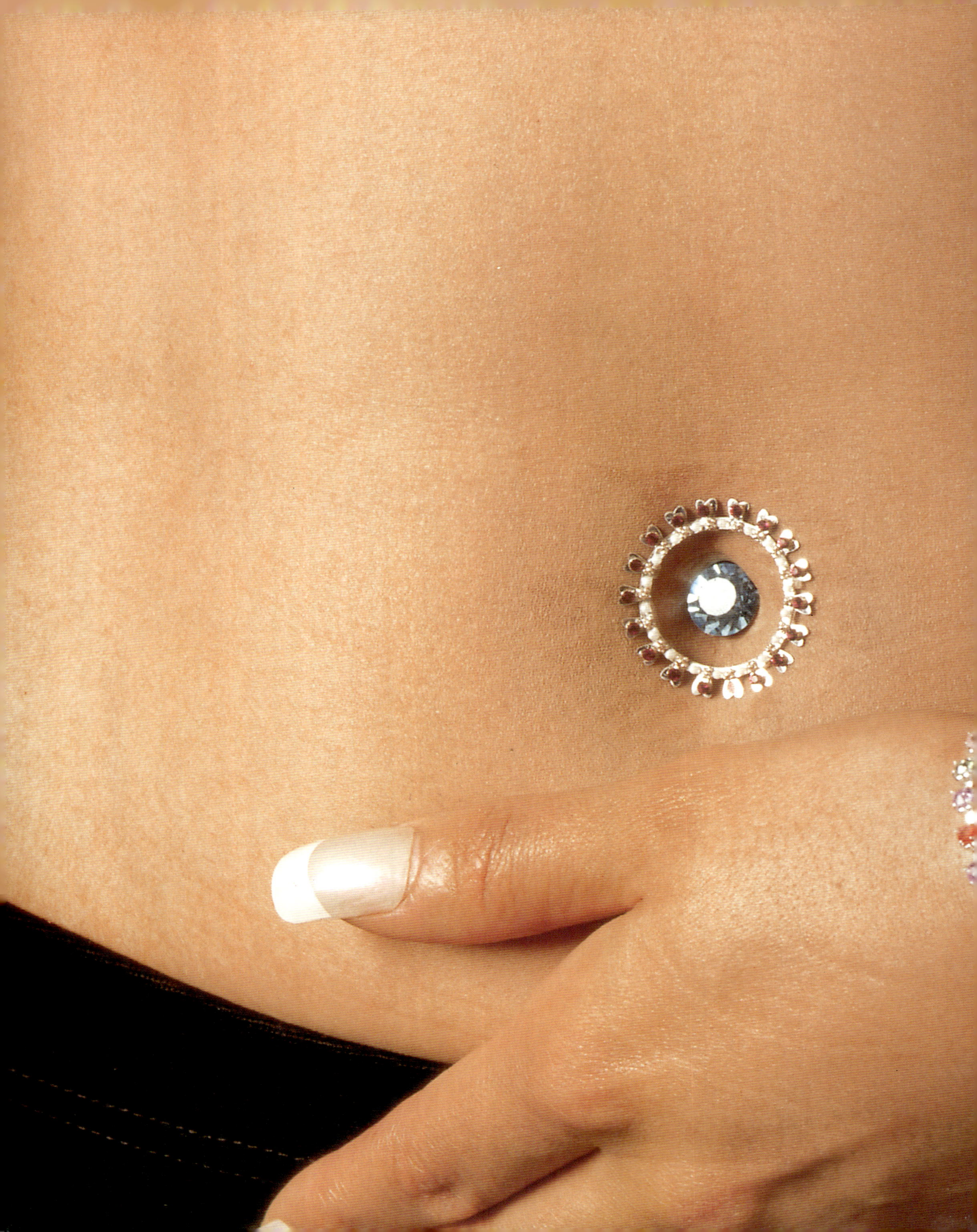

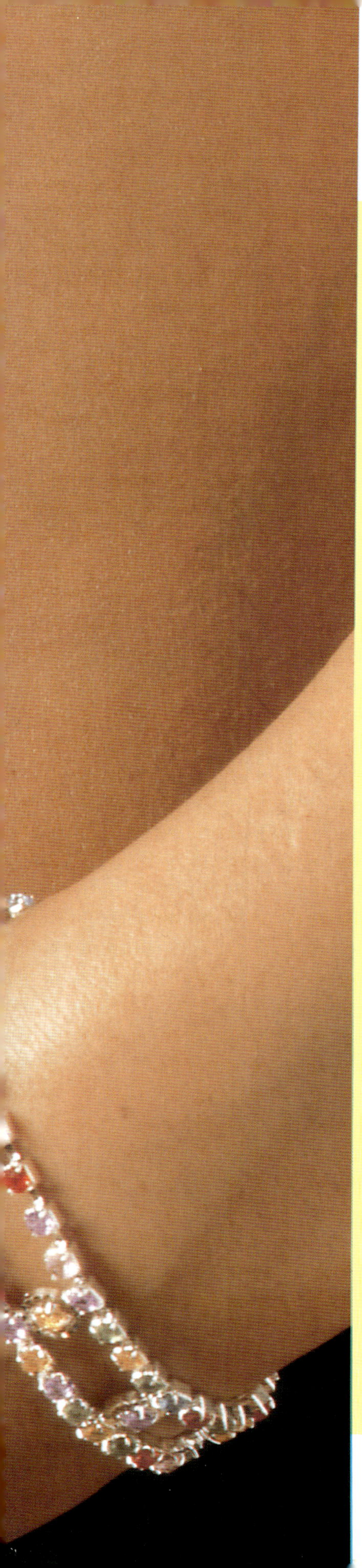

FINISHING touches

Bindis and body jewellery

Bindis are available in a variety of colours, sizes and designs, including butterflies, flowers, hearts and animals. They are applied either to clean, dry skin or to freshly applied make-up.

The simplest jewels and gems can be added to brighten up a temporary tattoo, henna design or stencil pattern, and more complex designs can be used as body art in their own right.

The bindi jewellery illustrated in this section is all beautiful and simple to apply. They are easily removable, and as long as you take care in removing them, they are all reusable.

Simple bindi

This jewel is ideal for positioning in the traditional place between the eyes.

YOU WILL NEED
- Bindi

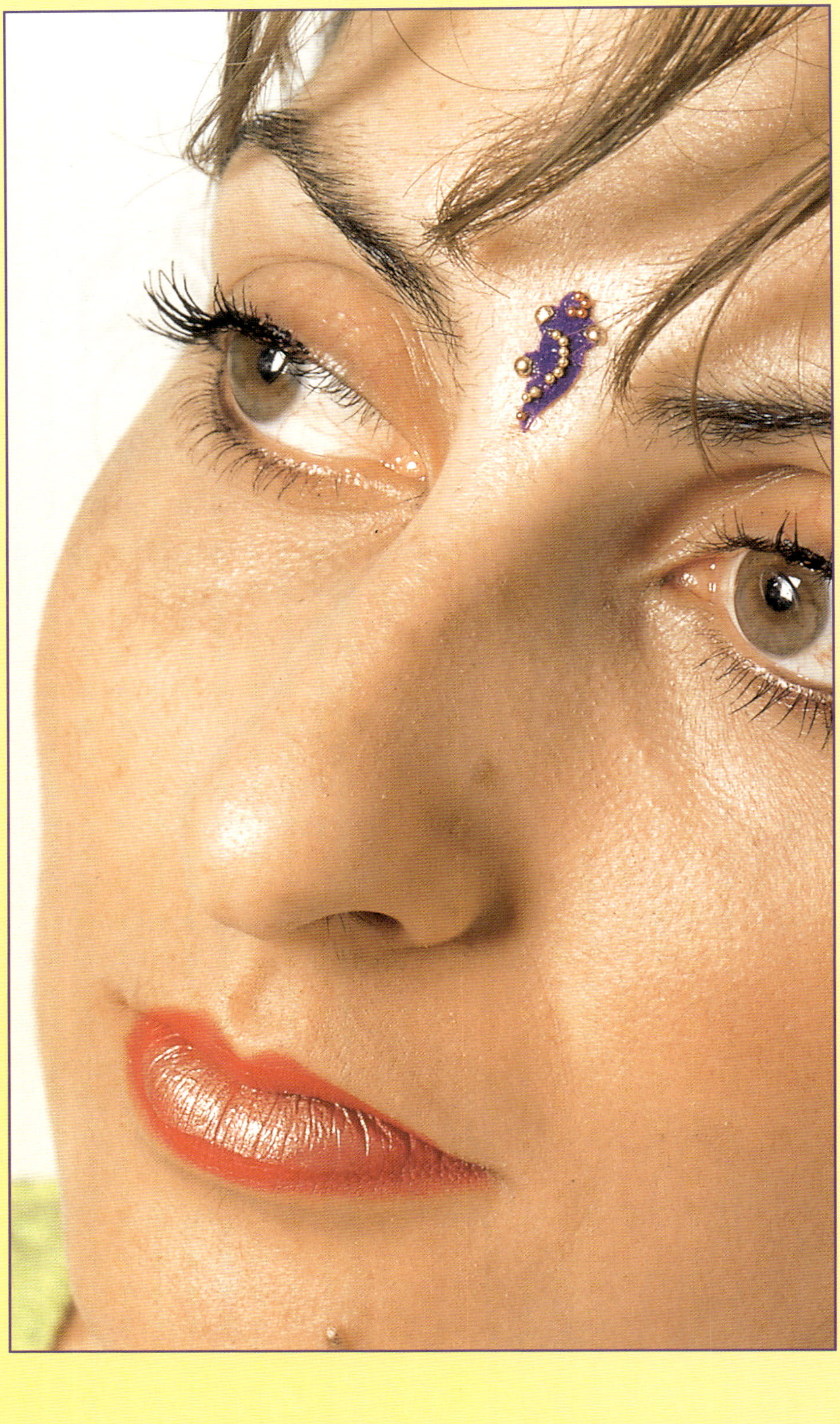

1 Unless you have applied make-up to your face, wash and dry the area to be decorated to ensure that it is completely oil-free.

2 Carefully separate the bindi from the plastic backing, making sure that it adheres to your skin.

3 Gently press the bindi onto your skin and hold it there for about ten seconds to warm the adhesive.

4 Remove the transparent tape carefully to ensure that the bindi remains fixed to your skin.

Green jewels

Eye jewels, which are sold in a wide range of designs and colours, can be bought individually or as a complete design. They have a self-adhesive backing which sticks to your skin.

YOU WILL NEED
- Eye jewels
- Tweezers
- Cotton bud

1 Unless you have applied make-up to your face, wash and dry the area to be decorated to ensure that it is completely oil-free.

2 Carefully peel back the self-adhesive and then gently position the eye jewellery on your skin (you may find this easier using tweezers).

3 To secure it, gently press a cotton bud onto the eye jewellery.

4 You could make this simple design more elaborate by adding more eye jewellery.

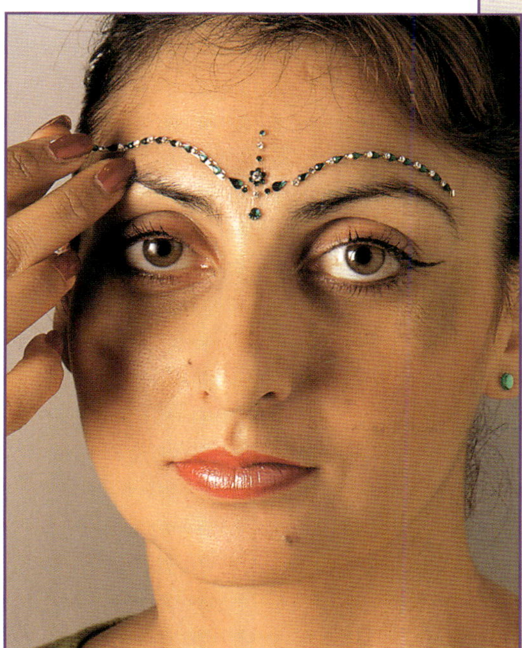

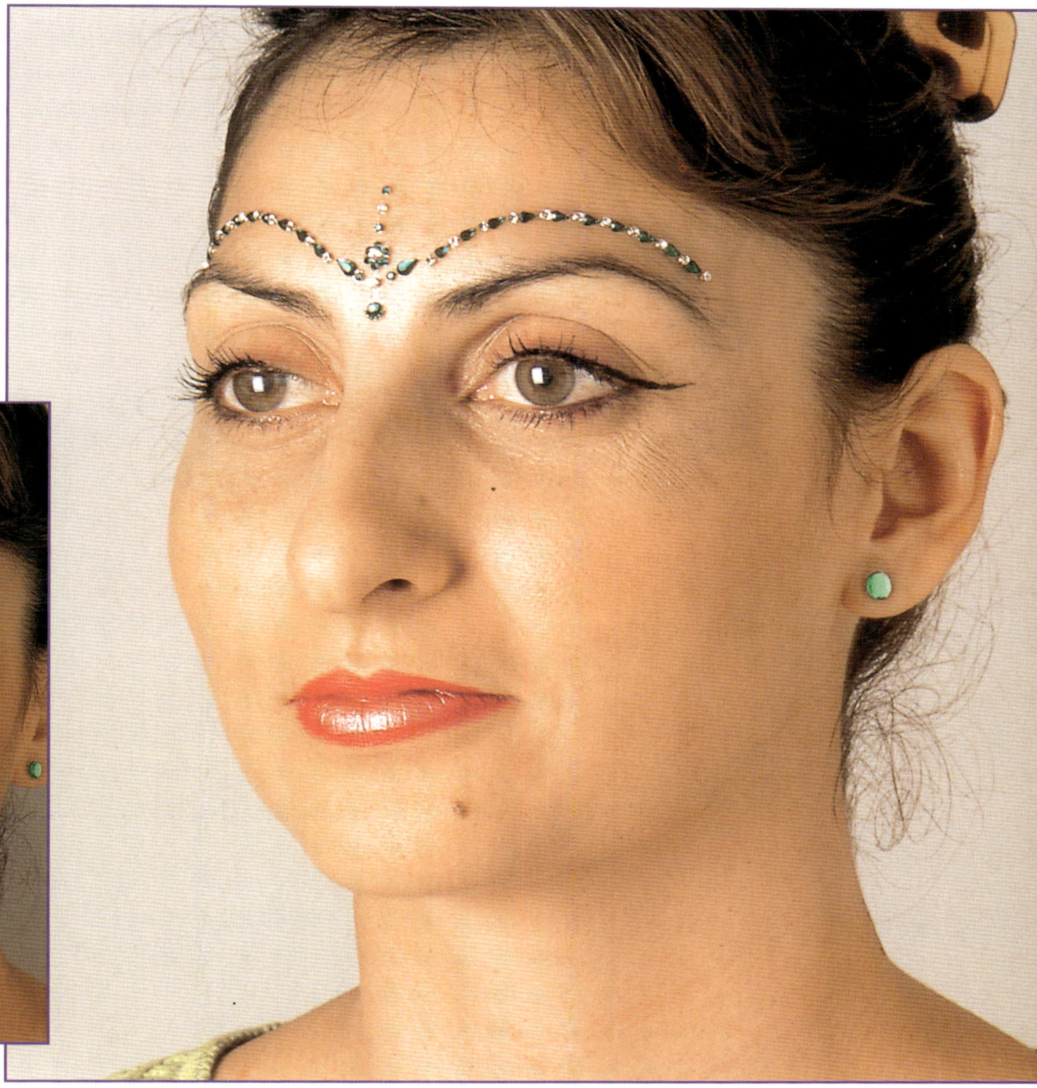

Simple body jewellery for the arm

Body jewellery comes in different kinds suitable for all parts of the body.

YOU WILL NEED
- Body jewel

1 Wash and dry the area of your arm to be decorated to ensure that it is completely oil-free.

2 Carefully separate the body jewellery from the plastic backing, making sure that it adheres to your skin.

3 Gently press the jewellery onto your skin and hold it there for about ten seconds to warm the adhesive.

4 Remove the transparent tape carefully to ensure that the jewellery remains fixed to your skin.

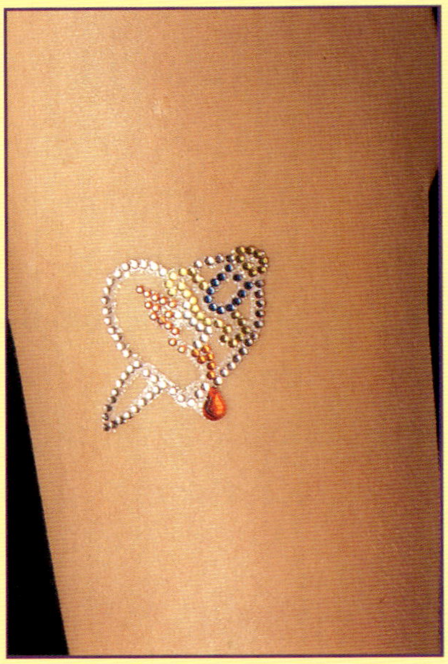

Belly button jewellery

This jewellery perfectly fits the belly button, and looks excellent with a stone fitted into the navel. Accessorise with matching bracelets.

YOU WILL NEED
- Body jewel
- Navel stone
- Accessories

1 Wash and dry the area of your arm to be decorated to ensure that it is completely oil-free.

2 Carefully separate the body jewellery from the plastic backing, making sure that it adheres to your skin.

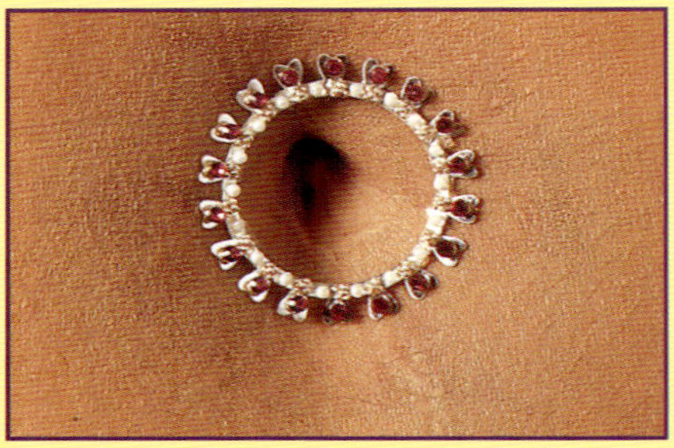

3 Gently press the jewellery onto your skin and hold it there for about ten seconds to warm the adhesive.

4 Remove the transparent tape carefully to ensure that the jewellery remains fixed to your skin.

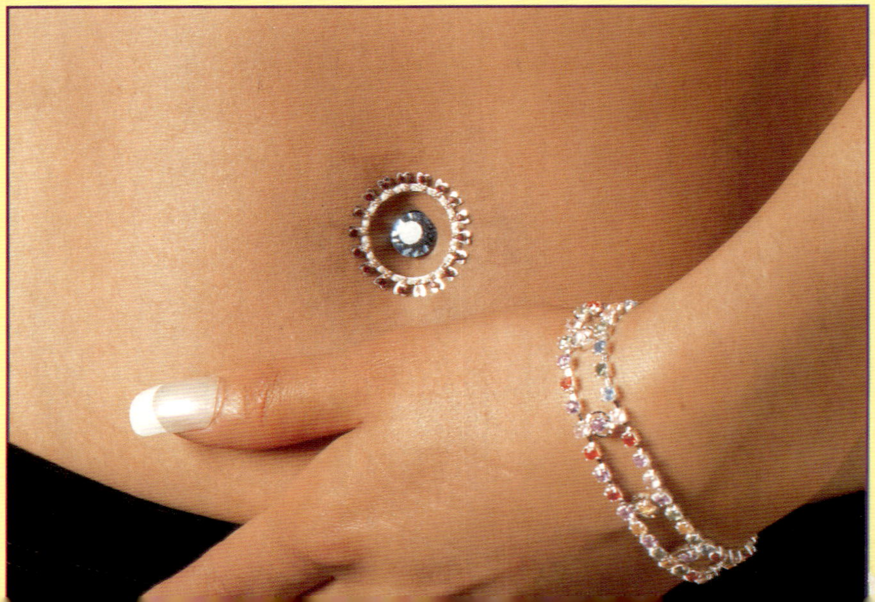

Body badges

Body badges are available in all sorts of colours and shapes and may also be decorated with gems. Place them wherever you like – on your arms, neck or shoulders – and wear them either to accessorise your clothes or just for fun!

YOU WILL NEED
- Cotton pad
- Alcohol solution (witch hazel)
- Body badge
- Tissue

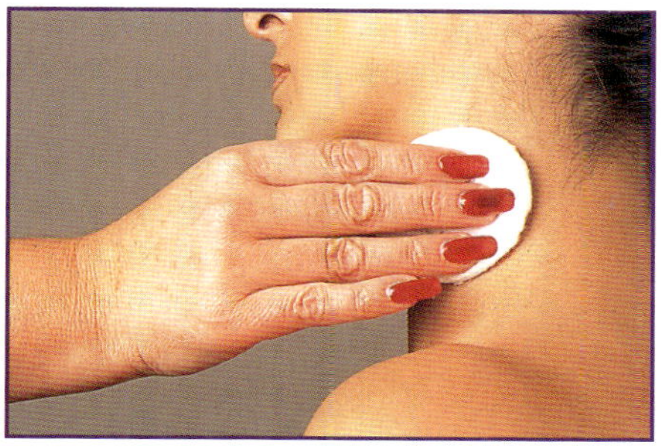

1 Ensure that your skin is oil-free by wiping it with a cotton pad dipped in alcohol solution and then let it dry thoroughly.

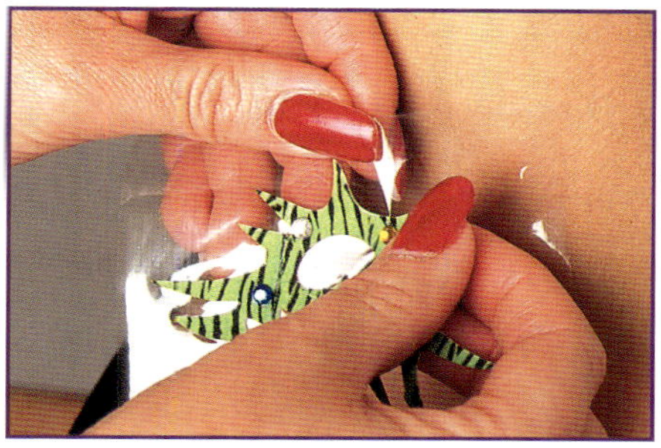

2 Peel the body badge from its self-adhesive backing and carefully position it on your skin.

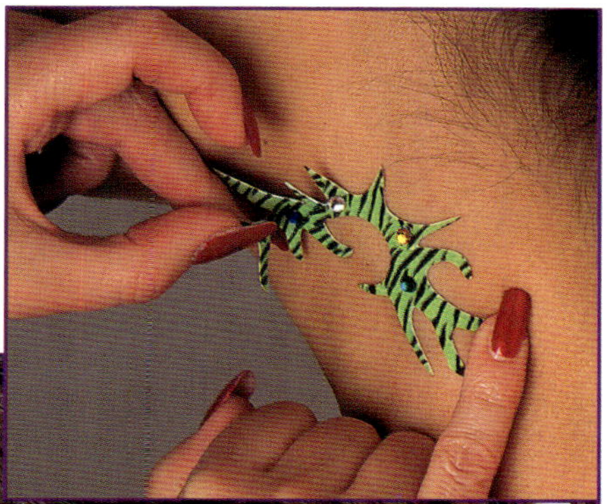

3 Press it into place with a tissue (don't use a cotton pad in case it sticks to the fabric and spoils the effect).

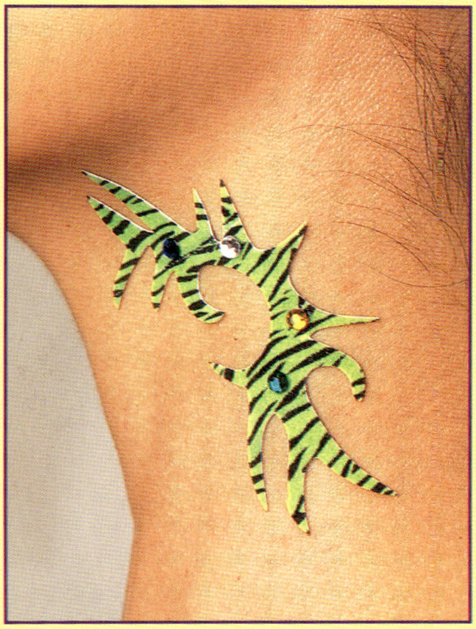

4 The body badge should adhere firmly.

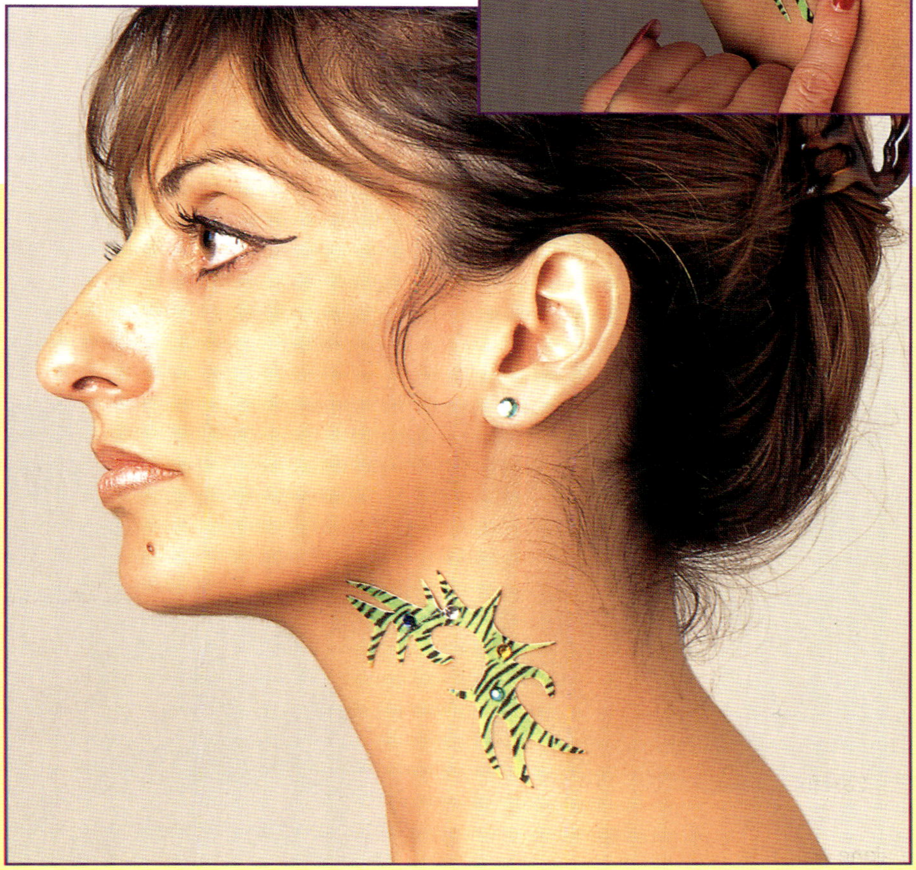

Hair tattoos

Hair tattoos can be a fun way of enlivening a party or special occasion. Note, however, that they suit longer, one-length hair better than shorter, layered hair. Remove hair tattoos by brushing your hair thoroughly and then shampooing it.

YOU WILL NEED
- Hair tattoo
- Cotton pad
- Water
- Hairspray

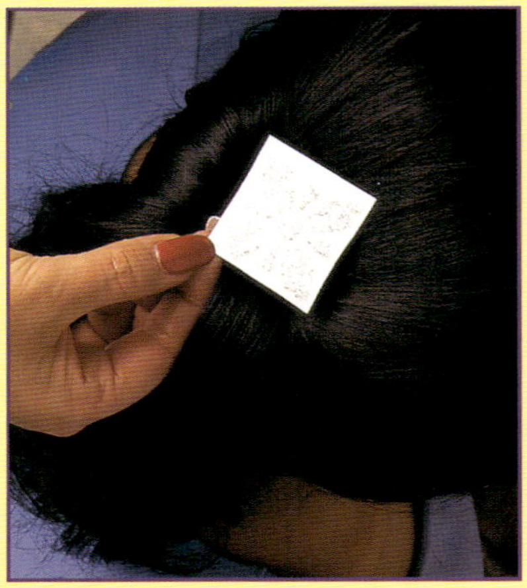

1 After styling your hair, remove the hair tattoo's protective sheet. Place the tattoo firmly on your hair, tacky-side down.

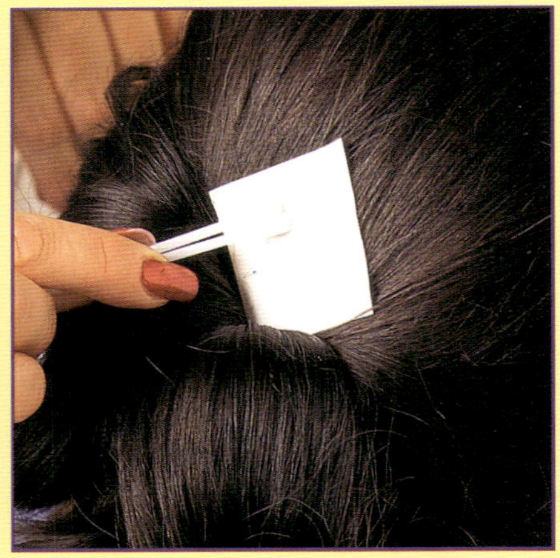

2 Carefully wet the back of the tattoo with a damp cotton pad. Try not to wet your hair until the tattoo becomes visible.

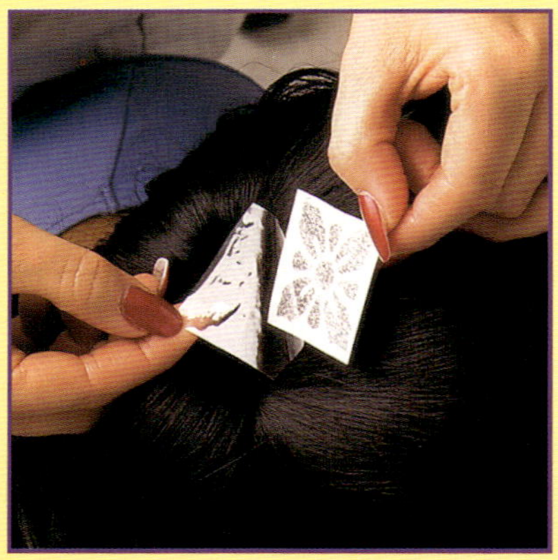

3 Gently peel away the backing paper.

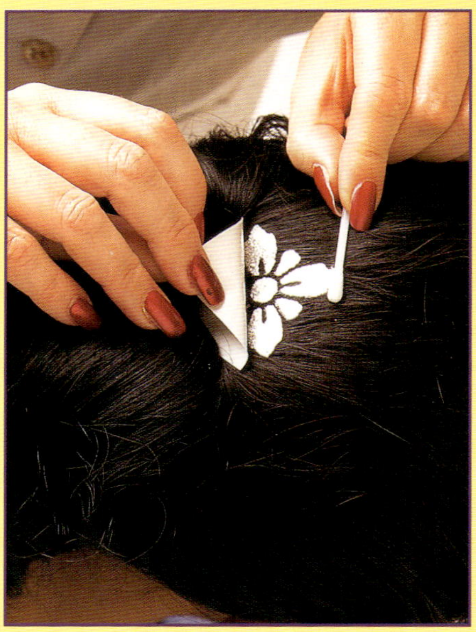

4 Use a cotton bud to help keep the hair tattoo in position.

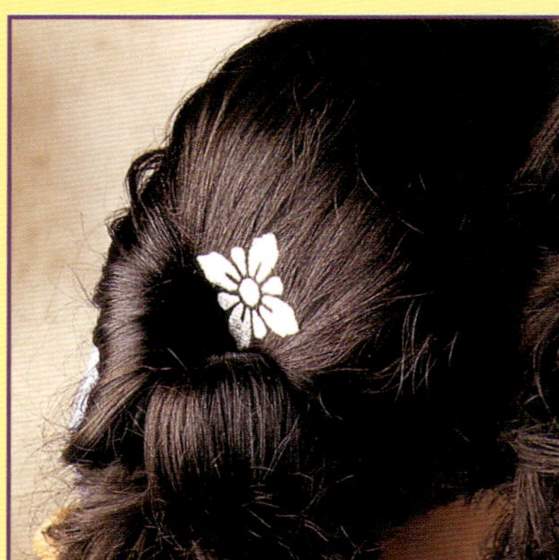

5 The design should be clear and sharp.

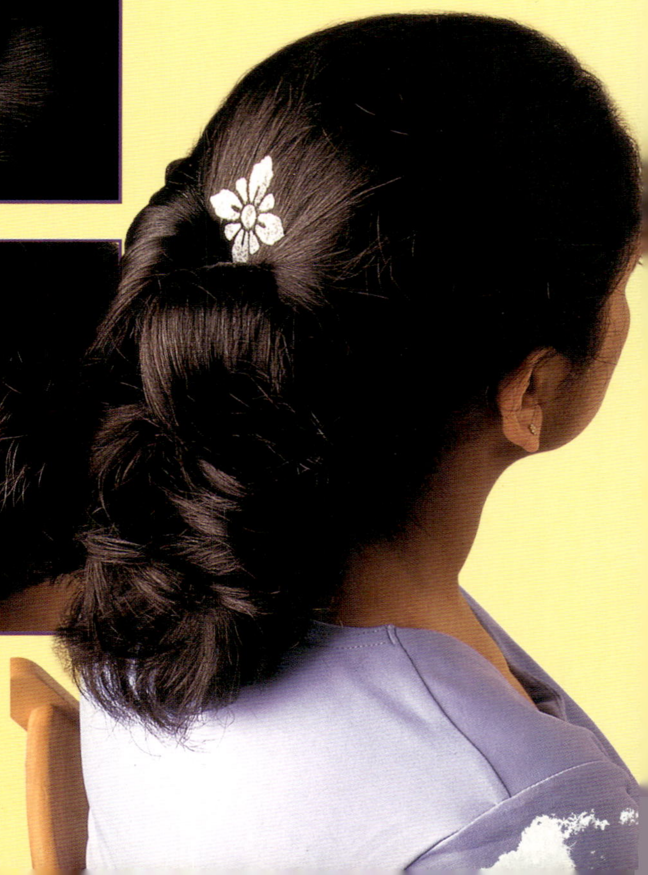

Bridal diamond bindis

Bindi face jewellery is traditionally used on brides for their wedding day. The jewels can be used in many different ways, and with different clothes and accessories for a stunning look.

YOU WILL NEED
- Green diamond bindis

1 Unless you have applied make-up to your face, wash and dry the area to be decorated to ensure that it is completely oil-free.

2 Carefully separate the two pieces of foil, making sure that the stones adhere to the transparent sheet.

3 Gently press the bindis onto your skin and hold them there for about ten seconds to warm the adhesive.

4 Remove the transparent tape carefully to ensure that the bindis remain fixed to your skin. Continue your design across your eyebrows, pressing the bindis into position.

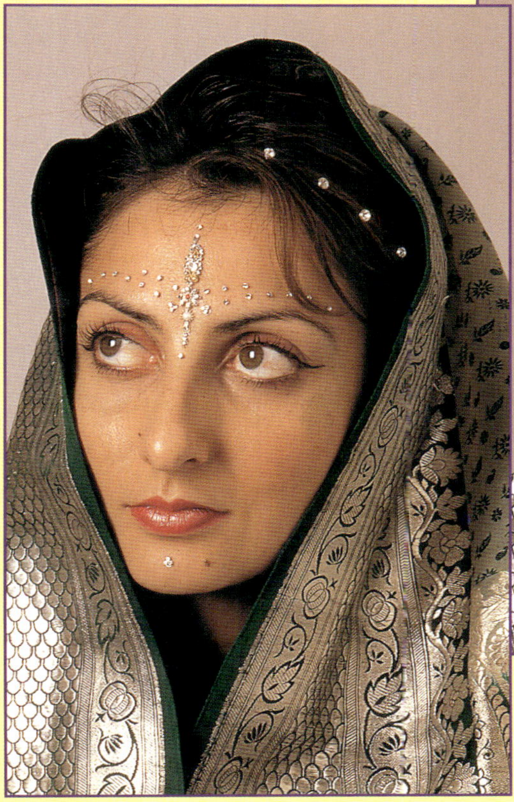

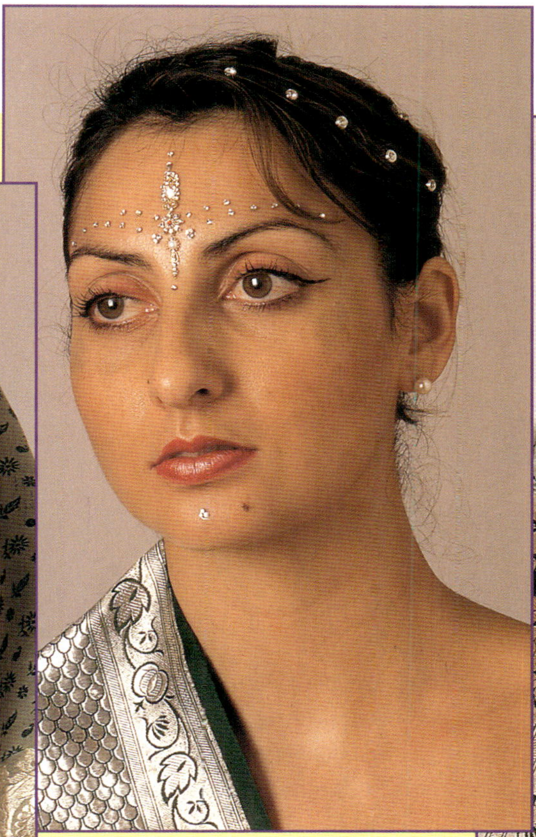

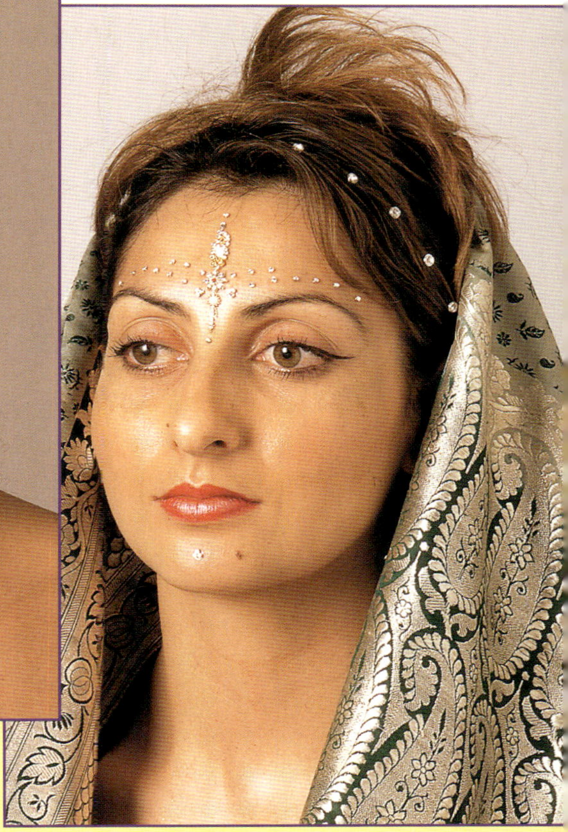

Index

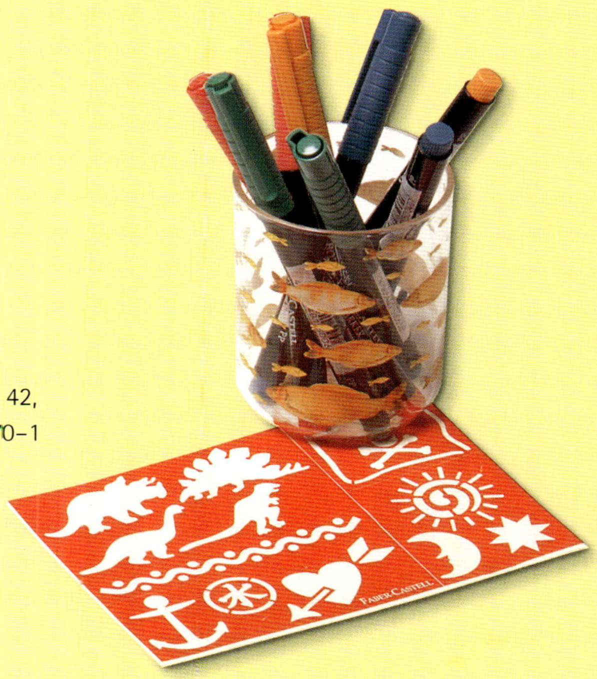

Credits and acknowledgements

Special thanks to the models, Danielle James and David Pollard, for their time, patience and dedication in helping to create the body art in this book.

Also a special thank you to the Henna artists Ronald Gomes and Reena Halai.

Special credits to SMG International Ltd UK for supplying henna and materials as well as Jazzy Bindi Ltd for supplying Bindis on pages 24, 34, 42, 90, 93.

Additional thanks to the nail-art supplier Star Gazer for supplying semi-permanent tattoos, body jewellery and bindis.

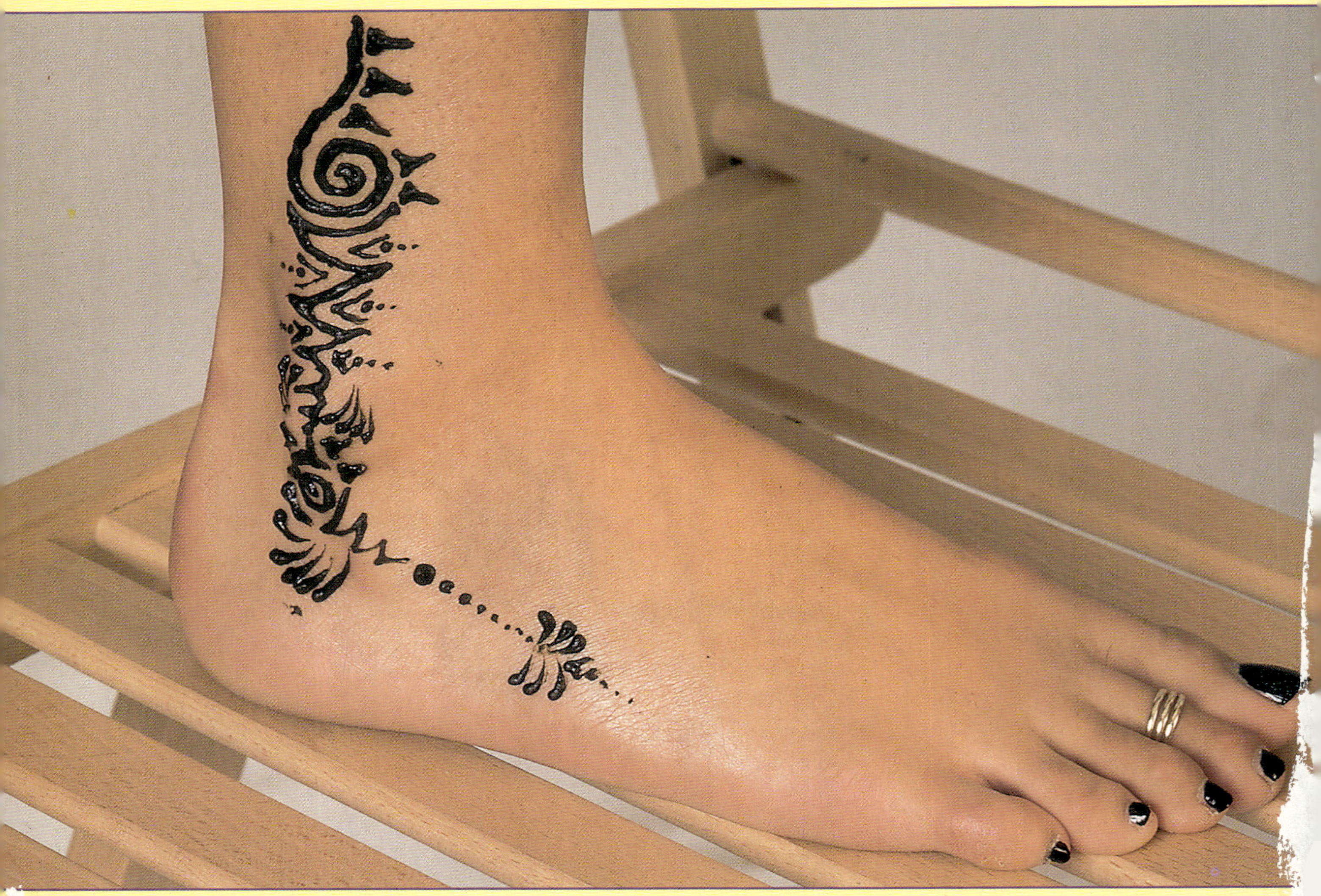